Politics in Hard Times

A VOLUME IN THE SERIES

Cornell Studies in Political Economy

EDITED BY PETER J. KATZENSTEIN

A full list of titles in the series appears at the end of the book.

Politics in Hard Times

COMPARATIVE RESPONSES TO
INTERNATIONAL ECONOMIC CRISES

PETER GOUREVITCH

CORNELL UNIVERSITY PRESS

Ithaca and London

First published 1986 by Cornell University Press.
Third printing, Cornell Paperbacks, 1988.

International Standard Book Number (cloth) 0-8014-1973-5
International Standard Book Number (paper) 0-8014-9436-2
Library of Congress Catalog Card Number 86-47631
Printed in the United States of America
Librarians: Library of Congress cataloging information
appears on the last page of the book.

The paper in this book is acid-free and meets the guidelines for permanence and durability of the Committee on Production Guidelines for Book Longevity of the Council on Library Resources.

For Lisa, Alexander, and Nicholas

Contents

Preface

Seven fat years, seven lean ones—the biblical story expresses the notion of economic cycle. Applied to capitalist economies, Pharaoh's dream may be wrong about the length of each particular phase, but in the notion of cycle it captures an important aspect of reality. Over the past two centuries levels of aggregate production in the world economy have certainly risen, but the gains have never come without intermittent periods of sharp decline. Business cycles, long waves, shocks, and busts, along with booms and upward spirals, have punctuated the evolution of the industrial economy.

The fat years and the lean ones are, of course, interconnected. Growth means change. In the prosperous years new industries emerge, populations shift, values and outlooks alter, age, and are rejuvenated. Lines of cleavage may develop, along with ambitions and hopes, points of possible conflict, and areas of disagreement. The good times will thus produce their own challenges over new ways of organizing society, new values, and rising aspirations. And they create fault lines that may emerge in the next downturn.

But more obviously, it is the crisis years that put systems under stress. Hard times expose strengths and weaknesses to scrutiny, allowing observers to see relationships that are often blurred in prosperous periods, when good times slake the propensity to contest and challenge. The lean years are times when old relationships crumble and new ones have to be constructed. It is then that institutions and patterns are built which will persist long into the next cycle.

History has its points of critical choice, moments of flux when several things might happen but only one actually does. For years afterward, that winning alternative will preempt other possibilities, and things will seem more closed. Economic crises create one such set of

9

points of choice, and it is on them that I have focused this book. Moments of flux are fruitful for evaluating theoretical debates and for analyzing historical patterns.

This book has two goals. One is to compare the policy responses of different countries to the same "stimulus," the crises of the international economy. I have chosen to examine the responses of five countries—the United States, the United Kingdom, France, Germany, and Sweden—to the three most recent convulsions of the world economy: the long deflation at the end of the nineteenth century, the Great Depression of the 1930s, and the wide gyrations of the 1970s and 1980s. What these countries did—what they chose in terms of policies—deserves explanation. Comparison allows us to stage a confrontation between competing explanations in the social sciences, arguments about state structure, social forces, ideology, international state rivalries, leadership, and the like.

The other goal is to trace, across countries and within particular countries, how alliances among societal actors form, crumble, and reform in each crisis period. We can learn much about the distinguishing features of a country's political life by determining how groups common to many countries relate to each other and around what policies they coalesce or conflict.

The organization of the book reflects the constant tension between these goals. Chapter 2 sets out a typology of policy options and a typology of policy choices. Chapters 3 to 5 link the historical trajectories to the explanatory arguments. Chapter 3 makes a particular effort to probe the various arguments in such a way that their distinctive features can be carried over to the remaining cases. Chapter 1 provides a short overview of the whole argument, while Chapter 6 analyzes the results of the discussion.

Readers process material differently. Some prefer to glean the author's perspectives through the cases before reading the theoretical commentary on approaches and understanding. Others prefer to examine the concepts before reading the cases that have been shaped by them. Both modes have their advantages, and either will work with this book. Those who prefer the former approach may reverse the chapter ordering, beginning with the cases of Part II in Chapters 3 to 5 and returning to the account of approaches and policy outcomes in Chapter 2 before taking on the conclusions of Chapter 6.

My decision to focus on economic hard times may have been influenced by autobiography, and in particular by the experience of refugee parents who fled the cataclysms of two world wars and the disasters of the years between. Certainly the book was begun in an intellectual atmosphere quite different from our own. In 1970 the United States faced war in Vietnam, issues of race and poverty, and the dollar "overhang." These and other issues contributed to a desire to question and examine. Curious to situate America's difficulties in a comparative context, a group of faculty members then at Harvard University put together a collectively taught course, "The Political Development of the United States." I proposed to lecture on the critical election of 1896 in comparative perspective, linking political economy quarrels over the American tariff to comparable debates in Europe. That lecture led to an article, "International Trade, Domestic Coalitions and Liberty."

While I was working on other research problems, my interest in comparative responses to economic crises continued. I wanted to see what happened to the coalitions that crystallized around the crisis of the 1880s and 1890s when hit by the Great War and then the Depression. As I read on those years, the atmosphere around me changed. The political-military issues of the war in Vietnam receded while economic matters loomed larger. Indeed, in the seventies and eighties so much of what I read in the daily newspaper resonated with the events of earlier periods that I could not forbear from continuing the comparison.

The result of these influences is a rather grandiose project, a comparison of five countries over three crisis periods. I was inspired by the work of Barrington Moore, Jr., whose *Social Origins of Dictatorship and Democracy* continues to influence reflection and scholarship. I have followed Moore's method of tracing different responses in various countries to the same event. Moore looked at the commercialization of agriculture. Under the influence of his colleague Alexander Gerschenkron, I have examined the stress of international competition on different "branches" or "sectors" of the modern economy.

My deepest intellectual and personal debt is to those who encouraged me to undertake this enterprise, despite its size and analytic difficulties. Particularly helpful have been James Kurth, who helped coax me to develop a lecture at Harvard into an article on tariffs in the nineteenth century, and an article into part of this book; Martin Shefter, who was always willing to exchange ideas as he pursued his own American and comparative interests; Peter Katzenstein, a thoughtful and critical reader, journal editor, and series editor; and Stephen Krasner, who also encouraged me, whatever our disagreements on interpretation. Barrington Moore, Jr., and Stanley Hoffmann have provided the best kind of support: intellectual stim-

ulus and tension, creativity and productivity, the challenge to think
about their ideas combined with the freedom to pursue one's own
interests and reach one's own conclusions.

In mentioning these individuals I risk offending those who have
helped greatly in various ways. These are many, and their assistance,
whether encouragement, criticism, or reading, has been substantial.
Those who have read large portions of the manuscript include
Suzanne Berger, Peter Cowhey, Bruce Cumings, Tom Ferguson, Peter Hall, Albert Hirschman, Miles Kahler, Robert Jervis, Robert Keohane, David Laitin, Charles Maier, Michael Mandelbaum, Victor Per-
ez-Diaz, Harvey Rishikof, Sidney Tarrow, and John Zysman. Those
who have read pieces of the manuscript and given useful comments
over the years include Perry Anderson, Neal Beck, David Bloom,
Stephen Bornstein, David Cameron, Stephen Cohen, Ellen Comisso,
Michael Doyle, Robert Gilpin, Richard Gordon, Patrice Higonnet,
Charles Kindleberger, Peter Lange, Andrei Markovits, Andrew Martin, Molly Nolan, Joseph Nye, George Ross, Charles Sabel, Janice
Stein, Michael Stein, Theda Skocpol, Tony Smith, Immanuel Wallerstein, and members of the Political Science Department at the University of California, San Diego.

Several institutions have given me valuable research support. A
National Endowment for the Humanities fellowship allowed me to
tackle the vast problem of the 1930s and to block out the comparative
contours of the book. A German Marshall Fund fellowship allowed
me time to write the book as a whole, and the Fund also contributed
support to some seminars organized by James Kurth at which I presented an early version of the case of the 1930s. A Lehrman Institute
fellowship proved extremely useful in creating a seminar that gave
criticism of several chapters; I found those meetings stimulated me to
rework ideas and organization. I particularly thank Michael Mandelbaum for his intelligent chairing of those sessions, as well as for his
own comments, and thank all of the participants.

My understanding of recent events has different sources and involves other debts. The Ford Foundation sponsored a project on
trade union responses to the economic crisis of the 1970s, on which I
worked with George Ross, Peter Lange, Andrew Martin, Andrei Mar-
covits, Stephen Bornstein, Maurizio Vannicelli, and Chris Allen. Our
planning meetings, field research, and writing sessions were wonder-
ful examples of the stimulating benefits of collaborative research
which helped me considerably, not only for the British case that I
coauthored with Stephen Bornstein but for my thinking about the
current period and the theoretical issues more generally. The fruits

of those labors are two volumes published by Allen & Unwin: *Unions, Change and Crisis: French and Italian Union Strategy and the Political Economy, 1945–80* and *Unions and Economic Crisis: Britain, West Germany and Sweden.*

Another collaborative effort helped me with the French case. I organized some papers for an International Studies Association conference and then worked with Stephen Cohen to edit them for Butterworths as *France in the Troubled World Economy.*

The Center for European Studies at Harvard has been an important source of not only financial but intellectual and psychological support; Abby Collins, Guido Goldman, Leonie Gordon, and Stanley Hoffmann have been the most conspicuous elements of a larger system of support. Additional assistance came from the Committee on Research of the University of California at San Diego, from a UCSD sabbatical leave, and from McGill University.

I am also very grateful to the organizers of and participants at various seminars where portions of the argument were discussed: seminars at the universities of Lund, Umeå, Stockholm, and Uppsala in Sweden; the University of Madrid; the Groupe de Sociologie des Organisations in Paris, where Martha Zuber, Pierre Gremion, Catherine Gremion, and Annique Percheron were particularly helpful; the Center for European Studies at Harvard; and groups at Cornell, Columbia, and Stanford universities, the University of Washington, and the University of California campuses at Berkeley, Los Angeles, and Santa Cruz.

Vital staff support came from many sources: the staff of the UCSD Department of Political Science, and particularly Lee Dewey, Betsy Faught, Judy Lyman, Betsy Ogden, and Monica Paskvan; the Center for European Studies at Harvard University, and particularly Abby Collins; the Fulbright Offices in Stockholm; and the libraries at Harvard and McGill universities and UCSD.

Editorial help came from the editors and reviewers of *International Organization*, which published an early version of parts of Chapter 4 as well as a theoretical essay, "The Second Image Reversed: The International Sources of Domestic Politics," *International Organization* 32 (Autumn 1978); and of the *Journal of Interdisciplinary History*, which published an early version of Chapter 2. At Cornell University Press, Walter Lippincott and Roger Haydon were particularly helpful.

Families are part of one's work, and mine has been both encouraging and helpful. Lisa Hirschman, my wife, has given not only intellectual sustenance and nourishment, but those extra hours on evenings and weekends which it takes to finish something. My children, Alexander and Nicholas, are too young to read this book, though I hope they may derive satisfaction someday from reading the work that took away some of my time with them. My mother, Sylvia Gourevitch, has provided intellectual commentary on substance and practical help in manuscript preparation. I am sorry that my father, Alexander Gourevitch, is not alive to read this book, as it was in large part inspired by my desire to comprehend the forces that so shaped the lives of my parents. My wife's grandfather, Nicholas Chapro, would surely have provided some memorable remark about a book whose development he watched and encouraged over so many years.

To all these people I render my thanks. The errors remain mine. The benefits are ours.

PETER GOUREVITCH

La Jolla, California

PART I

THE POLITICS OF POLICY CHOICE

CHAPTER ONE

The Politics of Economic Policy

Policy requires politics. Ideas for solving economic problems are plentiful, but if an idea is to prevail as the actual policy of a particular government, it must obtain support from those who have political power. Economic theory can tell us a lot about policy alternatives, but unless our economics contains an understanding of power, it will not tell us enough to understand the choices actually made.

In prosperous times it is easy to forget the importance of power in the making of policy. Social systems appear stable, and the economy works with sufficient regularity that its rules can be modeled as if they functioned without social referent. In difficult economic times this comfortable illusion disintegrates. Patterns unravel, economic models come into conflict, and policy prescriptions diverge. Prosperity blurs a truth that hard times make clearer: the choice made among conflicting policy proposals emerges out of politics. The victorious interpretation will be the one whose adherents have the power to translate their opinion into the force of law.

The 1970s and 1980s have been difficult years, years in which economic problems have made visible the importance of politics in shaping economic policy. Records have been broken. The early 1980s saw the most severe business-cycle depression in fifty years, the late 1970s the worst inflation in thirty years and the most persistent unemployment in the countries of Western Europe for two generations. The 1970s also gave us the most severe shock from a single source in the international economy since the banking collapse of 1931, in the OPEC price boost of 1973–74, and the unraveling of the monetary regime created in the 1940s, starting with the American dollar drop of 1971. As I was finishing this book in the mid-1980s, the American economy had, to the envy of Europeans, created millions of jobs, but the halcyon days of the fifties, when it seemed that economic growth, price stability, and full employment might be realized collectively, had not returned. Over the international economy of the latter 1980s hang the tremendous U.S. budget deficit, sucking in huge amounts of foreign capital, the gigantic debts owed by certain foreign governments, severe international competition, and massive reductions in manufacturing employment—outward signs of acute policy problems.

With economic dislocations have come significant political changes as well. The late 1970s and the 1980s have produced some of the largest swings in partisan politics since the 1930s. In 1981, for the first time in its history, France gave an absolute electoral majority to the Socialists in the National Assembly and elected the first Socialist president ever chosen directly by universal suffrage. In the United Kingdom the two-party system crumbled as Margaret Thatcher and the British Conservatives beat Labour twice while social democrats broke away to form a new party. In 1976 the Swedish social democrats lost power for the first time in over forty years, but in 1982, with commentators predicting a rightward shift in Europe, they came back under Olof Palme to win. In West Germany the governing coalition fell apart when the Free Democrats switched alliance partners. In the United States, Ronald Reagan led the Republicans to strong victories at the presidential level and to strong gains in voter identification at all levels. In Portugal, Spain, and Greece dictatorships fell, and in the latter two countries socialist governments took office.

These political shifts have been accompanied by major changes in economic policy debate. Out of the traumas of the Depression of the 1930s and of World War II the countries of Western Europe and North America had forged a "historic compromise." Bitter enemies had worked out a truce built around a mixed economy, a kind of bounded capitalism, where private enterprise remained the dynamo but operated within a system of rules that provided stability, both economic and political. Demand management to promote full employment, the welfare state, an extensive system of economic regulation, institutionalized industrial relations, free trade—these were the policy approaches of this bounded capitalism, and they departed strongly from the market orthodoxy of pre-Depression days. Political power was shared as well, and to a far greater degree than before the war.[1]

With the crisis of the 1970s this compromise has come undone. As the economy turned sour, so discord grew about causes and remedies, and the policy debate widened. Older interpretations, thought dead, have come back to life, sometimes in new language, while the doctrines of the sixties, once challengers to orthodoxy and then its successor, lost their intellectual predominance. Challenges to the historic compromise—among them nationalization of industry, industrial democracy, protectionism, and industrial policy—have returned to the policy agenda in recent years, and some have been tried in practice. In the first year of François Mitterrand's government, for example, France nationalized more industry than any Western country had done since 1945. Reagan slashed taxes and domestic spending more drastically than any U.S. president in generations and increased military spending dramatically for a nation not at war. In international trade a widespread return to protectionism has pierced the worn fabric of the General Agreement on Tariffs and Trade.

Economic crisis, policy debate, and political experimentation are surely somehow connected, and their connections are the subject of this book. Economic crisis leads to policy debate and political controversy; out of conflict, policies emerge. Policies, whether innovative or traditional, require politics: that is, the responses to the economic crisis require political support. To understand policy choices, therefore, we must understand the politics that produces them.

In this book I wish to gain an understanding of the politics of policy choice through a "political sociology of political economy"—that is, by looking at the politics of support for different economic policies in response to large changes in the international economy. When national economies are interdependent, crises are international. No country escapes, for a crisis is a stimulus to which all must respond. By examining what countries do, by looking at how their responses vary, we can learn something about the countries themselves and about the factors that lead them to choose particular policies.

Comparison is particularly useful for such an enterprise. The current crisis of the international economy is not the first, and two earlier experiences seem especially telling for our era. In the crisis of 1873–96 prices plummeted, levels of employment gyrated widely, production soared, profits were squeezed, some businesses exploded in size while great numbers of others collapsed, millions emigrated from Europe, new parts of the world entered the industrial economy, and countries wrangled over what to do. The crisis of 1929–49, beginning with the Great Crash, occurred in the context of deep problems in the system of payments (with German war debt and reparations for World War I) and that of trade and production (with the emergence of new products and new techniques). Much can be learned by comparing the current crisis to these earlier ones.

The three crises can be seen both as distinct historical periods and as recurrences of similar events. Each crisis combines three properties: a major downturn in a regular investment/business cycle, a major change in the geographical distribution of production, and a significant growth of new products and new productive processes. These three properties operate at an international level that deeply implicates domestic economies and so link conflicts over national policy within each country to international trends.

This book analyzes the response to the three international crises in the choices made by five countries: France, Germany, Sweden, the United States, and the United Kingdom. For at least a century, all five countries have had complex economies, part modern, part backward; part industrial, part agrarian; part oriented toward aggressive competition on a world scene, part oriented toward sheltered home markets. All five have at times converged, at times diverged, in their policy choices; all five have been capitalist through the period that interests me. And, with the conspicuous exception of the Nazi years, all five have had politics at least partly shaped by constitutional procedures.

From a comparison of the choices among policy alternatives which these countries have made, something can be learned about the importance of power in shaping policy. Ultimately, policy choices are made by politicians, by individuals who occupy institutional positions; power comes from the formal authority of those institutions. But somehow political leaders have to get into those institutional positions and hold on to them. And whatever they decide, their policies, to take effect, require compliance or even enthusiasm from countless individuals who work or invest or buy. When politicians make choices, therefore, their choices are constrained by the need to mobilize or retain support. Politicians have to construct agreement from among officeholders, civil servants, party and interest group leaders, and economic actors in society. My goal is to map out the patterns of support which have formed around the various programs of economic policy that countries have adopted in response to severe disruptions in the international economy.

Many accounts of these crisis periods make reference to coalitions that formed in conjunction with policy packages: the marriage of iron and rye, the Weimar coalition, the Populist revolt and the Gold Democrats; the New Deal coalition, the French Popular Front, the Swedish "cow trade" of the 1930s. These coalitions provided the support needed to get policies adopted and implemented. Our understanding of policy choices requires a political sociology of these historical coalitions: Who was in them? Around what substantive terms of trade did they form? How were they put together; that is, to what degree were they assembled by political figures, to what degree did self-motivated individuals converge out of particularistic calculations? Were other combinations possible; that is, could the same coalitions have sustained different policies, could different coalitions have produced the same policies? How loosely or tightly do coalition, political formula, and policy package fit together?

Unpacking what was involved in the formation of past coalitions tells us something about the political sources of policy choice. Several factors interact to bring such coalitions about and to cause their collapse. In an economic crisis social actors, affected by their situation, evaluate alternative policies in relation to the likely benefits or costs. One major analytical tradition of political economy therefore examines policy support by examining the placement of social actors in the economy itself.[2]

Economic conditions rarely operate directly on policy disputes. Other factors mediate them. Those factors include, first, the mechanisms of representation—political parties and interest group associations that try to manage the linkage of economic actors to the state. Second, politics is affected by the organization of the state itself: the system of rules (electoral laws, balance between legislature and executive, legal powers, and so on) and institutions which comprises the bureaucracy. Third, economic actors are influenced by ideology, which provides models of the economy and of the economic motives of other actors. Finally, coalition politics is influenced by a country's placement in the international state system of political-military rivalries.[3]

Each of these factors influences the interaction of societal actors. Each has also acted as a focus for important theoretical traditions of explaining policy and politics, some of them in strong conflict with my own concern for the economic situation and preferences of economic actors. It is, I believe, important to explore these traditions of interpretation to see where they can take us and where they are limited. This book attempts a description of policy choices which evaluates the connections among different arguments currently used to link the international economic environment to national politics.

THE ARGUMENT IN BRIEF

Each crisis involves a sequence of events which can be summarized quickly. In the prosperous years preceding the crisis, a policy approach and support coalition developed. Then came crisis, challeng-

ing both policy and coalition. Crisis opened the system of relationships, making politics and policy more fluid. Finally a resolution
was reached, closing the system for a time, until the next crisis.[4]

The Crisis of 1873–96

When the first crisis began, free trade had been spreading across
Europe's industrializing countries. Buoyed by growth, those countries
had accepted the concept of comparative advantage, which promised
greater aggregate wealth if countries specialized according to world
market conditions. In 1873, however, prices slumped; they would
continue falling for years. Many producers, sorely pressed by new
conditions, began clamoring for tariffs and other forms of aid. Of our
five countries, only the United Kingdom continued with its free-trade
orientation, which dated from the celebrated repeal of the Corn Laws
in 1846. Elsewhere protectionism prevailed, and with it the reshuf-
fling or reinforcement of particular alliances among societal actors. In
Germany, France, and Sweden both industry and agriculture were
sheltered. Agricultural tariffs would have been meaningless in a
United States whose farm production was swamping Europe, so in
America only industry received protection.

The simplest explanation of these outcomes lies with the way that
the new economic environment affected the major groups of industry, agriculture, and labor in each country. As the first industrial
nation, the United Kingdom led the world in most industrial products. It pioneered large-scale manufacturing first of textiles, then of
iron and steel. With the profits from those industries the United
Kingdom developed a very large financial/trading sector deeply attached to world trade. British agriculture had already begun adapting
to the pressures of international specialization. Labor, employed by
some of the world's leading industries, worried about the cost of food,
but after the repeal of the Corn Laws, labor also came to support free
trade. When prices fell after 1873, some farmers and some steel producers fought for protection. They were defeated by the larger
coalition.

The sharpest contrast to the British case is that of Germany. As a
later industrializer, Germany (its industries) faced stiff competition
from the British; its banks were linked not to international finance
and trade but to industries; and much of its agriculture was quite
uncompetitive and poorly structured for adaptation. Industry, led by
the heavy industries of iron and steel, and agriculture, led by the
grain-growing Junkers, came together in the famous coalition of iron

22

and rye in support of tariffs. An alternative alliance preferred free trade; it brought together export-oriented, high-technology industries such as chemicals and electrical equipment, farmers seeking cheaper grains to feed dairy and meat herds, and labor concerned about the price of food. The free traders lost.

This divergence in outcomes between the United Kingdom and Germany was reinforced by other factors as well. The well-developed Prussian-German state favored protectionist interests, for example, and the system of interest groups and political parties disadvantaged the free-trade coalition there. The German states had a stronger tradition of protection and a weaker tradition of free trade than the United Kingdom. Moreover, Germany's geopolitical situation on the European landmass, without extensive colonies or dominions, made it more vulnerable than the United Kingdom to dependence on the international division of labor.

When we bring the other countries into the comparison, however, we diminish the importance of these factors. France and Sweden had their equivalents of the iron-rye coalition, with industry and agriculture both facing stiff foreign competition and seeking protection. Yet the French state after the early 1870s was a rather weak republic open to social pressures, and Sweden lacked the powerful army and bureaucracy that made the German state so distinctive. In France and Sweden, indeed in all the countries including Germany, economic ideology appeared to shift rather rapidly with changes in economic conditions. In all could be found a range of viewpoints about policy, each view struggling for political primacy. In the United States, state structure, economic ideology, mechanisms of representation, and international situation were all quite different from their Continental counterparts. Nonetheless, protectionist groups in all four countries managed to prevail; in the United Kingdom they lost.

The influence of societal actors in this period appears to have been relatively naked and raw. To win policy debates, societal actors certainly had to operate through parties, the state, and ideology, and they certainly had to deal with international military considerations. But in this period these appear to have been instruments used as the societal actors saw fit. Whatever the system in which they operated, producer groups seem to have been able to get their way. It seems likely that even a republican Germany with a weak state, or an authoritarian France with stronger leadership, would have adopted the same policy. What makes the United Kingdom different from the rest is the profile of its national groups and their views; that is, sectors convinced that an open world economy operated to their advantage.

From these various policy battles emerged certain patterns in the interrelationships among societal actors. Though all industrialists had their conflicts with labor over wages, unionization, and other issues of property and power, some industries showed a higher propensity than others to make alliances with labor. High-technology sectors, for example, well placed in international competition, forged alliances with cheap-food-oriented labor groups. Heavy industry, faced with massive capital requirements and a need for stabilization of demand, as well as other industries facing stiff foreign competition, opposed free trade. They were more hostile to labor and to progressive political demands. Agriculture split between commodity crop producers and the growers of high-quality foodstuffs who used grain and other commodity crops as inputs. In Europe the latter had sympathy for free trade and industrial development, the former were protectionist. In America the commodity producers were antiprotectionist and also mistrustful of industry; the high-quality food producers were sympathetic to industry and accepted protection. Labor was a passive though not useless ally in these agreements. Unionized labor tended to be concerned with keeping down the cost of food; in Europe it tended to oppose tariffs, but in America, where food was cheap, it supported industrial protection. Nearly everywhere agriculture and labor found it difficult to cooperate.

In this first crisis, therefore, the international economy played a considerable role in shaping domestic politics. It did so by working through domestic actors, shaping their policy preferences and their propensities to conflict and to align with other groups. Elements of the national political system were the instruments through which group pressures made themselves felt.

The Crisis of 1929–49: The Depression

The crisis that began with the Great Crash of 1929 produced a massive attack, even greater than its predecessor's, on the classical economic views that dominated policy, and it led to the construction of new political formulas for supporting changes in policy. Long-standing relationships among social forces crumbled. Cut loose from their moorings, economic actors floated on a sea of confusing incentives, opportunities, and dangers. Policy and political experiments were tried, and some combinations, in particular that of Nazi Germany, led to disaster. Others produced a formula that became generally adopted around Europe and North America, though only after the cataclysms of totalitarianism, war, and occupation.

When economic depression spread after 1929, the universal policy response was the orthodox, classical prescription of deflation: cut all costs to encourage sales and investment, which meant cutting wages, taxes, and spending. But deflation failed to produce the desired result. Many alternatives were tried, among them socialization, protection, fiscal stimulus, and mercantilism. Every country gave up on deflation, but the degree of departure from orthodoxy varied.

The United Kingdom reversed its historic devotion to the classical line by devaluing the pound, reviving tariffs, developing subsidies and market regulation for agriculture, and granting some limited aid to industry. But the United Kingdom did not experiment directly or even rhetorically with demand stimulus. Sweden, Germany, and the United States adopted all of these measures, but they also began experiments with demand stimulus and macroeconomic management. Nazi Germany went farthest with deficit-led stimulus; Sweden and the United States experimented with it more loosely. France, after pursuing deflation much later than the others, tried fiscal stimulus under the Popular Front. When that collapsed, the country moved toward a less dramatic break with classical orthodoxy. In Germany political repression altered economic relations, because the destruction of labor unions changed the functioning of labor markets. The shift to military spending in the mid-1930s led to a much greater nationalization, albeit hardly of the kind desired by the left. Corporatist market regulation was tried in many countries; in Germany it became highly authoritarian.

Even in the horrors of the Nazi regime, then, it is possible to see some resemblances to the trajectories of other countries. The classical position held that deflation produces the best result in the long run. The willingness to sustain the long run varied, however. Agriculture everywhere turned desperate early, seeking some kind of substantial state aid. So did labor, both union and nonunion. Fairly soon, business fragmented in its attitudes: some stuck to orthodoxy, others agitated frantically for state action.

As the collapsing international economy disrupted older relationships among economic actors, new combinations became possible. Mass discontent created new opportunities for some elites, new constraints for others. Some capitalists wanted to abandon the deflationary prescriptions of the classical school but met strong resistance from their orthodox brethren. This resistance could be overcome by using the support of labor and the discontent of agriculture. By linking the various instruments of mass power (ballot box, workplace, street) with the various instruments of business (capital, ownership, legitimacy), coalitions formed which had considerable potential for action.

Such coalitions were also polymorphous—there were different

ways they could come together and different uses to which they could be put. The three experimenters with demand stimulus—Nazi Germany, Sweden, and the United States—were able to experiment because politicians fashioned new support coalitions. But the three experiments linked fiscal stimulus to different types of economic policy instruments and to different types of mass support.

It was in Sweden that the bargaining among social forces was most explicit. The Agrarian party and the Social Democrats formed the cow trade: subsidies for the countryside while retaining levels of unemployment compensation for the cities. Business groups were shocked by the deal, but when the election of 1936 demonstrated the failure of efforts to break it up, the high-tech, internationally oriented business groups struck a deal. In the Saltsjöbaden Accord of 1938 labor gave up its demands for socialization and agreed not to strike; business accepted high wages, labor union rights, and labor power in government; agriculture kept its subsidies. The whole accord was oriented toward international markets, whose discipline would be allowed to enforce concern for productivity and profitability. Macroeconomic policy would keep demand at levels high enough to prevent unemployment, and retraining would move labor from declining to growing companies.

In the United States the bargaining was far less clear and much more contorted. Labor and agriculture joined together around the Democrats, but the relationship of these two groups to business shifted. The first New Deal drove the internationalists out of their historic linkage to these groups, while their old enemies, the more nationalist industries that served domestic markets, combined with agriculture and labor to create the corporatism of the National Recovery Administration (NRA). Within two years that approach had disintegrated over its various internal tensions: business resistance to corporatist controls, antipathy to labor claims, tensions over foreign economic policy. The second New Deal put the pieces back together in a different way. It gave bigger concessions to labor in the Wagner Act, which helped promote and institutionalize trade unions, and Social Security, and it salvaged the agricultural programs from the wreck of the NRA. For business, it moved back toward internationalist foreign economic policy, stabilized markets through various regulatory devices, and contained radical agitation for the socialization of ownership. When the effort to balance the budget produced the severe slump of 1937, this new coalition provided support for an economic experiment— the first deliberate deficit, in the demand stimulus budget of 1938.

The Nazi coalition also broke with economic orthodoxy, and it also

26

drew for support on the intense discontent to be found in agriculture, labor, and business. But it drew on a sharply different *type* of labor support, and that difference was important to the gigantic difference in political formulas and program used to stitch the coalition together. Where in the constitutional countries the reformist coalitions used the existing representative organizations of union labor, in Germany the Nazis turned to the unorganized masses, to a wide range of groups including numbers of people working for wages. As an integrative ideology the Nazis used instead of social democracy a *völkisch* populism laden with racism and nationalism. Business was drawn in not as a part of a compromise among existing social categories but around a program of nationalism and imperialism. The new policy departures of demand stimulus and corporatism were thus linked to a very different political base and an authoritarian structure. Where in the United States and Sweden the need of governments for mass support led to a strengthening of trade unions, in Nazi Germany the need for mass support was used to destroy unions. A different political formula gave the Nazis not only the freedom to experiment with economic policy, including coercive corporatism, state enterprises, and strict control of foreign economic relations, but also the freedom to destroy peoples and countries.

In this crisis, as in the first, the policy preferences and coalitional proclivities of economic actors were strongly affected by their situation in the international economy. By contrast, the role of associations in mediating relations among social forces appears to have grown. In response to the first crisis a mass of organizations developed to handle the representation and governance of societal actors. As the organizational space of society "filled up," these organizations came to shape the way their members understood options and the way in which these options were expressed through politics. Specific decisions by organizational leaders loom large in the politics of the second crisis period: the willingness of the Swedish Agrarians to ally themselves with the SAP, the rejection by German and British labor parties of the deficit-financed public works proposed by the unions, the willingness of American and Swedish business groups to make alliances with labor and the rejection of such projects by their German counterparts. In some cases existing associations proved durable and adaptive, in others they were brittle and weak. New organizations rose up able to mobilize people in new directions; the Nazi party and its organs are the most spectacular example.

Differences in state structure also affected policy debates. The German case shows this most conspicuously: the weakness of the Weimar

Republic in the army, the judiciary, and other elements of the state bureaucracy contributed to the failure of constitutionalist accommodations. The weakness of the Weimar and Third Republic cabinets contributed to policy stalemates that ultimately favored the far right in both Germany and France. American federalism and loose party organizations weakened the labor-reform elements of the New Deal, facilitating the formation of a South-agriculture-Republican coalition that limited change.

Associations and state structure both played important roles; we can conceive of them as prisms through which the pressures of societal actors were refracted. It is hard to understand the policy debates without reference to them. Yet it also seems clear that their effects were not independent of the societal context in which they operated. There seem to be no characteristics of associations or state structure that can stand independently of social factors in explaining policy outputs. It is not the formal attributes of institutions which account for the outcomes, but the way in which formal structures interact with the objectives of societal actors and group leaders. Political context also strongly affected the differences in economic ideology and relationship to the international system which can be found among these countries during the Depression.

In crucial ways, then, policy and its political context turned on the accommodations that societal actors did or did not work out. Response to organized labor appears to have been pivotal. Where labor-allied parties and trade unions were drawn into coalitions, economic policy innovation could take place, and in a constitutionalist context. Where organized labor was repressed but another source of mass support was tapped, policy innovations occurred, but under fascist dictatorship. Where organized labor was excluded but not repressed, as in the United Kingdom and in France before and after the Popular Front, policy changes were more limited. This much is description. The explanatory problem arises in sorting out how different elements contribute to the packages of coalition, policy, and organization which prevail.

The Crisis of 1929–49: The Postwar Reconstruction

The Depression of the 1930s contributed to World War II by shaping the coalitions that took power in dealing with it. The war then reopened issues of political economy by shaking loose the political settlements of the 1930s. In the postwar years the policy debate resumed, augmented by the titanic consequences of the war itself. This time the countries of Western Europe and North America converged in their approaches to politics and economic policy, building in effect a compromise to end the battles of the thirties. They built accommodations, de facto or de jure, among societal actors.

Labor accepted capitalist management of an economy run on the basis of market incentives (even for nationalized industries) in exchange for a welfare system, high wages, employment-oriented macroeconomic policy, and constitutional protection of organizing rights. Agriculture kept the extensive system of market stabilization in exchange for its support of broad programs for labor and business. Business accepted these policy shifts in exchange for maintenance of many of the regulatory mechanisms that stabilized markets and control over investment and management. Under American leadership the compromise was attained in the context of an open world economy.

The path to this accommodation differs. In Sweden and the United States it came from internal political debates about the international system; in Germany it depended upon massive foreign interventions to restructure the society. But the end point was roughly similar. Studies of the postwar period usually pit the United States and Sweden against each other as polar opposites. Yet compared to the era before 1929, these two countries (and the others examined in this book) clearly appear after 1945 to be part of this historic compromise. Although policy mixes vary substantially, the character of state activism in economic management from 1945 onward diverges strongly from both the classical and the protectionist policy patterns that predominated in earlier decades. The system produced by this compromise sustained prodigious economic growth, and successes strengthened the accommodation—until things began to go sour.

The Crisis of 1971 to the Present

The very successes of the postwar boom sowed the seeds of subsequent difficulties. The revival of the West European and Japanese economies, the spread of industrial capacity to developing countries, and the emergence of new products and new processes, all paved the way for a wide-reaching crisis of international competition which can be dated to the early 1970s. This crisis has destroyed the compromise forged after World War II. Labor, agriculture, and business are having an increasingly hard time managing the terms of their accommodation. More precisely, those elements which forged the compromise are losing ground within each category to elements that dislike it.

The policy mix of demand management, regulation, and corporatism is no longer dominant either in rhetoric or in reality. Even where labor continues to participate in governing, policy has shifted toward the neoclassical. State intervention remains extensive, but the policy mix is changing. The interventions espoused by labor and stabilization-oriented industries are under challenge. Countries continue to vary widely in policy, but market considerations are pressing all of them to adapt in ways contrary to the patterns built up over several decades.

In the present crisis labor has lost its historic allies within business and agriculture. Business collaborated with labor in the postwar reconstruction to promote stabilization mechanisms and an open international economy, against the opposition of protectionists and nationalists. Now all business groups have accepted the interpretation that their international problems are caused very largely by labor costs, labor behavior, and the regulatory instruments that labor has supported. The principal way to modernize and rationalize national economies, business groups argue, is to improve profitability; hence they urge lower taxes, lower social charges, less regulation. The internationalization of production has thus reduced the link between domestic producers and domestic labor while at the same time it has moved international industry away from labor.

To agricultural interests, similarly, labor support is no longer necessary. Business no longer contests the system created in the 1930s. Instead, business now is willing to compete with labor in buying agrarian support with all sorts of subsidies. If it allies itself with business, agriculture can get these subsidies without having to pay for subsidies for labor. In the thirties, agriculture provided the fight against the classical approach not only with numbers but also with legitimacy: farmers are property owners. Without the farmers, labor has to fight against the core principles of the capitalist economy from its weakest ground, the claims of wage earners. Farmer support in the 1930s provided a populist base, not a socialist one. Today, as it was in the first crisis, the populist sensibility is quite antilabor.

Without these allies, labor has become defensive. Its policy approach seeks to defend existing positions in wages, social services, and jobs. But labor has difficulty in formulating a vision of how best to modernize a national economy in the face of new international economic conditions so as to allow it to mobilize broader support while retaining its own internal solidarity.

All social categories face the same general problem in devising political strategies—each has to balance the task of managing the economy as a whole against the task of asserting the particularities of its own situation. When business solidarity fragments under such conditions, as happened in the 1930s and 1940s, labor, agriculture, and other social fragments are able to play a considerable role in shaping policy. In the 1970s and 1980s, however, business strategies have converged on a neoclassical revival, and it is labor that has fragmented. This is likely to remain the case until policy problems in the international economy draw out intra- and interbusiness conflicts.

These changes in political relationships operate to constrain governments and to limit policy experimentation. The French Socialists under Mitterrand shifted away from nationalization, equalization, and fiscal stimulus, and toward austerity in state spending and the importance of market cues. These same pressures have constrained the Swedish Socialists and have contributed to fragmentation in the British Labour party, the Democratic party in the United States, and West Germany's SPD. At the same time the realities of contemporary electoral politics set limits to the application of market principles. Ronald Reagan and Margaret Thatcher have both drawn back from cutting the welfare state below levels that are considerably higher than prewar norms. Both countries continue to use considerable government intervention in the economy, albeit in untraditional forms.

Policy has fluctuated between the neoclassical revival on one side and market regulation and social welfare on the other. Between those two extremes there exists a considerable range in country responses. Sweden, though accepting the cues of the international market, intervenes far more than the United States does in labor markets and industrial restructuring, and it uses mechanisms of consultation to help along the process of adjustment. The West European systems of social services and labor-market restrictions remain far more highly developed than those in America. France uses industrial policy far more than the United States and the United Kingdom. The United States under Reagan has used far more than the Europeans the fiscal stimulus of massive deficits and the industrial policy of military procurement.

These differences can be partially understood in terms of the different relationships among societal actors country by country. By a number of measures the Swedish labor movement is far more powerful than its American counterpart. American financial, trading, and manufacturing groups, with the world's largest economy and the world's reserve currency, have resources and face incentives that differ from those of most of their European counterparts.

But we cannot understand the different relationships among societal actors without examining the organizations that represent these societal actors, the state structures, and the ideology. The strength of Swedish labor is intimately linked to its organizational forms, in particular the centralization of the Swedish trade-union organization and its links to the Swedish Social Democrats; participating in the government provides resources and incentives that then, in an interactive process, reinforce governing. In France the importance of nationalization as a policy option is linked to the position of the Communist and Socialist parties and trade-union movements; the absence of such parties and movements contributes to a different definition of alternatives in the United States. Thus the forms and the ideologies of the organizations themselves shape the ways in which societal actors choose options.

The strategies of societal actors are also shaped by the institutional frameworks created out of the second crisis. The five countries examined here differ considerably in the pattern of corporatist linkages which they developed to manage relationships among functional groups. Sweden may be less corporatist than Austria, but it is considerably more so than the United States. And the five countries differ considerably in the powers and mechanisms of intervention available to the state: France and the United States are the two extremes. The mere existence of these mechanisms does not serve to explain their use, of course, but it does affect the politics of policy alternatives involving their use.

In all three crises the military rivalries among states played a role in economic policy debates. In every case considerable increases in military spending accompanied certain policy approaches. And each time there has been a linkage between the advocacy of military spending and the advocacy of conservative political goals at home. The international system thus contributes to domestic debates about policy and politics. Rarely, however, has it been able by itself to explain the victory of one perspective or another.

CONCLUSION

Over the course of three crises in the international economy one can observe relationships changing among societal actors within countries and among the factors that shape economic policy. Societal actors divide and combine over time in ways that relate to their changing situations in the international division of labor. Critical realignments occur during crises, not only in the electoral arena but in the terms of trade among various economic actors.

In the first crisis, three types of coalition developed: an anti-corn-law pattern, typified by the United Kingdom, in which productive forces from industry, finance, agriculture, and labor sustained a policy of liberal adaptation to the international economy; the iron-rye pattern, exemplified by Germany, in which elements of industry and agriculture combined to interpose a stratum of protection against the international economy; and the antipopulist coalition, exemplified by the United States, in which industry and labor combined against commodity agriculture and traders.

In the second crisis, realignments took place. The social democratic pattern brought together labor, agriculture, and elements of business around the constitutionalist historic compromise through policies of demand management, welfare, and stabilization. The fascist pattern, by contrast, involved a different mixture of mass support, agriculture, and business which excluded organized labor and led to a savagely repressive regime. In its early days, nonetheless, the fascist variant pioneered policies that would spread to other countries after the war. Military intervention eventually destroyed the fascist pattern, opening the way to the spread of the social democratic model.

In the third crisis, tension has grown between the partners of the historic compromise. Business groups have drawn together in opposition to labor costs and extensive services, social agriculture finds little need for labor support, and pressure has built up to curtail state spending and interventions. Whatever the differences in partisan outcomes, all governments have been pressed in the same general direction. The differences in policy response have been strongly affected by differences in the mediating institutions, through which societal actors mobilize and apply power.

The descriptive element of these trajectories can be charted by following these relationships over time. More difficult is judging among alternative explanations of why these bargains occurred rather than some others and of the status of various factors in explaining the different bargains. Through all three periods, it appears, we must have some understanding of the impact that international and domestic economic situations have upon groups and their policy preferences. This need is surely constant. At the same time the relationship of economic situation to mediating institutions and ideologies does not appear constant. In the late nineteenth century parties and interest groups were relatively unformed. They congealed

33

around that crisis, and they became forever after part of what societal actors had to pass through. The second crisis both challenged these structures and considerably expanded them. State and society penetrated each other in exceedingly complex ways, making it difficult to judge how each shaped policy. When the third crisis began, the arrangements brought about during the second were in place to influence policy conflicts. Because these arrangements differed considerably across countries, however, their impact on politics varies as well. The relationship among causal factors thus varies across countries and within time periods.

The historically careful appreciation of contingency and balance specific to each case thus conflicts to some extent with the search for generalizations. Nonetheless, with careful pairings or triangulations of cases it is possible to explore some of the strengths and difficulties of the various analytical approaches. One can find limiting examples, comparisons that bring out a linkage, others that point another way. And so the tension between parsimony and elegance on the one side, accuracy on the other, remains powerful.

My epistemological claims, I stress, are limited. I have a healthy appreciation of the contingent. My mode of presentation, therefore, is the theoretically guided historical account. Systematic accounts of policy debates and choices allow the presentation of a story in such a way that the informed reader can evaluate the understandings of reality that lie behind broader generalizations.

I prefer to study crises rather than stable periods because I am interested more in comprehending the open moments when system-creating choices are made than in unraveling the internal workings of systems themselves. This book is intended to help us understand the range of choices, present and past, from which new systems emerge.

CHAPTER TWO

Explaining Policy Choices

In each crisis countries "choose" a policy or a sequence of policies. This is an anthropomorphic way to put it. The notion of choice implies consciousness, and the notion of policy implies coherence. Frequently in decision making we find neither consciousness nor coherence, though for the purpose of analysis we must use both notions. To compare what countries do, to find similarities or differences in their behavior, we need two sorts of frameworks: a typology of policy alternatives, and a set of explanations for interpreting choice among policy alternatives. These are constructs that we, the observers, impose. Policy options are generally messy, with fuzzy boundaries, and the same is true of explanatory modes. Only when options and explanations are made orderly can we chart disorderly reality, describe what happened, and then attempt to interpret it.

DEFINING POLICY OPTIONS

The goal of this book is to examine how and why countries chose particular policies in response to major disruptions of the international economy. Policy options must be defined, therefore, in ways that encourage comparisons across countries and across time periods. In looking at several countries, we need to conceive of the policy options in a general manner, as a set of possibilities from which any country might choose. In looking at several time periods, we need to pose the policy options in ways that make them, at least analytically, options for any of the periods. So we cannot define the policies in specific periods contextually, as orthodoxy versus radicalism, because the meaning of these descriptive labels may change from one period

35

to another: the radicalism of demand stimulus in the thirties, for instance, may become the orthodoxy of the eighties, when radicalism may come to mean the free-market ideas of the era preceding 1929.

Finally, we need to recognize that comparison requires some clear sense of the object to be compared, the outcome or the endpoint or what positivistic discourse would call the dependent variable. Without at least a rough sense of the object of comparison, we will find it impossible to engage in debate over explanations of policy choices. It is necessary therefore to simplify—brutally, deliberately, and at the cost of distortion.

There are two ways of constructing a typology of policy alternatives so as to meet the needs of comparison: deduction and induction. The deductive approach derives from economic theory a tightly formulated set of alternatives. This is the ideal method: theory permits precision in the determination of categories and their boundaries. Unfortunately, the deductive approach generates too many possibilities. Economic policy has many dimensions (fiscal, monetary, commercial, industrial, and labor are only the most obvious), and within each a number of alternative positions can be taken. These elements can be combined in so many ways as to make impossible any meaningful comparisons.

The number of combinations can be reduced to some degree by identifying theoretical contradictions: a free-trade commercial policy conflicts with intense government planning and nationalization in industrial policy; an encouragement of investment through low taxes conflicts with a need for high taxes to finance social insurance programs. But the conceptual limits are rather less strict than one might imagine—in Western Europe, for instance, free-trade countries in recent times also practice high degrees of corporatistic management of employment, investment, pricing, and marketing, and the private economies of some small democracies there also have very high taxes for welfare.

Defining policy packages by deduction (the logical combination of policy alternatives) thus will not work for our purposes here. We need to supplement deduction by induction, by looking at actual debates to find the limited number of combinations around which activity focuses. The clustering of options into policy packages, we find, derives from political circumstances. From the historical record, we can identify policy packages of a general sort which appear to form the focuses of political and intellectual debate. Countries, again speaking anthropomorphically, have usually argued about a specific set of policy responses to sharp changes in the international economy. Within

each of these options are many nuances of detail, and the broadness
of the following categories does not capture them—nor will the explanations pursued necessarily do well in explaining variance within the
categories. Nonetheless, the important policy packages have been
rather limited in number, both across countries and across time periods. There have been few identifiable schools, few lines of reasoning,
few interpretations of what is wrong and what is to be done. Relative
strength may rise and fall across countries and time periods, but the
options themselves have some uniformity.

We may identify five major policy alternatives: liberalism or neoclassicism, socialization of ownership and planning, protectionism,
demand stimulus, and mercantilism. Each is a general approach to
the problems of political economy, dealing with a large range of questions under a diverse set of circumstances. Our interest here is with
the policy prescriptions with which these approaches respond to a
severe disruption in the international economy—what to do when
profits fall and international competition becomes especially severe,
how to allocate resources to cope with severe shifts in the international division of labor. For some approaches, the formula for bad
times follows the same logic as that for good times. For others, the two
circumstances are quite different.

Option I: Classical Liberalism or the "Neoclassical Option"

Classical liberalism holds that the untrammeled free market—decentralized decision making in response to the incentive for private
gain—yields the greatest output and hence the greatest total wealth.
Because the greatest efficiency comes from private calculations, the
task of the government is to leave the market alone. The government
provides, at most, some services that are necessary for the market to
function properly but are in no one's private interest to supply. Defense, security, education, infrastructure, indeed a rather extensive
array of government services can plausibly be claimed as necessary for
the market, but by and large those who use the language of Adam
Smith seek instead to curtail the role of government action.[1]

In good times or bad the neoclassical solution to international distress is to allow the market to reallocate resources, and to allow it to do
so cheerfully. While the market destroys, it also creates. It knocks out
the inefficient but rewards the competitive. The revolutions in technology which drop prices, wipe out production lines, reorganize the
structure and the location of production—these are positive contribu-
tions to the creation of wealth. They are changes that contribute to

increased productivity, which means more output per unit of input, and hence more for everybody. The manufacture of buggies collapses because the manufacture of automobiles increases; slide rules give way to pocket computers, dial watches to digital ones, and so on. The decline of one use of resources happens because another one grows. A contraction of employment here leads to an increase in employment there.

Any effort to interfere with this process restricts the capacity of wealth, defined as the aggregate output of goods and services, to grow. If one protects the manufacture of phaetons and landaus, then one locks up resources, raising the cost of those resources to other uses that would produce more and absorbing a larger share of consumer purchasing power which could otherwise go to other goods.

The story is easily told for new products. For existing ones made by the same technology, the logic is the same: the shift in the geography of production from high-cost to low-cost areas. High-cost areas may feel a loss of jobs, say of shoes and clothing from New England to the South, but New England will be better off if it can shift its productive resources into products that the South still needs, such as education, computers, and research. Letting the South manufacture some products raises its income, so that it can indeed purchase goods and services in which New England remains competitive.

The rise and diffusion of a product follows a pattern modeled as the product cycle. A product is developed in a particular place that has the complex skills and markets to sustain it. Dominating the technology, manufacturers capture the market in their home country, then begin to export. Next the originating manufacturers begin to locate production in other countries, providing local substitutes for imports from their own core plants; other companies in other countries may also take up manufacturing. As the technology becomes standardized, requiring lesser skills, so it becomes easier to copy and diffuse. Production spreads widely, and the originating country ceases to be the cheapest producer.[2] Technological improvements may recapture the product, or the originating country withdraws from production, leaving the product to the developing countries and shifting resources into new products.

This is the concept of comparative advantage: everyone benefits from specialization. The classical formulation took two countries, A and B, and two products, wheat and wine. Country A may be more efficient than country B in producing both, but it will still be more productive with one than the other. The welfare of both countries would therefore be maximized if A agreed to specialize in one product and import some of the other from B. It is to the advantage of prosperous, technologically advanced countries to import products from less developed countries: buying goods from abroad puts money in the pockets of foreigners, who are then able to buy more domestic goods. The exclusion of imports deprives domestic exporters of potential markets and reduces the total output of the nation. To interfere with international specialization is thus to lose optimality.

This concept was developed by the British during the first part of the nineteenth century, when the United Kingdom was the world's dominant industrial economy. It has come to be used as a theoretical standard for all countries: developed and developing countries (and all the different kinds of each), agrarian and industrial, first-generation industrial and third-, fourth-, or n-generation, large and small.

It is also a standard used for all situations, good times and bad. The problem to be solved, it will be recalled, is how to absorb factors of production which have been dislocated by competition. In good times the message is clear: in a growing economy the expanding production of goods and services offered by efficient, competitive producers will absorb unemployed resources. Workers and capitalists can both find new employment because expansion creates demand for their resources. Ceding the production of some goods to foreigners (shoes, clothes, even cars and radios) helps promote the happy cycle, sending ways to generate revenue to those who are thereby enabled to buy more advanced products in which they have no particular advantage. Under these conditions the unemployment caused by foreign competition should be not feared and resisted but applauded and accepted as part of the intensification of the international division of labor, which, like all specialization, increases wealth.

What should be done, according to this model of political economy, in bad times? The classical answer is to let the market do its work, to let competition force readjustment even at the cost of unemployment and business failures. Bad times are part of the process that produces good times. From fruit trees, next year's crop can be increased by skillful pruning this year, and so too from the economy. In good times money and labor are drawn into creating a capacity for production which eventually outstrips demand, but in the meantime the inefficient are rewarded along with the strong. Business cycles knock out the weak and force factor prices back down.

Unemployment caused by shifts in the international division of labor is to the classicists no different from that of business-cycle shifts:

if another country or region can produce goods more cheaply, it can do so because its factor prices are lower, which means that the first country's prices have gone too high. Wage earners and the owners of capital in the first country are expecting too much: if they wish to regain markets, their prices have to come down.

The classical school thus has a policy prescription for a depression: *deflation,* helping the market force down factor prices. In periods of unemployment government should cut spending and cut taxes. It should balance the budget, and at the lowest possible level, to cut costs to business, because when business has fewer taxes to pay, it can allow prices to fall. Resources flow into private hands, and private actors can then respond to the incentives of lower factor costs. The pressure of unemployment will force wages to respond to market forces, and wages will go down. Prices fall to the point where the demand, by investors as well as by consumers, is revived, and the economy starts up again out of its downward spiral.

In commercial policy there can be no question of protectionism, for protection would interfere with the ability of international market forces to increase world efficiency. Currency values, however, must be preserved. For exchange rates, there can be no pure market, because a pure market would eliminate the discipline that avoids inflation. Government must intervene to sustain a fixed parity with gold or other currencies, guaranteeing the predictability of values needed to sustain international trade. With this single exception, interference with market forces, such as industrial policy or socialization, is of course excluded.

This policy stance is *procyclical.* It requires that government move with the business cycle, not against it, and that the disciplinary effects of falling demand be encouraged, not resisted. It admits of no government effort to provide compensation or to smoothe out the extremes of the downturn. Any such effort, it is presumed, will eventually have to be paid for, because it hinders efficiency. Surely deflation exacts costs, in unemployment and forgone profit, but these costs are necessary because the alternatives would cost more. Any reallocation of resources necessarily imposes costs, but it is the market that provides the best cues.

The interaction of many private, self-regarding actions thus produces a collective benefit greater than any that may be fashioned out of efforts to interfere with the market. To allow the market to regulate itself, to avoid using public policy to bring about alternative outcomes, such is the essence of the classical option.

Option II: Socialization and Planning

The classical socialist alternative to the classical liberal position proposes to replace private control of investment by public control and to replace the market by planning. The socialists reject classical liberalism on two grounds, its cost in noneconomic values and its suboptimal economic outcomes.

Capitalism is costly in social terms, the socialists argue, because it rewards only what is profitable to the investor. Other values, including community stability, family, solidarity of work and social relationships, aesthetic goals—a cluster of values that may be summarized as "organic"—are shunted to one side. Capitalism transforms human labor into a commodity. It treats each individual as an object whose social situation depends entirely on whatever he or she is able to sell in the labor market. Individuals must accept whatever wages the market offers for their skills, however weak the demand, however low the sum.

The second line of the socialist critique of capitalism turns against classical liberalism its own prime criterion, that of efficiency. The market, the socialists argue, is wasteful. The sum of particular, private decisions is a range of collective irrationalities: overinvestment chasing the lure of the big financial kill, financial manipulation, advertising. The logic of uncapped rewards to investors produces waste, in luxury goods, in pollution, in waste of natural resources. The privatization of profits goes hand in hand with the socialization of costs; so taxpayers pay for education, roads, and research, while investors get the profits from inventions produced and marketed by their companies. It is difficult to get done those things (health and education services, for instance) which all actors require for the system to work but which are not profitable for any one of them.

The socialist solution to the ills of waste and the damage caused to organic values is nationalization and planning. Nationalization gives the state power; the plan tells it what to do. If the state tries to plan without nationalization, it leaves private investors free to make other decisions. Nationalization without the plan, conversely, may lead to a different version of the market, one where only the identity of the shareholders has changed. In practice, socialized industries can be forced to operate under market conditions, and privately held companies can be forced to operate in a highly planned environment. These are relatively recent nuances, however, for historically planning and nationalization have gone hand in hand, paired features of a thorough rejection of the application of market principles to society, collective decisions, and the operation of the political economy.[3]

Socialism, like capitalism, has changed considerably in the postwar era. The power of the Bolshevik model—centralization in the economic sphere, authoritarianism in the political sphere—has weakened greatly among the socialist parties of Europe. To many socialists now, nationalization and the plan are no longer enough, nor, indeed, are they necessarily primary concerns any more. These democratic socialist reformers argue for democratization in both the economy and politics. In the economy they support industrial democracy, the active participation of workers in the governance of factory and firm combined with decentralization of decision making. In politics these reformers believe in constitutionalist political forms.

What unites the supporters of the socialist option is criticism of the unrestrained free market. Compared to other advocates of government intervention, the socialists support a greater degree of public ownership (especially of the "commanding heights" of the economy) and of centralized planning. Although the market has important functions, it should operate, the socialists believe, within redefined patterns of power and incentives.

Classical Liberalism vs. Socialization and Planning

Nationalization and planning have been socialist orthodoxy and an exact mirror of bourgeois orthodoxy since the last third of the nineteenth century. Where the latter urges that all social arrangements follow the logic of the market conceived as private accumulation, rewarding the decisions of private investors, the former wants to subordinate the market to objectives determined by constitutionally elected governments and, for one branch of socialists, workers' councils.

Each orthodoxy rejects the other, and each economic analysis (and, as we shall see, its political ramifications) requires sacrifices from the other. Both analyses are, in this respect, zero-sum. In times of crisis the bourgeois orthodoxy of deflation insists that the high wages and welfare benefits of the working class threaten profits. Owners of capital are discouraged from investing or even producing because wages and taxes eat up profits and prevent national production from competing with foreign goods. Wages and taxes must therefore be cut. Conversely, the socialist orthodoxy calls for the elimination of the owners of capital. If capitalists are unwilling to raise employment, or keep investment at home, or produce socially useful products, they must be replaced by decision makers who will.

Each position has political implications. In extreme cases, to attain the desired economic objective, it may be necessary to destroy the constitutional system. The deflationists may be tempted to try authoritarian government as a way of destroying labor's ability to resist wage cuts through strikes and its ability to resist reductions in welfare benefits through the ballot box. Conversely, the socializers may seek authoritarian government as a way of breaking private capital's hold on the economy (in particular, its ability to engage in a "capital strike") and of forestalling political moves by capital against labor organizations.

Economic ideologies, in short, carry with them considerable political meaning. They frame the sketch map of political objectives and requirements, of political friends and enemies, of political alliances and coalitions. As we shall see, political goals produce a need for economic ideas that induce coalitions to form in support of them, while economic ideas generate a need for political ideas to produce support. The two may, of course, be in tension.

The two economic orthodoxies of political economy which emerged in the nineteenth century polarized intellectual, political, and social relationships. Proponents of both argued that their view was not group-specific, that society as a whole would be better off if their view prevailed. But both perceived the economy in class terms—the socialists explicitly, the bourgeois theorists de facto. Capitalists and workers formed the group basis of the economy, and investing and selling labor power were the economy's key functions. It was not easy in the nineteenth century, nor is it easy in the twentieth century, for either group to mobilize mass support in a democracy around a pure version of its approach.

Other conceptions of policy posed the economic problem differently and thereby changed quite drastically the political implications of policy solutions. These other views called for "mixed games" instead of games that were zero-sum in relation to class; instead of pitting workers against capitalist, they allowed for compromises and conflicts across the boundaries of class.

Option III: Protectionism

Although liberalism came to embody the essence of nineteenth-century capitalist thinking, it was by no means able to preclude the development of other ideas, and even when intellectually hegemonic, it could not prevent the political triumph of other policies. Protectionism was an older idea, one that had preceded the liberalism developed by Adam Smith and the utilitarians. It had been policy every-where until the middle of the nineteenth century, when first Britain and then other countries adopted free trade. When the international economy turned sour, in the last third of the century, nearly every-body abandoned free trade; of the large countries, only Britain ad-hered to free-trade principles, along with a handful of smaller pro-ducers such as Denmark. Most nations experienced a revival of economic nationalism that led to the erection of rather high national tariff barriers. So prevalent was protectionism, so willing were the staunch supporters of capitalism to adopt it, that we may call it neo-orthodoxy—the orthodox deviation from free-market orthodoxy which is permitted in times of severe distress.

Protectionism operates most obviously through tariffs, though in the twentieth century countries have been ingenious in finding non-tariff forms of protection as well. Tariffs raise the price of foreign goods in relation to domestic ones. For some domestic manufacturers, those which are high-cost producers in relation to international com-petition, the tariff prevents bankruptcy. For others, even highly effi-cient and internationally competitive manufacturers, the tariff pro-vides the stability of a larger, more assured domestic market against which the amortization of extremely expensive investment can be planned.[4]

The boundary between tariffs and other forms of aid is often un-clear. Tariffs and quotas both raise the price of foreign goods; so does devaluation of the currency, but it is not usually analyzed as a form of protection. In the thirties, for example, John Maynard Keynes ar-gued that governments could choose one of three options—devalua-tion, protection, and demand stimulus—and *each one* would have much the same effects. The same is also true, we might add, of vari-ous forms of mercantilism, among them overt subsidies, marketing arrangements, regulation, sponsored research programs, and the building of new infrastructure.[5]

Devaluation was a heresy to the classical liberals, as bad as tariffs if not worse. The market could not operate well, the marketeers ar-gued, without a strong confidence on the part of investors in the stability of economic values (profits and costs). Because these rela-tionships are measured through an exchange medium, that medium must above all else be maintained at a fixed parity. This argument speaks against inflation at home, just as it opposes any cheapening of money in the international sphere, where the greater uncertainties of trade require a greater stability of currency values.

Protectionists need not necessarily be advocates of devaluation or of fixed exchange rates. Examples can be found in the case studies that follow of protectionists who supported devaluation and those who opposed it. Devaluation is nonetheless a break with orthodox market doctrine, a type of intervention which arises alongside of tariff protection, and for that reason I have placed it within this typology of policy alternatives.

Another boundary problem in defining these alternatives arises with cartelization. Tariffs and devaluation both provide shields against unstable prices and foreign competition. Cartels provide another, as producers combine to fix prices, share out production by allotting quotas to each company, coordinate sales by means of marketing boards, and make other, similar arrangements, either by direct collaboration among producers or through the medium of government sponsorship. The latter has the disadvantage of allowing government intrusion but the large advantage of providing the authority of the state to enforce rules against those who are tempted to break the agreement (the constant problem of cartels). Mild forms of private cartelization and loosely corporatistic government arrangements may be seen as an extension of the logic of protectionism to the domestic market. More intense versions involve something else—mercantilism, or industrial policy, or corporatism, addressed below.

Protectionism, like any economic policy, gets its justification partly out of formal intellectual arguments, partly out of particularistic self-advantage. Advocacy of the latter often fuels the creative imagination, leading to the articulation of the former. Those who are threatened by foreign competition, for instance, argue that without protection they will be ruined, and often that argument is sufficient—avoiding the ruin of business is widely seen as a legitimate end of government, requiring no further apologia. If this defense is challenged—as it is likely to be by those who are threatened by economic barriers—then other arguments will be necessary.

These come in two main varieties: arguments that work within the framework of economic efficiency, and those which turn to other values. Market theorists have always accepted that some conditions can justify protection. One obvious instance is the situation of infant industries—companies that are just opening their doors and launching the domestic production of certain goods. Start-up costs may create some period of time during which such firms cannot be competitive with older foreign producers, but after that period ends they will indeed be free-standing enterprises, needing assistance no longer. The wider policy implication of this line of reasoning is that selective protectionism may be legitimate if it is for specific products and for limited periods of time.

This line of reasoning has been expanded into a general argument about the special situation of whole countries that are seeking to industrialize in an environment where more advanced economies are already operating. Classical market theorists argue that specialization allows any country to develop its economy fully. Theorists of what was called nationalist economics in the nineteenth century and dependencia in the twentieth argue instead that the environment of the international economic system in which newly industrializing countries operate differs so profoundly from that of the earlier industrializers as to change drastically the character of development. If the newcomers throw themselves open to the world market, they run the risk of their development pattern becoming badly skewed. They may finish by exporting raw or basic materials and importing finished goods without their ever developing the capability to sustain industrial growth.[6]

Several policies may be derived from such reasoning, one of which is protectionism. For the newcomer to advance broadly, in a diversified manner, toward "self-sustained" growth, it needs some period of general autonomy from international market forces. Broad tariffs across a wide range of goods help by promoting the development of a dense network of forward and backward linkages within the national economy. After some considerable period of time the economy may develop the internal strength necessary to compete in a more open world market.

An extension of this argument focuses more explicitly on values other than those of economic efficiency: national strength, national power, national security. Because military strength is related to economic strength, the national economy must provide those capabilities which military strength needs, even at some cost to economic efficiency. In the late nineteenth century it was clear that military power required a great iron- and steel-making capacity, able to build weapons, railroads, and navies. Countries had to have this capacity even if foreign iron and steel were cheaper and could be delivered faster than the domestic market could provide them (whence stemmed the mercantilist justification of a state role even more active than sheer protectionism). More generally, imports might become difficult in times of war, and military planning therefore required advance consideration of which products should receive state policy directives in order to guarantee self-sufficiency for the nation.[7]

Military arguments were also made in support of agricultural protectionism. Food in wartime would surely be one of the most vital products in which to be self-sufficient. To many, moreover, and particularly to political conservatives, peasants and agricultural laborers made better soldiers—more suited to obedience and discipline, less ridden by disease and malnourishment, and radical political ideas, than their urban, industrial brethren. Agriculture could also draw strongly upon nationalist sentiment that defined the collective identity in attachment to the soil, to a specific, traditional, pastoral way of life.

One important characteristic of protectionism, vital to our understanding of the politics surrounding it, is that protectionism keeps the state's involvement in the economy at a distance: although the purity of the market has given way to government interference, that interference still works directly through the marketplace. Government action changes the structure of incentives through action on prices, but the state does not seek to change the way that economic actors respond to incentives. And though the market is affected by tariffs and devaluation, the government itself adheres to the traditional standards of household management: a balanced budget, a limited state, and restricted powers.

The relationship of protectionism to classical liberalism as a policy alternative is thus double-edged. Of the various policy alternatives available, protectionism is the most legitimate, the most orthodox in relation to the capitalist ideal. Though it deviates from that ideal, it does so less than other possibilities do. It can be understood as a second-best option, one for which a logic and theoretical underpinnings can be elaborated, without too much difficulty, inside the framework of capitalist economics. At the same time, of course, it does interfere with the market, and hence with the centerpiece of capitalist thinking. And the political-emotional charge of orthodoxy has been very intense, particularly, as we shall see, in the interwar period. Deviation from the ideal was understandable but a sign of weakness, of underdevelopment, of lack of maturity—it was something that only banana republics and emerging economies did.

The second interesting political element of protectionism is that it avoids a zero-sum political game with respect to the class divisions of society. In economic terms it pits domestically oriented producers against internationally oriented ones, and this is by no means a cleavage that brings capitalists and workers to confront each other. Rather, it joins the two groups together in conflict against another cross-class coalition. As an argument with a noneconomic base, moreover, protectionism is also able to appeal to ideals and emotions such as nationalism and national defense, which cut across class and other economic cleavages. Protectionism is not unique in this respect, but as an argument it combines the smallest deviation from capitalist orthodoxy with a substantial degree of collective, nationalist appeal. It is an argument that can be taken up by people at different points on the political spectrum, and it can be advanced in many different political contexts.

Option IV: Demand Stimulus

The fourth policy package, demand stimulus, is the most recent to have been theoretically elaborated, as it was worked out in the 1930s.[8] After World War II demand stimulus became so prevalent that it replaced classical market doctrines as the reigning orthodoxy of political economy among political decision makers, though perhaps not among managers and owners in the private sector. This political prevalence is what made demand stimulus vulnerable to the various economic shocks of the seventies and eighties; the doctrine now is paying the price of incumbency, being blamed for whatever goes wrong.

Demand stimulus consists of deficit spending by the government in order to prime the pump of a stagnating economy. Keynes's theoretical formulation stressed the insufficiency of the attention that market orthodoxy paid to the problem of demand. Keynes argued that equilibrium could be reached at a point considerably below the full employment of resources. In a deep business-cycle downturn, unused capacity grows. New investment is discouraged no matter how cheap money becomes (that is, no matter how far interest rates fall), because there is little point in building new capacity when so much old capacity is still available. The problem is thus not too little capital, as the classical school argues, but too much capital and too little demand. Keynes saw savings as plentiful, not scarce. The dearth was on the demand side: those who were willing to buy goods had no money. In this liquidity trap the economy could stagnate for many years. In the long run, as the classicists said, the economy would right itself, but, as Keynes's celebrated riposte noted, "In the long run we are all dead."

The proper response to severe stagnation was to reflate the economy by means of government deficits. Spending in excess of receipts would pour currency into the economy, increasing the demand for goods. Through a multiplier effect this spending would work its way through the economy, raising the overall level of demand, thereby triggering a beneficial, upward spiral of demand, leading to sales, leading to profits, leading to new incentives to invest. If this increased government debt, then so be it: the critical indicator was not a fixed policy norm but wealth, wealth defined as growth of gross national product (GNP), fall in unemployment, greater use of resources. Keynes "desanctified" policy instruments, turning them back into mere instruments again, into tools to be used to achieve economic goals rather than ends in themselves. Against the charge that their tactics would cause inflation, the demand stimulus theorists stressed the tremendous underuse of capacity in the economy. Not until full employment arrived would government budget deficits cause inflation or bottlenecks in production.

In some versions of demand stimulus, such as the ideas developed in Sweden during the 1920s, the notion of budget balancing was retained as a virtue but was "stretched out"—budgets were to be balanced over a longer period of time, in essence the rise and fall of the business cycle. In prosperous periods the government would run a surplus, building up reserves; in the downswing those reserves would be tapped for public works, thereby combining the production of useful public goods with the stimulus of deficit financing. Over the whole cycle the budget would be in balance. In practice, however, hardly any governments build a surplus during the good times.

Demand stimulus in the postwar era has been associated with the name of Keynes, but it has a healthy range of forebears; indeed, it was tried as public policy before Keynes published his famous theoretical elaboration, *The General Theory*, in 1936. A number of intellectual and popular traditions in Europe included notions of "underconsumption," an idea that stressed the maldistribution of income. Concentration of wealth left the mass of population unable to buy the output that modern production techniques made possible. Tremendous poverty limited consumption to basics (food, clothing, and housing). No income was left for products of higher quality, for newer products, or for the range of consumption goods that the factories of the industrial world were pouring onto national and international markets. Poverty was thus a limit on profits. If the poor could not buy, they would not stimulate the flow of profits leading to the incentive to invest, leading to employment, leading to the ability to buy goods which contributed further to the happy spiral. Some observers, John Hobson notable among them, believed that this tension led to imperialism, as the capitalists sought profits abroad instead of granting the higher mass purchasing power that would develop growth at home.[9]

Other ideas supported not only the redistribution of income but the notion of government spending to promote employment, public goods, and the general welfare. On the side of conservatives, European countries had long traditions of *noblesse oblige*, of elite responsibility for the welfare of the community, even its least important members. Bismarck and Disraeli represent two politically different versions of this notion, and their counterparts can be found in a wide range of doctrines and political contexts. On the side of radicals and liberals were other traditions that proclaimed the equality of all believers, the democracy of the primal community, the rights of the individual, the nobility of the worker, the claims of class and group. Public spending for socially useful projects, which also helped generate employment, has existed since the beginning of recorded history.

Like other policy packages, demand stimulus comes in many versions. Spending can go in quite different directions, to military or consumer goods, to government purchases or transfer payments. And budget deficits can be more or less intentional, more or less managed.

In contrast with both orthodoxies, classical liberalism and classical socialism, but similar to protectionism and mercantilism, demand stimulus has the capability to slice across class boundaries. It defines a collective game between labor and capital. Like all the options except mercantilism, it shies away from microeconomic issues. It does not call for interference with or even consideration of the internal organization of firms, markets, or industries. Demand stimulus at its core is a broad policy instrument, focusing attention on levels of aggregate demand.

Option V: Mercantilism

"Mercantilism," as I use it here, means state action in aid of specific industries or even specific firms.[10] Such action can take various forms: subsidies for individual firms, legal regulation of markets (through production quotas, price fixing, manufacturing standards, price supports, or marketing boards), reorganization of companies or industries, regulatory agencies for companies or industries, credit allocation, foreign marketing arrangements, and government purchases. Unlike other policy options, mercantilism can intervene at the microeconomic level, the level of the specific firm. The other policies operate at the level of the market; mercantilist policy, by contrast, concerns itself with problems of organization and of industrial structure.

Mercantilism is an old label with a historically specific meaning that is more restrictive than its usage here. In the seventeenth century it was linked to a bullion view of wealth. There was a fixed amount of wealth in the world, the argument went, states sought to get as much of that wealth as they could, and active state policy to create productive capacity as well as military capability was the best way to do so. Mercantilism thus predates laissez-faire capitalism as a theory of political economy. Indeed, it was mercantilism against which the theorists of the market economy, Adam Smith among them, railed in the eighteenth and nineteenth centuries; it provided the focal point for their arguments against the costs to optimality of the favoritism, corruption, and mistaken self-confidence to which they thought mercantilism inevitably led.

Despite their criticism, however, the policy has never disappeared. It began in association with luxury goods such as Dresden china, French tapestries, silks, and other textiles, and with military goods such as firearms, cannon, uniforms, and other war-related products. It continued through the nineteenth century as a way of doing important things quickly. British and some French railways may have been built privately, but most Continental railroad construction resulted from an act of state, either indirectly through financing or directly through government-owned companies. Military production has generally taken this form everywhere.

In the twentieth century mercantilism has taken other forms and other labels. Wartime production boards sprang up everywhere during both world wars. In the interwar period many countries tried a sort of mercantilist corporatism; the American National Recovery Administration, for example, sought to fix prices, standards, and production quotas, and industries have been regulated everywhere. Since 1945 the government's policies toward the condition of specific industries have increasingly come to be called *industrial policy*. The French distinguish between indicative planning, referring to informational elements, and industrial policy, referring to more explicit financial subsidies and organizational interventions. Japan has become famous for industrial policy, to which many ascribe the Japanese postwar boom. In the United States public and private officials deny that an industrial policy exists, yet to foreign and domestic observers alike it is plain to see in numerous mechanisms, from defense contracts to regulated industries, tax breaks, and research grants. It has existed since the days of public works at the beginning of the Republic, through the massive land grants to private railroad companies in the nineteenth century, to the research and defense contracts of the present day.

The concept of mercantilist policy need not be restricted to industry. In the 1930s nearly all countries adopted for agriculture such measures as price supports, production quotas, marketing boards, storage schemes, and education, training, and research programs. Some of these measures predate the 1930s (one thinks especially of land grants to agriculturally oriented universities, agricultural extension services, and health-related inspection schemes), and nearly all countries continue them down to the present. Even the budget-slashing British and U.S. governments of the 1980s have touched agriculture least of any interest.

The rationale for mercantilist policy is that the market by itself is inadequate to the economic task at hand. The reasons for this inadequacy vary. They include highly complex, expensive, perhaps unstable technology, carrying too much uncertainty about profits to support investment; a need for speed, as with defense production; structural inadequacies, where the rationality of individual gain leads to outcomes insufficient for the collectivity; and individual or cultural inadequacies, where private decision makers lack the skills or the intellectual outlook to make effective decisions.

The last point is often raised when it is argued that national capitalism is somehow defective. Entrepreneurs, the class of capitalists, may hold a set of ideas derived from earlier experiences, ideas that are no longer suited to contemporary economic needs. In France, for example, it has been argued that traditions derived from the aristocracy, the importance of land, and the mercantilism of Louis XIV and Colbert together produced an economic culture highly averse to risk, highly concerned with stability of market share and survival of the family firm, a culture in conflict with twentieth-century needs for rationalization of production and management, for the virtues of growth, for mass production on a high volume and low markup. What enabled the French economy to do so well after 1945 was the active intervention of the state in reorganizing the economic structure of several industries and replacing individuals who dominated the major economic levers of society with growth-oriented, dynamic modern managers.[11]

A recurrent theme in the justification of mercantilism is the specific problems of capitalism in different national situations. In Japan, for instance, mercantilism is seen as a response to Japan's acute backwardness at the time of its insertion into the world economy. In general, the argument holds, the later the industrialization in relation to others and the more backward the society when industrialization begins, the more inadequate are private forces or society as a whole to achieve modernization and the greater is the need for the state to play an active role. (Alexander Gerschenkron, Immanuel Wallerstein, and others have developed for us a set of propositions about this historical relationship among the timing of industrialization, the evolution of the international economy, the degree of backwardness of civil society, and the institutional and political base of the state.) Entering the game rather late, Japanese elites used the state to promote growth in ways that the market or straight protectionism could not have done. With a careful, complex policy that mixed the pressures and inducements of market forces with state planning, analysis, incentives, and penalties, Japan built up a highly diverse, advanced economy. In the twentieth century the country has come to exemplify the practice of contemporary mercantilism.[12]

Mercantilism requires very complex institutional mechanisms compared to the other policies (with the exception of the socialist alternative). The selective targeting of rewards and constraints requires an institutional machinery capable of making discriminations. If they are to reward winners and compensate losers, governments need to be able to figure out which are which. If government is to avoid conflict by organizing prior agreements, it must have the consultative mechanisms needed to do so. And if it is to enforce agreements, it must have regulatory powers. As the literature on democratic corporatism shows, the institutions devised to perform these tasks differ considerably from country to country.

In mercantilism, as in the other options, both form and substance affect the politics of policy quarrels. Policy alternatives stimulate controversy over their immediate content, that is, over who is helped or hurt. They also stimulate controversy over the effects of the mechanisms of implementation on the distribution of power in society, that is, over how they are to be carried out.

The Five Policy Options

To permit comparison across countries and across time periods, I have outlined five policy packages: (neo)classical liberalism, socialization and planning, protectionism, demand stimulus, and (neo)mercantilism. These packages differ in the policy prescriptions that they make for dealing with major stresses in the international economy, and they provide different answers to a common set of questions. What is the source of the problem, and what can be done about it? Who wins and loses from each policy, and who are thus potential allies and opponents? What institutional requirements are there for the implementation of the policy, and which patterns will thus be rewarded and which will cause controversy? These questions and themes that they raise have helped organize the case studies in subsequent chapters.

During any of the three crisis periods countries were, from an analytical point of view, free to adopt any one of these policy alternatives. As we shall see, however, countries, like individual decision makers, rarely canvassed all five possibilities at each moment of choice. Debates generally focus on two or three options in each period, although in each period all five positions had their advocates everywhere. To explain the choices that were actually made, then, we need to know something about power, about the resources available to advocates in the policy debates. The second section of this chapter examines the varying explanatory approaches available to us for exploring the linkage between policy position and power.

EXPLAINING POLICY CHOICES: SOCIAL COALITIONS, REPRESENTATION, AND THE STATE

There is a famous story about the Hawley-Smoot Tariff Act of 1930 which bears repeating. About a thousand economists, virtually the entire American community of professional economists at the time, signed a petition opposing the tariff on the grounds that it violated the principle of comparative advantage and thus hurt the general welfare. Congress ignored their advice. Hawley-Smoot raised tariffs on virtually everything manufactured within the United States, and a distinguished political scientist, E. E. Schattschneider, wrote an important book on the role of interest groups in bringing the act about.[13] Economic theories prevail, the story tells us, only when they have mobilized political authority, that is, only if those who believe the theories get the resources that enable them to take authoritative action.

To explain economic policy choices, we need to link policy outcomes to politics. Our explanatory approaches must have some way of accounting for the connection between policy and choice—between what could be done and the various factors that shape what decision makers actually choose to do. I have simplified the vast universe of theories provided by modern social science into five families of argument. The *production profile* explanation stresses the preferences of societal actors as shaped by their situation in the international economy and the domestic economy.[14] The *intermediate associations* explanation stresses the role of such organizations as political parties and interest groups in linking social preferences to state institutions.[15] The *state structure* explanation stresses the role of formal institutions, bureaucracies, and rules in mediating interests and, indeed, in defining both interests and intermediate associations.[16] The *economic ideology* explanation stresses the role of perceptions, models, and values in shaping the understandings of economic situation and political

54

circumstance which influence preferences and behavior.[17] Finally, the *international system* explanation stresses the impact of war, security issues, military procurement, and other elements of the state system in shaping economic policy.[18]

Each of these families of argument is sketched out briefly in this chapter, and together they shape the later presentation of material on the three crisis periods and structure the explanatory debate. At this point some readers may want a full elaboration of each theoretical approach. I have not provided one, however, partly because the relationships among the arguments are historically grounded and change from period to period, situation to situation; and partly because I believe that too much attention to theory before exposure to at least one case distorts the interactive way in which most people absorb and reflect on material. Thus I present a short version of the different explanatory approaches here and later probe their characteristic strengths and weaknesses in historical context.

The Production Profile Explanation

The production profile explanation concentrates on the preferences of societal actors as shaped by the actors' situation in the international and domestic economy. In an interpretation of policy making centered on interest groups, economic actors, whose preferences are shaped by their economic situation, apply pressures on governments. Desirous of a particular policy outcome, these actors form coalitions, involving bargains and tradeoffs, to mobilize the consent needed to prevail. Politicians act as the brokers of such coalitions, thereby having some impact on the shaping of the outcome. The options available to politicians turn on the pattern of social wants, and so to understand these options, it is vital to have a social "map" of the society with which politicians deal.

This mode of reasoning is a venerable tradition of political economy, and it exists in many versions. Between social pressures and policy outcomes are many steps dealing with the way these various traditions conceptualize society and the connection between societal actors and power. Where much of the literature examines pressure groups, I consider *societal actors* first and come to pressure groups after. Where much of the literature considers either very large aggregations (labor and capital) or very small ones (individuals or firms), I focus on a middling disaggregation (or aggregation), *sectors* or *branches*. Where many look at organizational forms of groups, I consider the *content* of the situation and preferences of groups. And where many look at the

55

domestic situation of economic actors, I focus on the *international* context of their situation.

When questions of public policy arise, the people affected by the decision to be made surely ask of any alternative, *Qui bono?*—Who benefits, and how will it affect my own situation? The answer to that question has a powerful effect on the policies that people prefer. What people want depends on where they sit, as theorists have argued since long before the time of Bentley and Marx.[19]

My interest here is in how countries respond to changes in the international economy. If we are looking at the policy positions that domestic actors take toward the international environment, then it makes sense for us to consider the situation of actors in that economy. Society may be disaggregated in two steps: first, between business, agriculture, and labor; and then, within each of those three broad categories, among sectors or product families (for the first two) and type of employment (for the third).[20]

For business, five main considerations appear relevant in shaping attitudes toward economic policy. The first is competitiveness in the international economy. Economic actors at the cutting edge of international competition are likely to support policies that promote open trading, not only for their own products but more generally for intensified specialization in international trade. Actors less well placed in international competition are more likely to support protection or modes of shelter or subsidy.[21] The second is vulnerability to fluctuations of demand. Economic actors exposed to wide and wild gyrations in market conditions are likely to want policies that shelter them from such swings. Companies with massive capital requirements, such as steel in the late nineteenth century, or oil in the 1930s, or mass-production industries in recent decades, may support tariffs or other government interventions that stabilize markets and allow more orderly planning of debt amortization.[22]

The third main point for business to consider is the role and character of labor needs. Industries requiring large numbers of relatively low-skilled workers will have intense conflicts with labor over wages, union rights, and social services. Industries that need fewer workers or a more diversified labor force may have an easier time accommodating labor demands.[23] The fourth point is the source of demand. The producers of mass-consumption goods have a concern for macroeconomic conditions, in their case the ability of the public to buy, quite different from that of the producers of capital goods who sell to other companies or to governments.[24] Finally, the structure of capital markets is important. Banking is an industry with its own sources of profit. Bankers' situation varies according to type: banking systems oriented toward commerce, capital flows, and reserve currency management are likely to be strongly internationalist, while industrial bankers are likely to split according to the situation of the industry to which each bank is allied.[25]

These various considerations do not necessarily converge to define a business situation in the economy: high labor costs may push one way, a desire for strong purchasing power for labor another. Other variables may have relevance; one need think only of industrial organization and marketing systems, for instance. Nor are these factors easy to operationalize. Nonetheless, to bear these considerations in mind will be of some use when we observe the preferences and political behavior of business in policy debates.

If the business category embraces manufacturing, trade, marketing, and finance, then the land embraces the rest. Like business, agriculture can be disaggregated, and two dimensions are important for our purposes. One is the market for products in terms of the buyers. A distinction can be noted between the world market for commodities (such as grains, cotton, tobacco) and more localized, urban industrial markets for high-value-added products of direct consumption (meat, dairy products, fruit, vegetables). Commodity producers conflict with the industrial economy over the terms of trade for their products; consumption producers do best as rising industrial incomes allow more people to consume more of more expensive products. The other dimension concerns the organization of production and adaptability to market changes. Between the agriculture of large estates (landowners with masses of laborers) and the agriculture of the family farm (owner-proprietors) lie many possible combinations. Some prove to be more rigid than others, less adaptable when swift changes in the international economy threaten organizational forms.[26]

The third term, labor, the sellers of labor power in the marketplace, can also be divided up. Two considerations are particularly noteworthy. The first is the scale and character of the enterprise and workplace. Those who work in large-scale, relatively standardized industries, on the one hand, and those who work in highly particularized, fragmented industries, on the other, appear to have different proclivities. Usually, the former are more likely to unionize, and as we shall see, the presence or absence of labor unions makes a considerable difference to behavior.[27] The second consideration for labor is the situation of the enterprise in the international economy. Workers employed in sectors at the cutting edge of international competition are likely to have attitudes toward policy issues different from those of employees in factories whose competitive position is deteriorating. All of the factors that influence business policy preferences are likely to affect those of labor as well.

Business, agriculture, labor—the definitions of these three elements can spread to embrace all of society. Of services, retailing, and the professions modern social theories have made much, but for our purposes, these are likely to resemble banking in that their situation is a function of how they relate to other elements of the economy. This treatment is surely unsatisfactory, but it will have to serve, because for analytical purposes, the modern economy could be disaggregated endlessly.

Our interest here is in policy preferences and political alliances. The behavior of economic actors is affected by preferences, and these in turn are affected by situation. The interaction of preferences and situation involves reciprocal effects as well as direct ones: tariffs on grains raise costs for industrial producers because they are then pressed to raise wages, which hurts the producers' competitive position. Agricultural producers buy industrial products and so prefer cheap goods, but they sell on industrial markets that need income to buy agricultural produce. Thus identically situated actors may adopt different policies depending on the preferences of other actors in the political system of which they are a part—workers in cheap-food countries and those in high-cost-food countries may think differently about tariffs.

So far, we have identified some categories of societal actors and some characteristics of their situation in the international economy which are likely to affect their policy preferences. These distinctions will allow in the historical case studies a systematic approach to sketching out the trajectories of alliance formation and the policy packages that go with them. Between sketching these trajectories and accounting for policy choices, however, quite a number of steps remain. Knowing preferences and coalitions is not the same as knowing power. Controversies turn on this point. After all, reductionism, by which I mean the reducing of politics to something else (here societal preferences), is at heart the overlooking of the question of transformation, of how preference through power becomes policy. Circularity is easy: advocates of the successful policy had the power because they won, and we know that because if they had not had the power, they would not have won.[28]

Where does power come from? In a significant way power is linked to economic situation; it *is* empirically circular. Economic situation arises from the functions that groups play in the economy. The economy operates by means of these functions—investment, management, labor, buying, professional services. Individuals and groups perform these functions, and power depends on the importance of the function to the economy and the resources that control of the function provides. Thus transportation workers and employees in power plants have far greater power over certain matters than do unskilled laborers, button makers, or dry cleaners. Control of capital, management of large corporations, practice of vital professional services such as medicine, all involve distinctive and considerable forms of power. Governments may chose a policy only to have economic actors reject it in the marketplace, thereby forcing a change in policy direction. The experience of the French Socialists, described in Chapter 5, provides one recent example of this process.

The people who actually perform each of these functions, vital to the economy, can be called societal actors.[29] I use this label in preference to the more frequent "interest group" or "class." Interest group generally refers to the associations that represent the functions (unions, business associations), but functions and institutions (or structures) are not the same. Capital, for instance, is a force independent of any association of investors; it does not take an association of investors or of speculators for capital to flee a currency when devaluation is feared. Although organization certainly does matter, it is not the same as function. Class directly expresses a type of function; the simplest formulation distinguishes between owning and managing capital on the one side, selling labor power on the other. This distinction is real but too general; there are too many conflicts among members of one side of the term, too many intraclass conflicts, for class to be analytically useful in many situations.

In sum, then, to explain a country's policy choice requires us to do some mapping of the country's production profile: the situation of the societal actors in the international economy, the actors' policy preferences, their potential bases of alliance or conflict with other forces, and the coalitions that emerge. When countries converge (or diverge) on economic policy, they are likely to do so because of the similarity (or difference) in the pattern of preferences among societal actors.

This line of reasoning has great power, because it calls our attention to an obviously important element in the political sociology of economic policy—the preferences of major societal actors in the economy itself. Yet the production profile approach also has difficulties. The danger of circularity has already been noted. The ambiguity of interests causes problems: preferences may derive from situations, but what if situations are unclear? Also troublesome are the roles of organizations (interest groups) and institutions (state structures): who or what connects preferences to actual policy outcomes, and how do these organizations and institutions mediate the process of "aggregation"? Finally, in the international sphere, alongside economic factors are political-military ones, the problems of security and rivalry. The problems of the economic interest approach thus lead to several other types of argument, which may solve many of the problems that the approach poses.

The Intermediate Associations Explanation

Functional position in society confers considerable power on societal actors, but position alone is often too blunt an instrument to achieve results. There are many other ways of shaping decisions, from influencing elections to lobbying, and these take organization. Between politicians and societal actors lies a vast network of associations designed to represent societal actors and to handle the linkages between government and society.[30] Political parties manage the presentation of choices to the electorate and the translation of those choices into policy. Interest groups manage the evaluation of options, the articulation of opinions, the mobilization of collective action, and a variety of functional tasks, some in the economy, some conferred by the state.

Such organizations have an effect upon policy which can be understood as autonomous from the individuals, groups, or forces that they represent. As Michels and other theorists have observed, parties and interest groups, in mediating the preferences of societal actors, acquire their own identity, their own existence, interests, perspectives, and concerns; they thus have their own impact on policy. Another problem is the ambiguity of interests. In Weimar Germany, for example, the fragmentation of the party system contributed to policy stalemate. In contemporary France the influence of the Communist party among trade unions contributed to François Mitterrand's decision to nationalize industry.

Countries differ in a variety of ways concerning their representative associations, and these differences have been used to devise whole theories of policy and politics. Particularly important are the linkages between interest groups and parties, the degree of centralization or dispersion of policy networks, the intensity of corporatist structures, and the internal organization of parties and interest groups. Other differences pertain less to systems than to the particularities of each party or group; they focus around ideology, leaders, and specific historical experiences.

The strength of the argument based on intermediate associations lies in the importance of organization for translating preferences into effective action. Associations obviously warrant our close attention. The difficulty for the argument is the problem for any mediating variable—its effects require linkage to the terms on either side, to society and to the state.

The State Structure Explanation

Societal forces and representative associations must act through the state to attain policy objectives. The structure of the state, its rules and institutions, can therefore have a very substantial effect on outcomes.[31] Rules shape the process of aggregation, and different rules favor different mixes. In fighting for tariffs, for example, the Junkers were favored by the three-class voting system of Prussia. Proportional representation in Weimar Germany, federalism and the separation of powers in the United States, the dual executive of the French Fifth Republic are all examples of rules that can affect the distribution of power. The institutions of the state—the bureaucracy, instruments of coercion and intervention, the judiciary, and so on—all affect the possibility of authoritative action. The powers and skills of the officials who occupy positions in these institutions allow them to aid one side or another in policy quarrels and to take the lead in mobilizing pressure and shaping opinion.

Countries obviously differ in the character of state structure, and policy similarities (or differences) among them derive from the similarities (or differences) among their state institutions. Arguments of this sort draw our attention to the differences between authoritarian and constitutional regimes, between centralized and dispersed systems, between highly developed bureaucracies with wide-ranging instruments of intervention and poorly developed or loosely integrated bureaucracies with limited modes of intervention, and, eventually, between "strong" states and "weak" ones.[32]

In pursuing the politics of policy formation, we began with a portrait of societal actors, then moved to the associations that represent them, then to the state institutions through which they work. The three elements clearly interact. Institutions and policy shape organizations, as the laws governing industrial relations indicate. Associations may shape the understanding that societal actors have of their own economic situation, and they may also play an important role in defining options. Many analyses collapse the three elements into two—a pattern of societal forces, and a pattern of associations or policy networks that mediate between state and society. Such simplification has virtues, but it has its costs as well. In constitutionalist systems, and in most authoritarian ones, society and the state have some autonomy from each other, and there must always be mechanisms for linking the two. These mechanisms remain distinct. State institutions, intermediate associations, and societal actors move somewhat separately. At times societal actors abandon the intermediate associations that seek to represent them; at times state officials bypass intermediate associations and turn directly to societal actors for support, while at other times they may use the associations to control society; at times social revolts run roughshod over both state institutions and longstanding intermediate associations. There is, therefore, some analytic utility in keeping the three as distinct categories.

The state structure explanation derives its force from the effects that decision-making mechanisms can be shown to have on the actual outcome of the aggregation of societal preferences and the lobbying of interest groups and parties: if society and associations are held constant, then different rules and institutions produce different outcomes. The weakness of the explanation is the great role it assigns to context. Just how rules and institutions produce varying outcomes turns on whom they affect, on the identity of the groups, with particular preferences and resources, that seek to work through the state. Rules and bureaucracies favor one side or another; state agents may shape social structure and representative associations. Rules can be changed, bureaucracies created or dismantled, authority generated or demobilized. The same institution can be used for quite varying purposes, as the example of German bureaucracy under the Nazis makes clear. Thus the impact of state structure, however great, cannot be shown independently of some understanding of the society it is meant to effect.

The Economic Ideology Explanation

Societal actors, I suggest, evaluate an economic crisis in terms of their own situations in the international economy. But often those situations are by no means clear. There is considerable ambiguity about economic reality, and ambiguity permits different interpretations. Different understandings or models of a situation shape to different ends calculations of the costs and benefits of action, its opportunities and disadvantages, and hence of behavior. Economic ideology may shape political calculations as well, by influencing under-standings of who the actors are, what they want, and what they will do.

Countries have varying traditions of economic analysis, not only among specialized elites but more broadly in the population. Some have traditions of active government involvement to promote eco-nomic development; others emphasize laissez-faire. In some countries traditions of free trade are strong, unemployment is feared, and so-cial services are accepted. Other countries are protectionist, fear infla-tion more than employment, and dislike social service systems.

The economic ideology interpretation of economic policy choices explains outcomes in terms of national traditions and values concern-ing the economy. Its strength lies in the reality of ambiguity. To the extent that economic reality is uncertain—which in real life is nearly always—cognitive elements affect decision making. The difficulties of the approach lie with comparisons with the rapidity of change. To compare countries in crisis is to suggest that similar traditions have supported different outcomes, different traditions have supported similar outcomes. Rapid changes within countries, moreover, such as the Junkers' Germany from 1872 to 1879 or the United States of Coolidge contrasted to the United States of FDR, undermine argu-ments that, like those of the economic ideology approach, stress con-stants over time.

The International System Explanation

Arguments that explain policy or politics by pointing to factors internal to a country are, in Kenneth Waltz's apt phrase, second-image explanations.[33] It is quite clear that the effects of the interna-tional environment run in the other direction as well. The third im-age, that is, or the international system, has a strong influence upon the factors that comprise the second image, or the domestic system. Hence it is important to reverse second-image reasoning and examine how international phenomena influence domestic ones.[34]

Two sorts of theorizing about the reverse of the second image can be distinguished; one stresses economics and the impact of market power, the other stresses political-military rivalries and the impact of force. The work of Gerschenkron and dos Santos, Cardoso and Wal-lerstein, illustrates the first approach;[35] that of Otto Hintze provides a classic example of the second.[36] The political economy school exam-ines countries' differences in relation to their position in a sequence of international development. Thus Gerschenkron developed the concept of early and late development to distinguish the roles played by the state in Britain, Germany, and Russia: the later the timing of development, he suggested, the greater was the importance of the state in economic development. The reason lay in the problem of competition. Development, Gerschenkron argued, is not a repetition of the same pattern, as W. W. Rostow and many Marxists have suggested, but rather a historical sequence of cases, because the existence of competitors changes the environment for those who follow. Development thus is like a market in that it rewards and punishes certain economic and institutional forms according to their utility in a process that is constantly changing.

Military theorizing at the system level examines the impact of war and preparation for war on the distribution of power in society. Hintze contrasts Britain and Germany, navies and armies, arguing that because armies allow for domestic intervention in ways that navies do not, the army tilted German development toward authoritarianism in a way inconceivable with Britain's navy. French centralization derives from the wars of Louis XIV, the Revolution, and Napoleon; the American state emerged with the Civil War and then World War II and the Cold War. As countries are drawn into military rivalries, in sum, they develop military machines that alter their political systems.[37]

The strong form of this type of theorizing, whether it concentrates on political economy or the military, sees the international system as totally constraining, leaving little as to choice for the units within it. In the dependencia literature, for example, country development is tightly constrained by the country's placement in the system, and nations have little choice over what to do. Those in the process of developing buy and sell in markets dominated by far richer and more powerful core countries. As a result, their development trajectories are shaped by the core countries, not by their own choices.[38]

It is not hard to find fault with the most sweeping versions of this argument. Rarely is international situation so perfectly clear, so totally unambiguous, as to be so completely constraining, rarely is there no range of alternative responses. Generally, it is clear, countries do have some choice over how to deal with their position in the international system. They may make alliances with one country or another, promote import substitution or commodity exports, stress agriculture over industry or vice versa, give free rein to foreign economic activity on their soil or seek to mediate or even control it. Such decisions require explanation that cannot come from the international system itself. Nonetheless, the line of reasoning based on study of development patterns captures important points. Sweden's divergence from German patterns of development, for example, was certainly affected by the limits that its small size imposed on autarkic or imperialist opportunities. The development of democratic corporatist elements in the small countries of Europe since the 1930s is certainly linked to the narrower tolerances that the international system allows those countries.

The issue, then, is not whether the international system shapes domestic politics but how and through what mechanisms. Unless the international situation is completely coercive, as may be case with foreign occupation, countries do have choices. The selection they make from among those choices depends on domestic politics, on the distribution of power within countries and the various factors that influence it—societal forces, intermediate institutions, state structure, ideology. The international economy affects national policies by acting upon domestic actors. As the international price of wheat falls, for example, it stimulates domestic producers to seek tariff protection or some other form of subsidy. As opportunities for export grow, on the other hand, other producers come to favor open international regimes. The system may be international, then, but in terms of national policy the effect of the system is felt through actors operating within the individual nation. Foreign companies may coopt comprador elites, but the more important point is that they have to find someone to coopt.

This book is about the impact of international crises upon domestic policy. To unravel that impact we must, according to the reasoning just formulated, examine the responses of domestic actors. Effects from the international economic system I therefore include in the first of the types of argument examined above, that of societal actors. International political-military effects do not appear directly in that category, however, and I shall consider them separately as a fifth line of analysis. As we shall see, international security concerns also operate through domestic actors and also impose some considerable objective constraints. Clearly Sweden can never defend itself in the same manner as the United States can. Nonetheless, Norway belongs to NATO but Sweden does not; interpretation varies by country as to what is appropriate behavior. Thus we need to consider the effects of international security considerations on domestic politics.

Security issues and domestic politics are linked also by the connection between military spending and economic policy. Ronald Reagan justifies U.S. budget deficits in part through reference to the imperative of defense. Victorian Britain's support of free trade has been

65

explained by some through reference to the preeminence of its navy, which provided the security that allowed the country to depend on foreign food and markets.

Relationship among the Explanations

Factors that plausibly may affect policy outcomes are legion, and the five summarized above could easily be expanded in number. The difficulty lies in establishing the relationship among them. The testing of alternative explanations and specifying their relative weights, a model derived from the physical sciences, cannot be used here, because satisfying the conditions of experimentation is impossible. So my task must be different. It is to clarify the nature of different arguments, their logic, and their internal characteristics. Then, having gathered the sorts of evidence appropriate to each explanation, I examine events from the arguments' points of view. At that point it becomes possible to clarify the relationship among the arguments, by careful patterning of comparisons among the cases. By judicious, focused comparisons, by select pairing of country behaviors, it is possible to obtain some leverage on the choice of policy outcomes.[39]

The relationship among the variables is not a constant. Relationships alter with circumstances and with periods; that is, they are not theoretical but sociological. The world changes the balance between ideology and force, between institutions and economic interests.

Each historical case study starts with the relationship of societal actors within countries to the international economy. Economic changes do affect economic actors, of course, and, moreover, I found strong support for the approach in looking at the first case, the late nineteenth century. I then became interested both in how well the argument would work for later cases, and in what happened to the relationships established in that crisis as the economic environment developed.

By giving pride of place to explanation based on international economic situation, I have both privileged and disadvantaged it. It is privileged because the ranking suggests priority of attention, but this priority also disadvantages it, because priority will attract criticism. Valuable books could be written to tell the same story beginning not with the international economy but with ideology or with the state. Wherever the story begins, though, there the attacks will be sharpest, for the first point can always be shown to be underdetermining.

I shall specify at the start, therefore, that ultimately all the arguments presented here are underdetermining. The historical reality of each case is too open, too uncertain, too plastic to sustain the reductionism involved in tracing outcomes back to one feature or even one combination of features of the system. Crises are particularly plastic— indeed, that is what makes them interesting. It is why I have chosen to focus on them rather than on the patterns of stable systems. Just how the elements that shape policy choices actually combine in a given historical situation turns on conjunctural variables—leadership, entrepreneurship, circumstance.

This book is an examination of the conditions in which political entrepreneurship and circumstance operate. It aims to specify materials, the constraints and the opportunities, from which politicians forge outcomes. Any political outcome involves the variables that I consider here: the support of societal actors, the linkages among intermediate associations, state structure or organization, ideology, and international military influences. How those variables combine turns on what individuals in actual historical situations are able to do with them.

The Choice of Countries and Crises

Following the usages of macrohistorical comparison, I have chosen countries with reasonable similarities in what I wish to explore. Since the 1870s, the first crisis I examine, all five countries have had complex economies—part modern, part backward; part industrial, part agrarian; part oriented toward aggressive competition on a world scene, part oriented toward sheltered home markets. Thus all five have had economic actors with rough similarities of placement in the world economy. Countries that made similar policy choices can be compared to see if there are similarities in the social attributes of their winning coalitions, in their intermediate associations, in their state structures, economic ideology, and position in the international state system.

My choice of countries is related to these variables. Because of the importance of international-domestic linkages that express the relationship of societal actors to the international economy, I wanted countries that had comparable mixtures in industry, agriculture, and labor. All, that is, had to have some industry in the late nineteenth century involved in export, agriculture split between grains and high-quality foodstuffs that consume grains, and labor involved in both industrial production and consumption. Second, I wanted countries that differed in outcomes during the crisis periods. Third, I wanted differences in other variables of importance, especially state forms, economic ideology, and international military situation. Fourth, I wanted countries both with some openness in political process (so that the role of societal actors, ideology, institutions, and the like could be examined) and with market economies.

Rather few countries fit all these requirements, but others could have been included. Japan, Italy, Spain, Canada, and Australia would have made particularly interesting additions; I omitted them only for reasons of economy. Several Latin American countries might also have made for interesting comparisons, but they were primarily agricultural in the first crisis and thus lacked the diversity of societal actors whose effects I wished to explore. I did not include Soviet-style regimes because the distribution of economic power there makes politics so different. Interest groups and societal actors exist in those countries, but they are so much weaker than state-party institutions in the West as to change the pattern of political advocacy.

In the case studies that follow, the treatment of the countries within each crisis period is not equal. Some countries get longer analysis than others, and different one are favored for each period. This tactic is deliberate: focusing comparisons on pairs or trios of countries allows an accentuation of specific elements in the explanatory discussion in order to sharpen the debate. Unequal as well is the space given to discussing the explanatory issues in each crisis period. The character of each type of argument is discussed at length in the context of the first crisis period, establishing the analytical groundwork for the next two, though the interpretative points are reexamined in the Conclusion.

Three great crises in the international economy affected these five countries: the downturn of 1873–96, the Depression of the 1930s, and the economic disruption that started in 1971. These crises involve an interaction between changes in the business cycle and changes in the basic structure of domestic economies. The first process involves regular swings between boom and bust following an investment cycle. The second involves major changes in the products that countries produce, in the organization of their production, and in the geographical distribution of efficient production within and among countries.[40] Although each crisis has its own characteristics, all three crises saw major changes in both processes.

Five countries, three periods—we seek to know what policies these countries selected, and that is our descriptive task. Simultaneously we seek to understand the application of different interpretative traditions to that selection, and that is our explanatory task.

PART II

HARD TIMES

CHAPTER THREE

Protectionism and Free Trade: The Crisis of 1873–96

When Richard Cobden and Michel Chevalier met in 1860 to sign the famous treaty between Britain and France which called for the lowering of tariff levels, the international economy seemed to be entering a new era. The 1830s and 1840s had been bitter and harsh. Industrialization had brought misery to millions through unemployment and hunger, overcrowding in hamlet and city, destruction of the old crafts, and riot and revolution. Was it an illusion to think that new technology would spawn new jobs and spread greater wealth? Many thought so, and the turbulent politics of those decades showed it.[1]

After the political tempests of 1848, however, the ship of the world economy righted itself. Prosperity did spread as the technological miracle took hold, and the happy spiral began to work: profit and demand chased each other to spur investment. Factories produced goods at ever cheaper prices, providing jobs and hence the income to buy their own output.

Britain began to ascend the spiral first. With textiles and iron it dominated the first two stages of the industrial era. In the 1850s other countries began to benefit as well: Britain bought their products (food, timber, and other raw materials), which permitted them to buy Britain's finished goods, which in turn allowed Britain to pay for its imports and have a surplus for investment. That investment spread abroad, helping other countries to launch their own industrialization. Belgium, France, the United States, and the various parts of what would soon become Germany began to copy British technology and then to create their own. The new economic ideas were working. Wealth was not a fixed quantity, as older doctrines had argued, to be allocated by power; wealth could be created through the application of new technologies. The prosperity of the great railroad-building boom of the fifties and sixties supplanted the hard years of the thirties and forties.

Prosperity encouraged the adoption of classical liberal economic policies. (That Britain was losing its monopoly on certain kinds of manufacture troubled no one, because the thirst for new products was so great that it seemed impossible to slake it.) This led to the Cobden-Chevalier treaty. Confident Britain, a free trader since 1846, persuaded protectionist France that it too would benefit from specialization. If France allowed in British and other exports while specializing on its own product lines, other countries would buy more French goods. The idea spread. In Germany, for example, first customs unions and then unification broke down many trade barriers. Free trade appeared ready to become the dominant doctrine of the international economy, not only in theory but also in practice.[2]

The optimism proved short-lived, however.[3] After more than twenty years of boom, and about ten years of liberal trade, troubles began to arise which in their turn would last two decades and more. The hard times that began in about 1873 derived in a direct way from the good times that preceded them. Technology and investment created overcapacity, and eventually the familiar logic of investment cycles caught up with the domestic and international economies. In that logic the race to make profit by investing in new plants so squeezes the profit margin that investment stops, and with it comes a falloff in demand which leaves all those new factories with a large capacity to produce but without buyers for their products. What happened, in Immanuel Wallerstein's terms, was that the original industrial core— the United Kingdom—drew semiperipheral countries into a new, larger core. World wealth increased, but the change caused tremendous structural shifts that required extensive and difficult readjustment.[4]

The boom decades had transformed industry and agriculture. In agriculture the new technology meant not only vastly increased output in what had been since time immemorial the most labor-intensive of economic activities but also a completely new geographical distribution of comparative advantage. The mechanical reaper and sower, fertilizers, drainage tiles, new varieties of wheat, and other changes made it possible to farm new lands in new ways. The great plains of North America, the pampas of Argentina, and the black earth of the Ukraine could now be sown with grains or used to pasture livestock. And because of new machinery, this could be done with a limited supply of labor.[5]

Equally important for agriculture was the revolution in transportation. When the British abandoned the Corn Laws in 1846, inadequate shipping acted like a tariff; there was insufficient shipping capacity available to bring the world's grain to British shores. By the 1870s the situation was completely transformed. The railroad had overcome the geographical limits of river systems to integrate the great interior land masses into the international economy. The motorization of shipping and the development of refrigeration got the produce from the great plains of North America, Argentina, and Russia to markets in Europe.

It is not too strong to call the effects of these changes cataclysmic. Prices plummeted. Suddenly, land-extensive and capital-intensive agriculture leaped ahead of labor- and land-intensive agriculture for a whole range of products. Most of Europe could not compete, and indeed, after several centuries as Western Europe's major source for grain imports, Prussia and other areas of Eastern Europe were now high-cost producers. Most of Western Europe did no better. Farmers in much of Britain, France, Germany, Italy, Scandinavia, and the Low Countries could no longer produce the same goods in the same way. Something had to change.

In industry also, two prosperous decades had transformed the world. British capital helped lay railroad tracks across the United States, Latin America, and Europe. Railroad building stimulated a tremendous growth in iron and steel making, not only in the United Kingdom, but in all industrializing countries. By the 1870s British dominance of that essential element of industrial development had vanished, and within a decade Britain would be overtaken by both the United States and Germany.[6] Textiles told a similar tale.

Prosperity, in industry as in agriculture, set the stage for problems. As railroad building tapered off, the supply of iron and steel began to exceed demand. In 1873 there was an especially sharp downturn in the business cycle. The curve would go up again, but not with its earlier strength; prices tended downward, and profits were squeezed.

For the next two decades and more the industrial economies of Europe and North America experienced considerable distress. We have no convenient label for what was going on, save perhaps to call it the downside of a Kondratieff long wave. Although there were several drops in the conventional business cycle, the period as a whole was not a business-cycle depression, for output increased, in fact considerably. Prices dropped, leading some to call it a period of deflation. To contemporaries, the nature of the problem was unclear. Some saw a crisis where others saw a limited, partial readjustment. Some thought it a temporary blip on the business cycle, others an epochal shift into a new historical era, one profoundly different from what went before. Some thought that it required nothing special in the way of action, others argued that it demanded major steps in government policy.

In its ambiguity, indeed, the crisis of the last third of the nineteenth century resembles more the crisis of the 1970s and 1980s than it does the Depression of the 1930s. The Depression was not ambiguous: it was a tremendous disaster, and it was understood as such. The argument was over what to do about it. But in the other two crises, disagreement at the time is as basic as whether anything was happening which required special attention or notice. That ambiguity affected the politics of the debate, making passive responses more plausible. It also lengthened the debate. The drama of the Depression lasted a decade and in some respects less than half of that.

Whatever we call the crisis of 1873–96, it was certainly one of the great periods of structural readjustment in the international economy. Big shifts had been occurring in the international division of labor—in the geographical location of efficient production, in the terms of trade among goods, and so on—and those changes caused considerable stress. That stress required adjustment, both extensive and intense. People, goods, and capital had to move around, change, collapse, or grow. In 1896, it is true, aggregate income was higher than in 1873, but this statistic, like all aggregate figures, masks tremendous suffering.

Those who suffered began to seek help. "Seek," in fact, is too weak a word; they demanded, insisted, shouted, clamored, screamed for help. Thus began a great policy debate: How should each country respond to this major change in the international economy?

Broadly speaking, two options presented themselves, the market and protection. The market or classical liberal solution urged acceptance of the new international division of labor, for all the familiar reasons. To intensify specialization would be to increase productive capacity (the ability to create wealth) and so to raise the gross world product. But to let the market allocate factors of production meant moving people and capital, closing factories and opening them, changing land use, abandoning housing and building it—an endless chain of events in an increasingly complex industrial economy.

The major alternative, protectionism, would use tariff barriers to shield European producers from cheaper foreign goods. In agriculture the tariff would allow people to stay on the land; perhaps they could not do things entirely the old way, but at least the process of readjustment would be slowed. But even the productive farmers of

Europe found that lower prices menaced their livelihood. For these producers in the new territories of cultivation, tariffs would do no good. Their grievances demanded other remedies, such as cheaper money, regulation of shipping, marketing cooperatives, and so on.

For industry, in its own "search for order," tariffs were also the main policy solution desired. For industry as for agriculture, tariffs would at least slow down the pressure to change, at least keep companies and jobs afloat long enough to allow either modernization of production or the shifting of labor and capital. Even efficient companies might desire tariffs in order to guarantee enough stability in the domestic market to amortize expensive investments.

Tariffs were not the only policy instrument available to governments, nor was government intervention the only way of altering the operation of market forces. Companies could and did create cartels and mergers in order to "create order"—that is, to fix prices and market shares. Governments could help out with tax policy, purchases, regulation, public works, and social insurance. In this period, though, the centerpiece of policy debate was protection vs. free trade. It is, therefore, tariff policy that I shall seek to describe and explain. In descriptive terms, every country except Britain erected tariff barriers. (See Table 1.) France, Germany, and Sweden put tariffs on both industrial and agricultural products; the United States, an efficient agricultural producer, put them on industrial goods only. Britain experienced an attempt to reverse the decision of 1846, to restore the Corn Laws and impose industrial tariffs at least against those beyond the empire if not against countries within the empire as well. But those efforts failed, and Britain remained loyal to the free-trade creed that it had helped develop.

Why this result? Why did republican America and France, imperial Germany, monarchical Sweden, and most of the rest of Europe abandon the free-trade hopes of Cobden-Chevalier in favor of protectionism? Why, alone among industrial nations, did Britain diverge from this trend, joined only by a few small agricultural countries such as Denmark? In the previous chapter I noted several ways of answering these questions—the preferences of societal actors deriving from their economic situation, the system of representative associations, the institutional structure of the state, economic ideology, and the international state system. To confront these various arguments with historical experience, we shall look at the policy debate in the five countries, exploring the evidence that the different arguments require us to consider.

This chapter is constructed around a focused comparison of the

Table 1. Tariff levels in industry and agriculture, 1880s–1914

		Industry	
		High	Low
Agriculture	High	France, Germany, Sweden	
	Low	United States	United Kingdom

United Kingdom and Germany. These two industrializing countries differed sharply in policy outcome: continuing free trade for the former, a shift to tariffs for the latter. They differed also in ways relevant to the explanatory variables: Britain's leadership in the industrial revolution vs. Germany's tardiness (production profile); a constitutionalist order in Britain, with low levels of centralization and bureaucratic institutionalization, vs. Germany's authoritarian state, with a well-developed bureaucracy and strong centralized controls (state structure); Britain's free-trade tradition vs. Germany's more statist and nationalist tradition (economic ideology); and security through the navy for Britain vs. perceived insecurity in relation to other land-based powers for Germany (international state system).

THE UNITED KINGDOM

Britain was the only industrialized country in our sample not to raise tariffs on either industrial or agricultural products in this period. An interpretation based on societal actors would have us look at Britain's *production profile*—the situation of the nation's economic actors in the international economy and the way that their situations relate to policy preferences.

By the early 1870s the British economy was highly evolved. In industry the iron-steel and textile sectors were world-dominant until the beginning of the crisis, with a host of forward and backward linkages (to manufactured goods and to mining). Banking and shipping formed a highly articulated, distinct, and world-dominant economic sector separate from industry. Banking stressed the financing of trade and foreign portfolio loans, not domestic investment banking, and shipping and insurance were also oriented toward high volumes of world trade.

In agriculture there was a fairly high concentration of ownership, but the sector was thoroughly commercialized within the market economy and oriented toward the production of high-quality goods for industrial markets. Considered as a percentage of the national economy, agriculture was already falling faster in Britain than in any other country. Finally, Britain had the largest percentage of industrial workers of any advanced country. Employed mainly in highly competitive industries, British labor had already undergone considerable craft unionization.

How did these groups respond to the new economic conditions after 1870? Industry and agriculture both split over whether to raise the tariff. Within each camp emerged protectionists seeking to reopen the debate that the repeal of the Corn Laws had closed in 1846. In each camp the free traders fought back, however, and in alliance with other groups managed to win.

Within industry, the strength of the free-trade position in the United Kingdom seems easily explicable by Alexander Gerschenkron's famous distinction between early and late development. Gerschenkron attacks the notion that development is the same for each country.[7] Rather, the first developer, the United Kingdom, grew in an environment without rivals, while followers have a competitor to contend with. The consequence for tariff policy is to orient leaders toward free trade and followers toward protection, because leaders are likely to dominate world markets and hence to benefit from an open trading system, but followers need shelters behind which to build up their competitive abilities.

The contrast between the United Kingdom and Germany seems to fit this pattern quite well. Dominant for several decades, British manufacturers felt confident in their ability to prevail in international competitive struggle. By keeping its borders open, the United Kingdom encouraged international specialization, importing lower- and exporting higher-value-added products. The policy had worked splendidly during the prosperous years of the 1850s and 1860s and seemed worth continuing.

But the new conditions of international trade after 1873 caused problems for British manufacturers. Other countries began to substitute their own products for British goods, compete with Britain in overseas markets, penetrate the British domestic market, and erect tariff barriers against British goods. These problems led to demands for tariffs, either direct or within the context of the empire. A fair trade league was formed, and politicians, notably Joseph Chamberlain, sought to organize a new majority of industry and labor around a policy of imperial preference.[8]

77

Protectionist agitation was blunted by several factors. Although competitive pressures were real, other sources of income and of sales existed. Despite Canadian and Australian tariff barriers, the rest of the empire sustained a stable demand for British goods; so did overseas investment, commercial ties, and prestige. As markets fluctuated widely, British steel and other industries made relatively low investments in plant modernization, cutting down on risk and keeping up profits even if in the long run also preventing recovery of competitive leadership.

Most striking about the British situation was the country's rising income from international banking and shipping, which helped conceal the relative decline in sales. Britain was reaping the rewards of early industrialization: fortunes made in textiles and iron created the capital for the nation to become the world's banker. Financial services became an industry, a sector by itself. Lacking strong ties to domestic industry, the finance-trading sector could accept—even welcome— further specialization, and it favored anything to keep the international economy open for trade and capital flows. Bankers and traders thus led a lobby against protection. They were joined by manufacturers of finished goods, consumers of iron and steel, who wanted to keep the costs of inputs low, and by manufacturers of various speciality products in which the United Kingdom continued to do well on world markets.

Agriculture saw similar battles over policy. As British grain growing had by now become uncompetitive, free trade after 1873 meant cutting back on domestic grain production while expanding the production of high-quality foodstuffs such as dairy, meat, fresh fruit, and vegetables. Cheap foreign grains would be an input, both as feed for the animals that produce milk, meat, and other materials, and as cheaper bread for consumers who could then spend saved income on higher-quality goods. Modernizing farmers would benefit strongly from industrial growth, because as consumer income rises, so the proportion going into higher-quality foods rises. Gerschenkron calls this path the Danish model.[9]

Conversely, a protectionist policy would block or deter specialization and modernization. Tariffs on grain would help preserve domestic production of a traditional product and allow traditional ways of growing grain to persist. Protection would thus preserve a larger agricultural population, and it would prolong national self-sufficiency in food.

In the United Kingdom there were advocates of each position. Some landowners did push for protection, particularly those hurt by the plummeting prices for grain. But the support for protection among British farmers was weaker than among those of Germany and France. Why, in particular, did the British landowning aristocracy fail to match the Junkers and their French counterparts in striving ardently for protection? British aristocrats, after all, held a privileged position in the national political system, being significantly overrepresented in Parliament and local administration, and they had wealth and prestige. The answer is that the advanced state of British industrial development had already altered the structure of incentives in agriculture. Much land had already been shifted into producing higher-value goods for urban industrial markets. Although landowning was concentrated, the land was rented out, in sharp contrast with the land tenure system on the Junker estates. It was mainly rented, moreover, to skilled yeoman able to adapt to the complex skill requirements of animal husbandry and truck farming.[10]

British industrial development affected how British aristocrats evaluated the post-1873 situation in another way. As they were far more deeply involved in industrial development than their Junker counterparts, the decline of farming did not threaten their livelihood as deeply. Many generations of British aristocrats had invested in mining, manufacturing, and trading. Urban growth built over land they owned, and raw materials were discovered under their land. Meanwhile their younger sons and impecunious daughters had intermarried with the rising industrial bourgeoisie, thus blurring further the boundaries between these groups. At least some British aristocrats thus derived income from a wide range of sources and had strong psychological linkages to the new industrial order.[11]

Differentiation within the landed interest thus provided some basis for splits over policy toward industrial issues, from the Reform Bill of 1832, through the repeal of the Corn Laws, down through the policy quarrels that reopened in the 1870s. For a large fraction of British landowners, the interests of advanced, free-trade-oriented industry and those of modernizing farming converged. If specialization through free trade was good for industry, it was good for the specialized farmer. And to farmers as consumers of industrial products, free trade in industrial goods was good because it lowered costs.[12]

Labor, by the 1870s, was quite strong in support of free trade. In the 1840s anti-corn-law activists had argued that labor ought to support free trade in order to keep down consumer costs, especially the price of food. Labor activists at the time were more skeptical, seeing tariffs as a middle-class concern that distracted attention from the broader political demands of Chartism. Liberal economic policies

79

seemed also to threaten jobs, and many workers remained to be convinced that free trade meant rising living standards for all.

It was only after experiencing the prosperity of the 1850s and 1860s that British labor accepted free trade. As Liberals and Conservatives vied for mass support in their efforts to gain power, the Liberal position came to predominate among labor groups. Cheap food in the workshop of the world furthered the interests of the working man—this became a tenet of the political economy for British labor and grounds for alliance with a segment of British industry working through the Liberal party. Joseph Chamberlain tried through the Tories to form an alternative alignment based on deference to Church and Crown and imperial preference. He had some success among English workers in iron-steel areas, but he failed among most English workers and in Scotland and Wales.

In Britain's production profile, then, we can identify a considerable range of forces aligned in favor of continuing free trade. We can represent policy preferences towards high or low tariffs in industry and agriculture in a simple table, locating groups according to their preferences. (See Table 2.) The farther a group lies from the intercept or origin, the more intense are its preferences; the closer, the more ambiguous. Most groups, it will be seen, congregate in the quadrant that describes the actual policy outcome: low agricultural tariffs and low industrial tariffs.

A second explanation of Britain's low tariffs during the late nineteenth century examines the political parties and *interest groups* that sought to link society and government. In this period such organizations grew prodigiously. At mid-century European politics had revolved around loose political parties, business associations that looked like clubs, and trade unions like fraternal orders. Organizations in many areas were almost nonexistent, provoking Marx's characterization of French peasants as potatoes in a sack. In the last third of the century, however, partly in response to the crisis, organizations grew explosively and became institutionalized. Also responsible were the growth of mass society, the extension of the franchise, the growth of cities, factories, and large-scale economic units. These various changes provided powerful incentives to organize—to change government policy to favor or oppose tariffs (or for any other goal) required the mobilization of support at many levels and the capacity for representation at the centers of power.

In most countries this was happening during the crisis. As organizations were new and rapidly changing, it is difficult to isolate their impact on the political debates of the day. In the United Kingdom,

Table 2. Policy preferences toward tariffs in the United Kingdom after 1873

	Agricultural Tariffs	
	High	Low
High **Industrial Tariffs**		Iron-steel manufacturers
Low	Grain farmers	Most labor High-quality product farmers Finished manufacturers Bankers and shippers **The Outcome**

though, political parties had already acquired both organization and substantive content. They had developed strategies for linking leadership elites with the masses in ways that affected the tariff debate. In the various controversies of mid-century the Liberals had forged a new coalition that blended political reform (gradual democratization), religious freedom, and free-trade economic policy. That coalition linked Midlands industrialists eager for export and trade, the bankers and shippers of the City, and large chunks of the emerging working-class electorate drawn by religious nonconformism and the quest for cheap food.

As controversies over the tariff reopened in the last part of the century, the Liberals led the fight to hold to the course adopted in 1844. In electoral competition they compromised classical laissez-faire at home (with welfare legislation) in order to maintain mass support for free trade in foreign economic policy. Even the Conservatives never fully accepted free trade. Joseph Chamberlain tried to organize a coalition with a family resemblance to Bismarck's, grouping of industrialists, farmers, and workers hit by foreign competition. But Disraeli's formula for the Conservatives held: gradual democratization of suffrage through the reform bills, unity of Anglicans of all social classes in support of the high church, growth of empire, and at least verbal acceptance of social responsibility for the suffering caused by economic change.[13]

The contrast with Germany is sharp. Britain had two major political parties, well developed and with strategies for broad social coalitions, both committed to constitutionalist, democratized monarchy, and both defending free trade. As we shall see, Germany had no such political parties. German politics was much more a direct struggle among social categories unmediated by associations, a struggle in which individuals, preeminently Bismarck, could play important roles as power brokers.

Societal actors and intermediate associations must ultimately work through the state, and so a third line of interpretation examines *institutions*. Since the destruction of the royal bureaucracy during the English Civil War,[14] the British state had lacked the capacity to impose the views of a narrow band around the court upon society. So state policy followed shifts in society—the aristocracy and its allies made policy, not the masses, to be sure, but nonetheless, in sharp contrast to Prussia or Japan, England had a system that was constitutionalist and nonbureaucratic. The army and other instruments of coercion were relatively undeveloped.

When industrial interests grew rapidly in the eighteenth and nineteenth centuries, therefore, it would have been difficult for the British state to do other than what it did—accommodate and change. Although the aristocracy was certainly privileged, it could not impose its wishes unilaterally upon the nation (and, most important, it did not appear to want to). When social preferences moved to favor reform and free trade, the state expressed those shifts. The British state is thus noteworthy, in relation to the tariff controversy, for its relatively high permeability to social influences.

Another explanation of the continuation of free-trade policy after 1873 looks to *economic ideology*, to the strength within British political culture of free-trade ideas. As the first industrial nation, Britain had developed the concepts of comparative advantage. British theorists gave voice to Britain's situation in the international division of labor, and British prosperity strongly reinforced the credibility of their doctrines. It was small wonder that the ideas were widely shared; indeed, so strong was the British example that other countries, as Charles Kindleberger has argued, followed these doctrines even when they received rewards less obvious and immediate than in the British case.[15]

When economic conditions changed after 1873, the new situation was at least unclear. Contemporaries did not know whether they had reached a turning point in the history of the world's industrial economy, and in ambiguous situations ideology usually looms large in shaping understandings and behavior. The British were armed with an understanding of economic policy choices which had brought them world dominance; why should they change? British society, from interest groups and producers to politicians and civil servants, continued to analyze the United Kingdom's options in terms similar to those of previous decades, and so they neglected signs of strenuous competition and the possible utility of tariffs in stabilizing markets for modernization. Free trade persisted after the conditions that made it rational had disappeared, and all the more so because economic theory, then as now, continued to view free trade as optimal.[16]

The final explanation stems from *international state system.* Free trade involves specialization in the international division of labor, sloughing off weaker industries to push resources into industries that capture comparative advantage. This specialization means dependence, on foreign supplies of needed domestic goods and on foreign markets for home-made-ones. Dependence in turn involves security, particularly for food. Only secure countries (or totally vulnerable ones, for instance Denmark) can specialize and hence accept free trade. Britain had security because of its navy, which could provide stability of trade, guarantee sources of overseas food, and protect orderliness of markets, capital flows, and loan payments. Free trade and the navy reinforced each other.[17]

And so the United Kingdom continued with free trade. It is not clear that Britain was best off doing so—in retrospect, this period saw the beginning of that languorous decline in domestic industrial production which continues to the present day. Through politics, decisions were made during this first economic crisis in favor of a particular economic policy. Each of the five interpretations examined here is able to explain why, and looking at Britain alone makes it hard to sort out the interpretations one from another. Comparison with other countries is needed.

GERMANY

Germany was the first European country to adopt tariffs in response to the economic downturn that began in 1873. The social coalition of iron and rye, the role of Bismarck and the privileged position of the Junkers in the German state, the weight of nationalist ideology, and the rise of German militarism all figure prominently in the history of that country as tariff barriers were being erected. It is thus a useful case for exploring these interconnections.

To explain German tariff policy by reference to societal actors and interest groups, one needs to know Germany's *production profile*—the relationship of societal actors to the international economy and the way in which it related to their policy preferences. A simple model of

German society, adapted from Gerschenkron's *Bread and Democracy in Germany*, contains four major groups: agriculture, made up of Junkers or aristocratic estate owners and peasants or small farmers; industry, split between manufacturers in heavy, basic industries producing largely for domestic consumption and manufacturers of finished goods and export products; labor, consisting of both unionized workers in large enterprises and individual workers or employees; and finally, a mixture of other groups, including shopkeepers and artisans, shippers, bankers, and professionals. Each of these four groups had particular interests in relation to the new market conditions that prevailed after 1873.

For agriculture, there is one key question: Why did Prussian Junkers resist so intensely the modernization solution followed in Denmark and accepted by British landowners? High-quality foodstuffs were best produced by high-quality labor. Small units, managed by owners or long-term leaseholders, seemed best able to provide the skilled husbandry needed to produce meat, dairy, fruit, and vegetables for nearby urban markets. Landless laborers, be they serfs or wage earners, working for a squirearchy, seemed least able to handle these sorts of products. Conversely, grain, cotton, and other basic crops could be produced effectively on great estates. (I note that this is not a proposition about these crops general for all times and places but specific to certain ways of producing agricultural products at certain times.) In the United States, by contrast, meat could be raised extensively by hired hands on the rangeland, grain by family farmers (with enough capital for machinery). In the Europe of the late nineteenth century, however, the shift to higher-quality foodstuffs seemed to have an affinity with decentralized production in which autonomous farm "managers" owned or leased land and played an important role in the organization of production.

These differences in organizational form had considerable implications for the politics of agricultural modernization. Where small units of production already predominated, modernization would be easier. Where farming involved low-skilled hired help, recently or currently serfs, on the other hand, modernization would be far more difficult, because it would require not only considerable investment in equipment and education but also extensive reorganization of social and economic arrangements in the countryside.

The advantages of small-scale farming for modernization in these years can be seen clearly in the example of Denmark. When the crisis of 1873 began, Denmark's socioeconomic organization was suited to the new type of specialization. Denmark, like much of Western Europe, had evolved very differently from Prussia east of the Elbe:[18] the small farmer, the household, the managing tenant—the yeoman or kulak of other eras—these remained economically significant and, as democratization trickled down, politically important. A major shift in production into dairy and meat products could be undertaken without large scale social reorganization. Modernization involves risks, of course, and though the structure of Danish farming made landowners more receptive to change, it did not do so entirely spontaneously: the costs had to be socialized to some degree, that is, they had to be born collectively by the state. The Danish government helped farmers by loaning capital, providing education and technology, and sponsoring cooperatives.[19]

In Germany east of the Elbe the situation was quite different.[20] It was not that Junker estate owners had little experience with international markets—on the contrary, they had been integrated into a Europe-wide economy since the fifteenth century. (Indeed, many historians see that integration as the root cause of the reassertion of serfdom there as serfdom was crumbling in western Europe.) Rather, it was the character of the internationally oriented market economy in east Prussia which made it different from Denmark; that character demanded labor-intensive grain growing by servile labor on great landed estates. It was not well suited to the situation that emerged so dramatically in the eighth decade of the nineteenth century.

It was certainly not impossible for the Junkers to change. The soil, which was poor, and the climate, cool and damp, were certainly obstacles, but surely some agricultural product from the area could have found market in the world economy, as Polish hams do today. But that product could by no means have sustained the same population, in the same organizational forms, at the same rate of return. Some drastic reorganization would be required, at once social, infrastructural, and financial. The Danish model, in which high-quality goods were produced in small autonomous units managed by extended families, ran headlong into the latifundia form of social organization. The problem was not large landowners: in Britain, after all, an aristocracy continued to concentrate landownership in a few hands, but it subdivided the actual farming through long leases among many free farmers. In that respect the British countryside resembled the Danish and was thereby enabled to shift into the new forms of specialization.

The American trans-Mississippi region offered other models of efficient agriculture in that period: land-extensive, capital-intensive family farms for grain, and the open range for cattle supervised by small numbers of cowboys. The Old Northwest (east of Illinois) along with the older farming areas of the Northeast followed the Danish path, producing high-quality foodstuffs that consumed grain and were sold to the urban Northeast. But either American model would have required a vast reorganization of Junkerdom, reshaping the way land was farmed, changing the size and character of the work force, building infrastructure, providing farm machinery, organizing information, marketing, and finance, or, to make range land, driving off most of the population.

So unrealistic were these "alternatives" that the Junkers fought hard for protectionism. Tariffs would make it unnecessary for them to change dramatically. Sheltered behind the high walls of tariffs against the flood of foreign goods, life could go on as before. The Junkers could still raise low-quality grains and other materials and sell them within the empire—a large population, growing larger and more prosperous rapidly. Germany was a market big enough to absorb Junker production, provided foreign imports were kept out. With tariffs, adjustment to new conditions of the international division of labor could be gradual or nonexistent.

There were, of course, costs to the protectionist alternative: the German consumer would have to pay higher prices, directly in higher prices for grain and the products that consumed it, indirectly in lost demand for industrial products and the higher costs that filter through the economy when inefficient agriculture retains resources. How these costs affected the policy preferences of other groups in Germany society will be discussed below. Here my point is that the domestic costs of protectionism were not born by the Junkers. In a broad, long-term view it could be argued that adjustment made sense, but in practice adjustment seemed the least desirable option.

The Junkers were the most ardent advocates of protectionism among agriculture, but they were not all of German agriculture. In the west and south of the empire constructed in 1871, the pattern in the countryside resembled that of France, England, Denmark, and the Low Countries: great lords and independent farmers, laborers and leaseholders, cities and towns, old middle classes and new ones, huge factories with the latest machinery and traditional artisans—the old and the new living side by side in a tremendously diverse and increasingly complicated society. The "life chances," in Max Weber's phrase, of the peasants in the west were quite different from those in the east. In the west some became landowners, with plots of varying size; others became leaseholders or renters; yet others, landless laborers. Peasants could rise or fall. They could acquire more land through skill, luck, and marriage, owning or renting with an eye toward profit in the market; or they could fall through constant division of inheritance into subsistence farming, owning dwarf plots barely able to keep a family alive, let alone selling a surplus for cash.

The farmers of the German west and south were thus situated quite differently from the Junkers in relation to international economic conditions after 1873. As they were in structural terms more similar to the Danes, so the Danish solution to the crisis, modernization through intensified specialization in the international division of labor, was more of a possibility for them. Grain would become an input for modernizing farmers, and such farmers could be expected to oppose tariffs on imported grain.

Gerschenkron supposed that the small farmers of the south and west would be "natural" members of a free-trade coalition, but he observed that German agriculture in general supported protectionism. Gerschenkron supposed, therefore, that the viewpoint of one segment of agriculture, the Junkers, suffocated that of another, the smallholders. The need for an explanation led Gerschenkron to consider political entrepreneurship, ideology, and organizational sociology: the smallholders accepted Junker leadership apparently because the Junkers had the time and resources to engage in political activity, because they were able to control the agricultural associations, and because of the ideology of German self-sufficiency and rural autonomy which they were able to call on.

More recent scholarship dissents from this analysis in important ways: it sees the smallholders' acceptance of grain tariffs not as a misunderstanding of situational interest but rather as a sensible response to the pressures of uncertainty, intense competition, and economic distress. The Danes modernized not just because the market required it, but because the Danish government offered them incentives to do so. It was far from clear that German smallholders, lacking such help, should have undertaken the risks involved in shifting from one form of farming to another. Smallholder support for Junker protectionism was not therefore a simple case of coercion, political or cultural.[21]

At best, then, we must conclude that the situation of the smallholders of western and southern Germany was ambiguous. In contrast to the Junkers, for whom the alternatives to protectionism were sure to be costly, the smallholders could make their decision on the basis of what politics and the market were offering as incentives. They could specialize if properly encouraged, or they could continue grain production as before, sheltered behind the tariff walls so ardently desired by the Junkers.

So far we have examined the implications of the crisis in the international economy for the attitude of agricultural producers toward agricultural products. We cannot stop there, however, for the situation of the countryside is profoundly affected by developments in industry. Agriculture is simultaneously a consumer of industrial products and a seller to industrial producers. Lords, smallholders, and landless laborers all buy items such as nails, pots and pans, and machinery, and to industrial producers they all sell foodstuffs and a variety of raw materials used for manufacturing.

In this sense the city and countryside are in constant conflict. The city wants cheap food and raw materials but wants high prices for its own goods. Owners and workers are drawn together by the desire to keep food costs down: the latter because they are the bulk of consumers, the former to keep down labor pressure for higher wages and to free purchasing power for industrial goods. Agricultural producers, conversely, want to sell their produce for the highest possible price, whatever that costs the consumer, and they want to buy needed industrial goods at the lowest price, whatever that costs the producer. One result is a strong divergence on tariffs: farmers want high tariffs on agriculture but low tariffs on industrial products, manufacturers want the reverse.[22]

As the business-cycle downturn of 1873 turned into a broader crisis, the industrialists of Germany divided. For some, the new international division of labor afforded opportunities to move ahead and dominate production; for others, the new conditions meant considerable distress, requiring active help. The battle between free trade and protection took a new turn in German politics, contributing to an important realignment in policy as well as in politics.

Among the strongest advocates of protectionism were the producers of textiles and iron and steel.[23] In both product sectors Britain had been the world's dominant producer since the beginning of the industrial revolution. German industrial development occurred, therefore, in an environment very different from what Britain had known. Germany, and all later developers, had to promote economic growth in the shadow of a more advanced, more efficient producer. (Gerschenkron formalized this distinction in the dichotomy between "early" and "late" development.)

The timing of development has considerable implications for the likely policy preferences of producers, according to where they are in the historical sequence. Manufacturers able to dominate world production, through their position in technology or factor costs, are likely to be favorably disposed toward free trade. Manufacturers overshadowed by stronger competitors are likely to seek tariffs or other forms of government assistance. This rather simple rule provides considerable assistance in mapping out the policy behavior of German industrial sectors in the nineteenth century. Manufacturers of textiles and iron in Germany were consistently protectionist. To them, free-trade doctrines meant accepting the continuance of British domination. Without tariff protection, they would never be able to emerge from the British shadow.

In part this was the familiar infant industry argument, a legitimate case for protection in the framework of the market. Economic development of an industry entails start-up costs in capital and knowledge. During the early days competition from established producers threatens to smother newborn producers before they have the opportunity to become viable, independent adults. Tariffs are justified to protect entrepreneurs until they can compete on their own. Once these infants reach industrial maturity, however, tariff protection can and should be removed. A developmental argument articulated within the framework of liberal economics, this made a case on grounds of efficiency. Other goals extended the justification for tariffs: industry as the base for national power; industry as promoter of skills and values; market results as source of too much suffering. And in the nineteenth century one can already find many advocates of what in the twentieth would come to be called industrial policy on behalf of "creating comparative advantage"[24]—those who believe that market forces are *never* reliable instruments for promoting industrial modernization.

All of these arguments were made by German industrial protectionists. In textiles, it is true, British and other foreign competitors were quite strong, but the behavior of the iron and steel industry deserves our further attention. True, Britain had dominated world production, and as German ironmakers sought to catch up, they claimed the need for economic protection. In this they came into conflict with the Junkers, who wanted industrial free trade. Indeed, animosity over economic policy was one of the major obstacles to unification in the middle of the century. But the British lead makes it appear an easy matter to understand the continuation of protectionist sentiment among German iron and steel manufacturers after 1873.

The trouble with this line of reasoning is that German iron and steel manufacturers were rapidly becoming the world's most efficient. In the last decades of the century they not only caught up with the leaders but, with the United States, raced ahead of them. Germany and the United States poured huge sums of capital into new technology, developing an immense iron- and steel-making capacity. German iron products were of high quality and competitively priced. They penetrated markets everywhere around the world, even in the United States and the United Kingdom. Why, then, were German iron and steel producers in the forefront of German protectionism? Why, then, did they participate so energetically in the iron-rye coalition of 1879?

The answer may lie in the structure of investment in iron-steel technology. Making iron, and later steel, was very capital-intensive. As mass-production techniques replaced artisanal manufacturing, the capital needs involved in building foundries grew rapidly, dwarfing the requirements of, for example, the textile industry, and as the technology progressed, so did the capital requirements. Iron and steel became huge consumers of capital, as did their main customers, the railroads. By mid-century the ability to produce iron and steel involved the organization of capital as much as the acquisition of technology. And indeed, a key element of Gerschenkron's thesis holds that the advantages of backwardness are in part organizational—the mercantilist state, too heavy-handed for the decentralized origins of the industrial revolution in textiles, proved useful later, when extensive centralized coordination was an advantage.[25]

Lateness proved an advantage as well in exploiting the latest technology. Britain had taken the lead in iron, but as technology progressed, it devalued that lead. British capital was sunk in machinery that was outmoded; American and German capital went into new, more up-to-date equipment. The advantage of efficiency was gained only through massive infusions of capital.

With the thirst for iron and steel round the world apparently unquenchable, massive amounts of money poured into production in the sixties and seventies. Then the market went soft. The combination of massive new capacity and uncertain markets makes the protectionism of the efficient more understandable. Vast investments had to be amortized over a long period of time, and they were inflexible. They could not fluctuate with the vagaries of the business cycle compounded by the stress of overcapacity in world markets. Investment of such a size required the assurance that some minimum amount of production could be sold at specific prices. There were various ways of getting that sort of guarantee: cartels, mergers, government purchase, and tariffs. Behind tariff walls, efficient producers would be assured some degree of long-range predictability, at least some knowledge of return on investment, sufficient to justify the stupendous sums required. From a secure domestic market, manufacturers could compete more ferociously in the international wars, their oligopoly profits allowing them to use price cutting, dumping, and the rest of the arsenal of international competition. Iron and steel manufacturers were, as we shall see, in the vanguard of protectionist movements everywhere, even in Britain, the scene of their only failure.

If iron-, steel-, and textile makers led protectionist sentiment in Germany, they did not speak for all of German industry. In some areas of the international division of labor Germany was in the vanguard of innovation and production. In chemicals and electrical equipment, particularly, German companies, backed by German science, were developing new products and new processes. Chemical dyes, chemical materials used in processing, machine tools, the machinery for a new energy source, electricity, and electric motors—in these areas Germany was able not only to compete with the first industrial country but to outstrip it.

For companies in these advanced industries, the deepening of international specialization could be only an advantage. If all countries followed the principle of comparative advantage and allowed free trade, these industries would have the world as their market. As leaders, they would make considerable profits. Tariffs, conversely, would constrict markets. If Germany threw up tariffs against textiles, iron, grain, and other products, other countries were likely to respond in kind. The German home market might be large, but it was still smaller than the world market, particularly the combined market of other industrial countries. For leading German industries, then, British notions of sloughing off weaker companies and products, importing from abroad, and shifting resources into areas of higher value added all made sense. Nor were the emerging German giants in chemicals and electrical goods alone in seeing benefits in free trade. For the producers of consumer goods, iron and steel frequently were inputs for the manufacture of the products they wished to sell. Textiles and food, moreover, were basic consumer items for the salaried labor force; higher costs there meant lower purchasing power for other goods.

Different sectors of German industry, then, were situated quite differently within the new international division of labor which emerged after 1873. Older industries, such as textiles, and second-generation ones, such as iron and steel, faced severe problems of overcapacity and slackening demand which troubled even the most modern, efficient manufacturers. Newer industries, such as chemicals and electrical equipment, and the makers of finished consumer goods were surely affected by the difficult economic environment, but for

91

them, international trade afforded real possibilities. These two groups diverged on the question of foreign economic policy.

When we compare country debates over economic policy, therefore, it is important to pay attention to the patterns of economic development within those countries. The various industries, branches, or sectors that comprise an advanced economy are not likely all to have the same relationship to the international economy. Some industries are likely to be more or less ahead of the competition than others, some are likely to have greater or lesser needs for stability of revenue to handle large-scale investments, and so on. As a result, they are likely to disagree on economic policy.

So far we have looked only at manufacturing under the rubric of industry. Other kinds of capital existed, and in particular the banking, shipping, and retail sectors. There are other categories within the industrial work force, such as professionals and workers. What was their situation in relation to foreign economic policy?

Banking in Germany developed quite differently from its British counterpart.[26] In the first industrial nation, banking developed separately from manufacturing. The textile industry was able to generate its own capital through a relatively simple, decentralized banking system; new investment could draw on the substantial earnings of this rapidly growing group of businesses in the early stages of the second generation of industry. For iron and steel at the start, that is, capital requirements were still relatively low and could be mobilized through the great profits accumulated by the first generation. Banking in Britain developed as an instrument of commerce, trade, and portfolio investment, and it financed shipping, agriculture, trade, overseas infrastructure, and absentee share investments for domestic trust portfolios. As such, British banking developed a specific situation in the international economy, one distinctly different from that of British manufacturing.

Advanced technology was already much more capital-intensive when Germany launched its development drive, particularly in iron and steel. Vast quantities of capital had to be mobilized, and quickly. This was done in Germany, before and after unification, by banking with help from government. German banking from the beginning thus had an intimate relationship with German manufacturing. (Generally, Germany formed investment banking rather than the commercial or merchant banking of the United Kingdom.) As a result, German banking had neither a situation nor an outlook distinctly different from that of its industries. Banks worked closely with specific firms in specific industries to analyze, define, and articulate their collective interests.

The same could be said of the various professions. Lawyers, accountants, managers, scientists, professors, all worked for different employers in different situations; as their situation varied, so did their outlook. Shipping, conversely, developed a situation that drew it toward the free-trade position: more international trade, more imports and exports, meant more business for shipping lines. Railroads and canal and river shipping firms, on the other hand, whose business lay largely within Germany, found protection satisfying as a way of building up the domestic economy.

Retailing sought to promote sales. Cheap prices for the goods that retailers sold were the likeliest way of expanding a mass market. Low food prices and low raw material costs, moreover, would increase the purchasing power of the consumer. On the other hand, free trade could cost some employment (from retailing's point of view, "reduce the number of consumers") in some industries. Here we must analyze the situation of labor.

Labor is of course a very broad category, as large as that of capital and situationally, therefore, quite diverse. As sellers of labor power, workers are very broadly in conflict with employers. Generally, workers desire higher wages and better working conditions, while employers prefer lower wages and cheaper working conditions. At a wide range of other points conflict occurs, from the status of trade unions and the nature of labor relations, to safety and welfare, to the role of workers in management, and the definition of property rights.

But on some issues the interests of some elements of labor and some elements of management may converge. Both may seek low food costs, for example, workers to save money as consumers, employers to deflect pressure for higher wages as well as to free purchasing power for the consumption of industrial items. At such times labor and industrial capital may converge in a conflict with agriculture over agricultural and industrial prices.

Business-labor relations have a further element of complexity: business, as we have noted, is by no means uniform in its policy positions. Business may generally agree on the need to keep down labor costs and demands, but on specific issues of foreign economic policy there may be considerable conflict within the ranks of business, as we have seen. On free trade vs. protectionism, each side may seek allies for the battles over economic policy. Each may try to manage its policy disagreement with workers over wages in order to mobilize labor support. When this happens, labor must also make decisions about its own internal disagreements and conflicts. As an aggregation of consumers, the labor movement has a generalized interest in cheap prices. As a congeries of producers, however, labor may find its interests split, those who work for protectionist employers sharing their bosses' outlook, those who work for free-trade employers allowing their producer and consumer interests to converge.

Labor, then, can take various attitudes toward policy, depending on which of its conflicting preferences predominates. We need to examine more closely, through comparative analysis, just what conditions seem to encourage one choice of behavior or another.

In Imperial Germany the labor organizations, trade unions, and Social Democratic party by and large supported free trade. They opposed Bismarck's course after 1879 and became part of the coalition that Chancellor Georg von Caprivi drew together from 1890 to 1894 in seeking to reverse Bismarck's line. Some elements of the labor movement were drawn toward protectionism, but the "freer" trade course predominated.[27]

The last few pages have examined the policy preferences of various groups in German society toward the "economic crisis" of the last third of the nineteenth century and have made some suggestions about the ways in which those preferences relate to the situation of each group in the international economy. These preferences can be summarized in diagrammatic form. Table 3 shows each group's position in relation to tariffs, agricultural and industrial. Political behavior is a matter not only of preference, however, but of intensity of preference. We may surmise that the greater the range of plausible responses, the more "cross-cutting" are the cues from situation; hence the more ambiguous and thus the less intense the preference will be. Intensity can be suggested in the diagram by proximity to the axis: closeness to the intercept suggests ambiguity in the group's interest, distance suggests clarity and intensity of interest.

The actual policy outcome in the law of 1879 was tariffs on both industrial and agricultural imports. No single group wanted that outcome; rather, the law was a compromise among sectors. This result seems to fit quite easily with a societal actor explanation of policy outcomes. Logrolling, or horse trading, is something we expect of interest groups.

Nonetheless, a different outcome—*low* tariffs on both types of goods—would also have been compatible with an interest group explanation. Logrolling could have drawn together those parts of industry and agriculture which had a plausible interest in low tariffs: manufacturers of finished goods and their workers, shippers and dock-workers, shopkeepers, consumers, and the farmers of the west and south. Such a coalition may even have been a majority of the electorate at times, and at certain moments it managed to obtain some

Table 3. Tariff policy preferences in late nineteenth-century Germany

Agricultural Tariffs

		High	Low
High Industrial Tariffs **Low**		**The Outcome** Small	Heavy industry Workers in heavy industry farmers
		Junkers	Workers in finished manufacturing Finished manufacturers

policy success. Under Chancellor Caprivi, between 1890 and 1894, reciprocal trade treaties were negotiated and tariffs lowered. Clearly this coalition lost over the long run, but of what did its weakness consist?

One answer is provided by the explanatory tradition that looks to the parties and *interest group organizations* of Germany. Although political parties were growing rapidly in a newly unified Germany with universal suffrage, none had developed the capacity to make broad appeals, linking together diverse elements of the German people. German parties lacked the organization, experience, tradition, and ideological arguments of their British counterparts. No party, in particular, had developed a framework for combining capital and labor around liberal economics, constitutional government, and better working conditions and wages. The Socialists grew in strength, but in ways that made such an appeal difficult. Liberal formations in Germany, weak even before the economic crisis began, got weaker under the divisive strains of debate over economic policy. As a result, this answer claims, we can ignore Junker manipulation and downgrade the importance of organizational strength: Junkers and small farmers alike supported protection because of the harsh economic conditions in which they operated.[28]

Another interpretation of tariff policy looks to the *institutional arrangements* of Germany which favored protectionist forces at the expense of free traders. In particular, it focuses on institutions, such as weighted voting and the bureaucracy, and the preferences of key political actors, such as the chancellor and the Crown—elements of the organization of the state which comprise *state capacity*.[29] In all these domains the protectionists, especially the Junkers, had real advantages. Having dominated Prussia, which now dominated Germany, the Junkers had a special place inside a vital element of the state, the army. The elite positions of the Prussian Army, now the German Army, were monopolized by members of the Junker aristocracy. Middle-class individuals could rise into the officer corps, it is true, but only if they adopted the values of the Junkers. The same was true of the civilian bureaucracy: if members of the Junker class did not actually staff the bureaus, they were able to shape their outlook. Careful controls over recruitment (known as the Puttkamer system) enabled German conservatives to ensure that the state apparatus remained safely in the hands of people who accepted their understanding of the constitution, both formally, in the primacy of the Crown and the executive, and socially, in the primacy of the social elite.

The constitution of Prussia affected the distribution of power as well. Although the Imperial Constitution of 1871 proclaimed universal suffrage, election to the Prussian Diet was organized into three electoral colleges, according to property. This division greatly weakened the mass electorate of the working class, small peasants, and artisans, to the benefit of the Prussian elite—of which, of course, the Junkers were an important fraction.

Among the major institutional levers for the protectionists during this period was the executive, and the relationship between Bismarck and the Crown deserves more detailed exposition. Bismarck and the emperor, both free traders before the 1870s, swung over to the position of the Junkers after prices began to plunge. In the German empire, having the executive on one's side was no paltry advantage. Technically, the Imperial Constitution called for a parliamentary system, and chancellor and Cabinet, if defeated on a motion of no confidence, would be expected to resign. In that sense the government was not independent of political forces—it had to find, organize, and maintain majorities in the Reichstag, like any other constitutional government. The institutional argument, which stresses the executive, neglects the point that the effects of rules are not separate from the society in which majorities must be organized.

But the German executive was not quite like any other. The accountability of the executive to the Parliament had never been confirmed through tests, battles, and showdowns. The most dramatic case of conflict between chancellor and legislature had been in the early 1860s, in Prussia, over the Army Bill; then Bismarck had defied the Assembly, continued to collect taxes, borrowed money, and went ahead with his policies. After the success of the campaigns against

Denmark and Austria the Assembly capitulated, authorizing money and army reforms after the fact.[30] Among the results was a weakening of the notion of executive accountability, in stark contrast with British politics since Stuart efforts in the seventeenth century to create a continental-style executive and, in the French Third Republic, with the triumph of the National Assembly over a strong presidency.

The German executive had tremendous authority as long as kaiser and chancellor agreed, which they did most of the time. Much of the bureaucracy, indeed much of the country, saw its obligations as lying with the kaiser and his ministers, not with some parliamentary majority. This was certainly true of the army. Indeed, various administrative changes made sure of it. Many aspects of army organization and policy were taken out of the hands of the minister in charge, precisely so that no technical way would exist through which Parliament could hold him accountable. Most of the apparatus of the modern state—army, police, civil service—looked to the executive, not the Parliament, for authoritative decisions.

That executive commanded tremendous resources. It had a well-developed police apparatus; it controlled tremendous funds with no parliamentary supervision; it had an ideologically congruent and coherent body of officials. Whichever group had that executive on its side would thus have a considerable resource in any policy battle—and the protectionists had both kaiser and chancellor. Bismarck was of course a Junker, with Junker worries about the profitability of his lands, but that is not an adequate explanation of his behavior. Indeed, Bismarck did many things that the Junkers disliked—such as unification, which they feared threatened their privileged place in Prussia, and the constitution of 1871, which for them was far too liberal.

For Bismarck, protectionism offered a political solution to a problem that had plagued him since he took office—how to fashion a compliant majority in the legislature. How, in other words, could he manage executive-legislative relations in a way that would give the political legitimacy provided by elections but without his having to give up substantial control over policy?[31] Bismarck was not willing to run a traditional dictatorship; he would not give the order, as one general said the king must always be able to do, to shoot the members of the Reichstag. Bismarck, whom Henry Kissinger called the White Revolutionary, understood the force of mass politics. Bismarck sought to gratify the German public substantively, not procedurally. He would give them many of their substantive demands, among them unification, industrialization, market liberties, subsidies, and control

97

of working-class organization, but he would not accede to their procedural demands for democratization of society and the political process, and he would tolerate no spreading of liberal, constitutionalist values.

In the 1860s the Junkers and much of the new middle class were on a collision course. The former feared unification and wanted to preserve a special place for themselves and for agriculture; the latter wanted a unified Germany and a free national market sheltered from outside competition. Then, for much of the population, the main purpose of the army appeared to be domestic repression—making the world safe for the Junkers. By using the army as the instrument of unification, Bismarck transformed the situation, but even after 1871 his situation remained unsure. There were plenty of dissidents about what had happened: liberals, Catholics, federalists, workers, democrats. The very hetereogeneity of this opposition was its major weakness, but nonetheless a coalition that could threaten Bismarck's authority was not impossible.

In the 1870s Bismarck used the Kulturkampf, the policy conflict about the role of the Church in the school system, to prevent the formation of a revisionist alliance. By attacking Catholics, he split the opposition, giving Protestants and liberal anticlerics a sense that he was on the progressive side of history. But that political formula made the government too dependent on politically unreliable liberals. Moreover, it excluded from the conservative coalition a group whose political outlook ought to have made it one of the coalition's cornerstones, the Catholics.

The new economic situation beginning in 1873 offered Bismarck just the new solution he was looking for. It allowed the refashioning of the conservative coalition on a new footing. Junkerdom and big bourgeoisie, the traditional and the new elite, agriculturalists and industrialists—these various elements of German society put aside earlier antagonisms in exchange for tariffs. Industrialists abandoned hostility to the Junkers and any lingering demands for more constitutionalist politics in exchange for tariffs, antisocialist laws, and their incorporation into the governing majority (and, later on, navy contracts). Catholics abandoned complaints about the constitution in exchange for tariffs and an end to the Kulturkampf, which was expendable because its integrative and divisive functions would now be played by tariffs.

The Junkers accepted higher prices for industry, and the claims of industry generally, but they got high prices for food and their privileged position in the system. Peasants got protection to ease their immediate distress, a solution perhaps less desirable over the long run than the Danish one but effective nonetheless. Labor was offered social insurance. The military obtained armaments, for which the iron and steel manufacturers received the contracts. The coalition excluded everyone who challenged the economic order, or the constitutional settlement of 1871, or both: socialists (the Social Democratic party was outlawed the same year as the tariff was introduced), federalists, supporters of *grossedeutsch* solutions, democrats, and liberals. This coalition would remain in power until 1918, with only a brief and limited hiatus in the early 1890s under Caprivi. Because of its importance in the reorganization of German politics, the tariff of 1879 has aptly been called the second founding of the empire.

Control of the executive allowed Bismarck to orchestrate the complex tradeoffs of coalition politics, for each partner had to be persuaded to pay for a share of costs of the coalition, especially the high tariffs on the goods of the other sectors. Control of foreign policy offered instruments for maintaining the bargain once it had been struck. Indeed, Hans-Uhlrich Wehler, following the intellectual tradition of Eckhart Kehr, stresses the primacy of domestic preoccupations in Bismarck's foreign policy. The chancellor used imperialism, nationalism, and overseas crises to obscure internal division and, in particular, to blunt middle- and working-class criticism of the regime—a strategy famous since antiquity and used to great effect recently by Margaret Thatcher in the case of the Falklands War. Nationalism and a vision of Germany surrounded by enemies, or at least harsh competitors, reinforced arguments favoring self-sufficiency in food and industrial production and a powerful military machine. As Wehler wrote, "From the early 1880's, imperialism became an ideological force for integration in a state which lacked stabilizing historical traditions and which was unable to conceal sharp class divisions between its authoritarian cloak."[32]

The protectionists had these various resources at their disposal in the struggle over foreign economic policy. What of their opponents, the free (or, more accurately, freer) traders? Their coalition operated under several handicaps. First, it was very heterogeneous. It sought to embrace diverse economic categories, including producers and consumers, manufacturers and shippers, owners and workers, city dwellers and peasants. Little in day-to-day life brought these elements together or otherwise fostered the pursuit of common goals, and much kept them apart: quarrels over property rights, working conditions and worker wages, credit, taxation. The low-tariff groups also differed on other issues that were not explicitly economic, such as religion, federalism, democratization of the constitution, and constitutional control of the army and executive. Unlike the protectionist alliance, however, the low-tariff coalition had to overcome its diversity without help from the executive. Only during Caprivi's four years as chancellor were the resources of that office available to the low-tariff side, and even then Caprivi was isolated from the court, the kaiser, the army, and the bureaucracy. Yet despite all these weakness, the low-tariff alliance had its successes. It did well in 1881, in the first elections after the tariff was imposed, inflicting a defeat on Bismarck which, Wehler argues, drove him further toward social imperialism. From 1890, moreover, Caprivi directed a series of reciprocal trade negotiations that led to tariff reductions. His ministry suggests what was needed to keep a low-tariff coalition together: at home a little more egalitarianism and constitutionalism (the end of the antisocialist laws), and in foreign policy a little more internationalism—not so much a lack of interest in empire or prestige as a greater willingness to insert Germany into an international division of labor.

The institutional interpretation of the protectionist victory, in sum, stresses the advantages that the structure of the German state conferred upon the high-tariff coalition in the battle over German foreign economic policy. The Prussian model triumphed under Bismarck's leadership, and Prussia's institutions had special weight in the new empire. Bureaucracy, army, and judiciary were staffed with staunch conservatives, respondent to the will of the executive as expressed by the Crown through the chancellor. The three-class voting system, the federalism that favored Prussia in German affairs, and vast financial and organizational resources all aided the chancellor.

These levers are substantial, and they make for a very plausible account of the outcome. Bismarck was surely the most skillful politician of the era, and the Prussian-German state the most highly developed. If "institutional capability" existed anywhere in the Europe of the period, it existed in Imperial Germany. That capability surely rendered an activist economic policy easier than it would have been for a weaker state. Moreover, that those in charge of the state favored the protectionists' demands surely made the tariff triumph easier.

Put thus the argument is strong but confusing on one critical question: How is Bismarck's behavior to be explained? Was his support of the protectionists a matter of institutional arrangement (state capacity) or a matter of his relationship to societal forces? The institutional argument roots the outcome in formal arrangements of the state—its rules, procedures, and bureaucratic forms. Yet telling the story demands repeated reference to the way that these formal arrangements affected societal groups. Bismarck's control of these arrangements surely gave him resources, but his tenure in office itself depended on his ability to mobilize support within elites and the mass electorate. The mobilization of support had many consequences—the formation of ideologies, programs, and policies that functioned (and were at in least in part designed) to obtain support for the government. This, then, is not an institutional argument but a political one, which is not at all the same. The distinction is worth remembering.

Another explanation for the success of the protectionist alliance looks to *economic ideology*.[33] The German nationalist school, associated with the ideas of Friedrich List, favored state intervention in economic matters to promote national power and welfare. More generally, free-trade and laissez-faire doctrines were not well entrenched in Germany. In Britain, by contrast, the mercantilist approach to economic development was a casualty of the Civil War: with the dismantling of the royal bureaucracy went both institutional capability for and the belief in state-organized manufacturing. The collapse of the Holy Roman Empire in Germany at about the same time did not end absolutism. There, many smaller entities, organized *à la française*, acted on the belief that profit-seeking individuals could not be relied upon to create wealth. The state therefore promoted manufacturing through deliberate policy. In contrast with Britain, in sum, Germany had developed neither a liberal society nor a liberal state. As the industrial revolution spread into Germany, it drew on mercantilist, interventionist traditions, not liberal ones.

Germany's political fragmentation, moreover, created a strong nationalist impulse in the nineteenth century. Unity, industrial development, and national power fused together around the conviction that as a late developer, Germany had to promote economic growth; it could not wait for "nature" to do the job alone. So it was, the explanation holds that when the international situation changed, German economic actors found it easier to accept state intervention in the form of protection than did comparable groups in Britain, where liberal ideology was far more potent.

The final explanation for tariff policy looks at each country's position in the *international state system*. A country's economic policy, according to this line of reasoning, derives not only from specific economic calculations but also from other national concerns, such as security, independence, and glory. International specialization means interdependence, and an open economy makes itself vulnerable to disruptions in supplies of food, raw materials, and manufactured goods, and to changes in foreign markets. Countries whose geopolitical situation is secure may take this risk; those which are threatened may not.

Britain thus could afford to rely on imports because it was an island and had the world's most powerful navy. If Germany were to do the same, however, would it not become vulnerable to that navy? In the debate over German foreign economic policy the international context figured large. Protectionists used national security to justify their preferences. Germany, they argued, was indeed surrounded by hostile powers that had seized empire, built industry, and created enormous military capability. Germany had to do the same. A balanced domestic economy, one that preserved a capacity to produce a whole range of products, was vital.

This line of reasoning points to position in the international system as an explanation of policy. It supposes that such position is objective, that its meaning imposes itself upon domestic actors. Usually, however, there are different ways of interpreting the international system, and a country's place in it, and the implications for policy. In late nineteenth-century Germany some argued that international trade in a framework of world peace would allow Germany to realize many of its ambitions. German industries were strong and competitive; Germany could absorb resources in competitive industries and import where costs worked against domestic production. That France, Britain, and Russia were drawing into alliance with one another was not, according to the internationalist school, some inevitable thing of nature. Rather, it was a response to aggressive German behavior. Were Germany to act more cooperatively, it could prevent such polarization against it.

The military rivalries of the international state system do not impose protectionism, therefore; protection is one possibility among many. Its triumph cannot be deduced from the international system, because the influence of that system is refracted through the prism of domestic politics. Protectionism involves conflict among different viewpoints and the triumph of one over others. To understand just how the international system affects economic policy outcomes therefore requires us carefully to examine domestic political conflict and the interrelation of issues, both international and domestic. Indeed, the conflict between these two viewpoints is a classic one. Each side represents an important tradition in German historiography and in international relations writing on the linkages between domestic and international politics.[34]

A different version of the international system explanation focuses on the structure of economic negotiation and bargaining among countries. Tariffs are interactive: if one country raises tariffs, others will almost always retaliate. Reciprocal trade agreements require careful negotiation, however, and it is not easy for a low-tariff system to be constructed and survive. The temptation is always present to "beggar thy neighbor"—to take a free ride on others' free trade. A low-tariff regime can be seen as an international cartel, an understanding to prevent deviation from a collective rule. To understand what happened in the late nineteenth century, therefore, we need to consider the conditions that allow such intercountry agreements to rise or fall. Some theorists argue that the key is the existence of a hegemon, a dominant international power able to organize the free-trade cartel and pay transaction and maintenance costs. Others argue that the agreements rise or fall with general economic conditions; a prosperous era can sustain free trade, a troublesome one cannot.

The late nineteenth century fails to satisfy both conditions. Britain lost its dominant position, and so the international economic system no longer had a hegemon. As the downswing occurred, moreover, the benefits of free trade faded while the costs were being felt acutely and intensely. One might even argue that Germany was driven to high tariffs by the protectionist behavior of other countries. The timing of reciprocal trade treaties in this period might demonstrate the point; the available evidence seems to suggest, however, that in Germany the shift from Caprivi's low-tariff policy in the early nineties to Bernhard von Bülow's solidarity bloc early in the new century did not result from changes in the behavior of foreign governments. Rather, the Bismarckian coalition of heavy industry, army, Junkers, nationalists, and conservatives mobilized to prevent further erosion of its domestic position.[35]

In sum, one might argue that all five explanations are compatible with German experience in the last quarter of the nineteenth century. Economic circumstances after 1873 provided ample inducements for major interest groups to support high tariffs. Intermediate associations accommodated societal pressures. Political institutions provided the protectionists with leverage while the support of the kaiser and the chancellor made sure that they would be used in a particular direction. German economic traditions helped justify the protectionist victory. International political conditions seemed to make protection a matter of national security. Are all these factors really necessary to explain the protectionist victory? Or is this a case of causal overdetermination? Let us reserve judgment until after we have looked at other countries and other policies.

FRANCE

The French case offers us a very different political system that produced a very similar policy result. As with Germany, the causal variables all point in the same direction. Looking at the interests of key economic actors, high tariffs for both industrial and agricultural goods are what we would expect to find. French industry, despite striking gains under the Second Empire and the Cobden-Chevalier treaty, was certainly less efficient than that of other "late starters" (Germany and the United States). Hence manufacturers in heavy, highly capitalized, or particularly vulnerable industries had an intense interest in protection. Shippers and successful exporters opposed it.[36]

Agriculture, as in Germany, was diverse. France had no precise equivalent to the Junkers, and in comparison to Prussia, even on the biggest farms, the soil was better, the labor force freer, and the owners less likely to be exclusively dependent on the land for income. Nonetheless, whether large or small, all producing units involved in the market were hit hard by the drop in prices of the 1870s; the large numbers of quasi-subsistence farmers, on the other hand, were less affected. The prevalence of smallholding made modernization easier than in Prussia, but it was still costly. For most of the agricultural sector, the path of least resistance was to maintain past practices behind high tariff walls.

As we would expect, most French producer groups became increasingly protectionist as prices dropped. In the early 1870s Adolphe Thiers, as president of the Republic, tried to raise tariffs, largely for revenue purposes, but he failed. New associations demanded tariff revision. In 1881 the National Assembly passed the first general tariff measure, which protected industry more than agriculture, but in the same year American meat products were barred on health grounds. Sugar received help in 1884, grains and meats in the tariffs of 1885 and 1887. Finally, broad coverage was given to both agriculture and industry in the Meline tariff of 1892. Thereafter, tariffs drifted upward reaching apogee in the tariff of 1910.[37]

French institutions and associations contributed to this policy response. Universal suffrage in a society of small property owners favored the interests of units of production over those of consumers. Conflict over nontariff issues were severe, of course, but they did not prevent protectionists from finding one another. Republican, royalist, clerical, and anticlerical protectionists broke away from their free-trade homologues to vote the Meline tariff in.[38] Some of these protectionists even hoped to reform the party system by using economic and social questions to drive out religious and constitutional ones. This effort failed, but cross-party majorities continued to coalesce every time the question of protection arose, and high tariffs helped reconcile many conservatives to the Republic.[39]

In the case of France protection is also the result we would expect

from the international system explanation, because international political rivalries imposed security concerns to preserve both a domestic
food supply and a rural reservoir of military manpower. Finally,
French ideological traditions abound with arguments that favor of
state intervention. The Cobden-Chevalier treaty itself had been negotiated at the highest political level, and the process of approving it had
generated no mass commitment to free trade to resemble what had
resulted from the lengthy public battle over the repeal of the Corn
Laws in Britain. The tariffs of the 1880s restored the status quo ante.

Two things stand out when we compare France with Germany.
First, France had no equivalent either to Bismarck or to the state
mechanism that supported him. The national compromise between
industry and agriculture was organized without any help from the
top. Interest groups and politicians operating through elections and
the party system came together and worked things out. Neither the
party system, nor the constitution, nor outstanding personalities can
be shown to have favored one coalition over another.

Second, it is mildly surprising that this alliance took so long to
form—perhaps that was the consequence of having no Bismarck. It
appears that industry took the lead in fighting for protection and
scored the first success. Agriculture was left out of the tariff of 1881
(while in Germany it was an integral part of the tariff of 1879), even
though it represented such a large number of people. Why did it take
another eleven years to get a general tariff bill? Part of the answer
may lie in the absence of leaders with a commanding structural position who were working to effect a particular policy. In any case, the
Republic eventually did secure a general bill, at about the same time
that the United States was also raising tariffs.

THE UNITED STATES

Only the United States of the five countries examined here combined low-cost agriculture and dynamic industry in the same political
system. The policy outcome, high industrial tariffs and low agricultural ones, fits the logic of the production profile argument. En-
dowed with efficient agriculture, the United States had no need to
protect it; given the long shadow of the British giant, industry did
need protection. But despite its efficiency, or rather because of it,
American agriculture did have severe problems in the later nineteenth century. On a number of points it came into intense conflict
with industry, and by and large industry had its way.

In monetary policy, for instance, the increasing value of money made the value of debt that farmers owed to East Coast bankers appreciate. Expanding farm production drove prices constantly downward, so that an ever larger amount of produce was needed to pay off an ever increasing debt. Cheap money schemes, however, were repeatedly defeated. In transportation, farmers were highly vulnerable to rate manipulation where no competition among alternative modes of transport or companies existed. Regulation eventually was introduced, but whether because of farmers' efforts or because of the desire of railroad men and other industrialists to prevent ruinous competition—as part of their search for order—is not clear.[40] Insurance and fees also helped redistribute income from one sector to the other.

Tariffs themselves hurt farmers, for the protection of industrial goods required farmers to sell in a free world market and buy in a protected one. In taxation policy, meanwhile, industry blocked an income tax until 1913; before income and corporate taxes were imposed, the revenue burden was most severe for the landowner. Market instability, in particular erratic prices, could have been controlled by government storage facilities, price stabilization boards, and price supports, but such tools were not provided until after World War I. Differential pricing practices (such as "Pittsburgh Plus," whereby goods were priced according to the location of the head office rather than the factory) worked like an internal tariff, pumping money from the country into the Northeast. The antitrust acts addressed some of these problems but left many untouched. Finally, in patronage and pork barrel, some agrarian areas, especially the South, fared badly in the distribution of federal largess.[41]

In the process of political and industrial development, defeat of the agricultural sector appears inevitable. Whatever the indicator (share of GNP, percentage of the work force, control of the land), farmers decline in importance; whether peasants, landless laborers, family farmers, kulaks, or estate owners, they fuel industrialization by providing foreign exchange, food, and manpower. In the end most of them disappear.

This can happen, however, at varying rates: very slowly, as in China today, quite slowly as in France, quickly as in Britain. In the United States, I would argue, the defeat of agriculture as a *sector* was swift and thorough. Some landowners were successful, of course. They shifted from broad attacks on the system to interest group lobbying for specialized clienteles. The mass of the agricultural population, however, lost most of its policy battles and left the land.

One might have expected America to develop not like Germany, as

Barrington Moore suggests (although that was certainly a possibility), but like France: with controlled, slower industrial growth, speed sacrificed to balance and the preservation of a large rural population.[42] But for that to have happened, the mass of small farmers needed allies willing to help them battle the East Coast banking and industrial combine that dominated American policy making. To understand their failure, it is useful to analyze the structure of incentives among potential alliance partners, as we did for the European countries. If we take farmers' grievances on the policy issues noted above (such as on money and interest rates) to be the functional equivalent of tariffs, then we make comparable the politics of coalition formation in the United States and in Europe.

Two alliances were competing for the allegiance of the same groups. The employers of the protectionist core of heavy industry, banks, and textiles persuaded workers that their interests derived from their roles not as consumers but as producers in the industrial sector. To farmers selling in urban markets, the protectionists made the familiar case for keeping industry strong.

The alternative coalition formed around hostility toward heavy industry and banks, appealing to workers and farmers as consumers, to farmers as debtors and victims of industrial manipulation, to the immigrant poor and factor hands against the tribulations of the industrial system, to farmers as manipulated debtors, and to shippers and manufacturers of finished products on behalf of lower costs. It sought lower tariffs and more industrial regulation (of hours, rates, and working conditions). Broadly, this "Jacksonian" coalition confronted the "Whig" interest, the little man opposed the man of property.

The progressive, low-tariff alliance was not weak. Agriculture still employed by far the largest percentage of the work force, and federalism should have given it considerable leverage: the whole South, the Midwest, and the trans-Mississippi West. True, parts of the Midwest were industrializing, but then much of the Northeast remained agricultural. Nonetheless, the alliance failed, and its failure turned on the critical realignment election of 1896. The defeat of populism then marked the end of two decades of intense party competition, the beginning of forty years of Republican hegemony, and the turning point for agriculture as a sector. Heuristically it is useful to work backward from the conjuncture of 1896 to the broader forces that produced the contest.

The battle of 1896 was shaped by the character and strategy of William Jennings Bryan, the standard bearer of the low-tariff alliance. Bryan has had a bad press historically, because his populism

had overtones of bigotry, anti-intellectualism, and religious funda-
mentalism. Politically these attributes were flaws: they made it harder
to attract badly needed allies to the farmers' cause. Bryan's style,
symbols, and program were meaningful to the trans-Mississippi and
Southern farmers who fueled populism but incomprehensible to city
dwellers, immigrants, and Catholics, to say nothing of free-trade-
oriented businessmen. In his drive for the Democratic nomination
and during the subsequent campaign, Bryan stressed the importance
of "free silver," yet free coinage was but one piece of the populist
economic analysis and not the part with the strongest appeal for non-
farmers (nor even the most important element to farmers themselves). For the city dweller, for example, deflation actually improved
real wages, while cheap money threatened to raise prices. In the
search for allies other avenues of attack on the industrial order could
have been developed, but silver overwhelmed them.

Even within the agrarian sector, the concentration on silver and the
fervid quality of the campaign worried the more prosperous farmers.
By the 1890s American agriculture was considerably differentiated.
In the trans-Mississippi region, conditions were primitive: farmers
were vulnerable, marginal producers who grew a single crop for the
market and had little capital and no reserves. Southern agriculture
was also marginal, though for different reasons. In the Northeast and
Midwest farming had become much more diversified; it was less dependent on grain, more highly capitalized, and benefited from greater competition among railroads, alternative shipping routes, and direct access to urban markets. These farmers related to the industrial
sector rather as dairymen did in Britain and most farmers did in
Denmark. Bryan frightened these farmers as he frightened workers
and immigrants. The qualities that made him attractive to one group
antagonized others, and like Sen. Barry Goldwater and Sen. George
McGovern more recently, he was able to win the nomination but in a
manner that guaranteed electoral defeat. Bryan's campaign caused
potential allies to define their interests in ways that seemed incompati-
ble with those of the agricultural sector, and it drove farmers away
rather than attracting them. Workers saw Bryan not as an ally against
their bosses but as a threat to the industrial sector of the economy in
which they worked. To immigrants, he was a nativist xenophobe.
Well-to-do Midwestern farmers, Southern Whigs, and Northeast
shippers all saw him as a threat to property.

The Republicans, on the other hand, were shrewd. Not only did
they have large campaign funds, but James G. Blaine, Benjamin Har-
rison, and William McKinley understood that industrial interests re-

quired allies, whose support they must actively recruit. Like Bismarck, these Republican leaders worked to make minimal concessions in order to split the opposition. In the German coalition the terms of trade were social security for the workers, tariffs for the farmers and the manufacturers, guns and boats for the military. In the American version McKinley et al. outmaneuvered President Grover Cleveland and the Gold Democrats on the money issue and then went after the farmers. Minimizing the importance of monetary issues, they proposed an alternative solution in the form of overseas markets: selling surpluses to the Chinese or the Latin Americans, negotiating the lowering of tariff levels, and policing the meat industry to meet the health regulations that Europeans had imposed in order to exclude American imports. To the working class, the Republicans argued that Bryan and the agrarians would cost them jobs and boost prices. Social security was never mentioned—indeed, McKinley ended up paying less than Bismarck had.

In 1896, then, the Republican candidate was tactically shrewd and the Democrat was not, but it might have been the other way around. One can imagine, say, a charismatic Democrat from Ohio with a Catholic mother, traditionally friendly to workers, known for his understanding of farmers' problems—the historical equivalent of Sen. Robert Kennedy in the latter's ability to appeal simultaneously to urban ethnics, machine politicians, blacks, and suburban liberals. This imaginary figure is unlikely but not impossible: even had he existed, however, such a candidate would still have labored under severe handicaps. The difference between Bryan and McKinley, that is to say, was more than a matter of mere personality or accident.

The forces that made Bryan their standard-bearer were built into the structure of American politics. First, McKinley's success in constructing a coalition derived from features inherent in industrial society. As in Germany, producers' groups had a structural advantage. Bringing together farmers, workers, and consumers was difficult everywhere in the industrial world, and in America it was made even harder by ethnic, geographic, and religious differences. Second, the industrialists controlled both political parties. Whatever happened at the local level, the national Democratic party was in the firm grip of Southern conservatives and Northern businessmen. Prior to 1896 they wrote their ideas into the party platforms and nominated their man at every convention. The Gold Democrats were not a choice but an echo, and even the Republicans thought so. After the election of 1892, for instance, Andrew Carnegie wrote to Henry Clay Frick: "Well we have nothing to fear and perhaps it is best. People will now think the Protected Manufacturers were attended to and quit agitating. Cleveland is a pretty good fellow. Off for Venice tomorrow."[43] A Bryan-type crusade was structurally necessary, because only action out of the ordinary would wrest the electoral machine away from the Gold Democrats. But the requirements of that success sowed the seeds of the failure of November 1896.

Why, in turn, did the industrialists control the parties? The Civil War is crucial to the answer. The Republican party at its inception was an amalgam of entrepreneurs, farmers, lawyers, and professionals who believed in opportunity, hard work, and self-help; these were people from medium-sized farms. They disliked the South not because they wished to help blacks or even to eliminate slavery, but because the South and slavery symbolized the very opposite of "Free Soil, Free Labor, Free Men."[44] By accelerating the pace of industrialization, the Civil War altered the internal balance of the party and tipped it toward control by industrialists. By mobilizing national emotions against the South, the Civil War fused North and West together, locking the voter into the Republican party. Men who had been antibusiness and Jacksonian prior to 1860 became members of a coalition dominated by business.[45]

In the South the old Whigs, in desperate need of capital, fearful of social change and contemptuous of the old Jacksonians, looked to Northern industrialists for help in rebuilding their lands and restoring conservative rule. Only the hostility of the Radical Republicans made it impossible for them to join their Northern allies in the Republican party. Instead, the old Whigs went into the Democratic party, where eventually they helped sustain the Gold Democrats and battled with the Populists for control of the Democratic organization in the South.

There were, then, in the American system certain structural obstacles to a low-tariff coalition. What of explanations based on economic ideology and the international system? Free trade in the United States never had the ideological force that it possessed in the United Kingdom. Infant industries and competition with the major industrial power provided the base for a protectionist tradition just as farming and distrust of the state provided a base for free trade. Tariffs had always been an important source of revenue for the federal government. The slogan "Free Soil, Free Labor, Free Men" had a powerful appeal in America. Ideological consistency would have added "free trade," but economic circumstances pushed preferences in the other direction.

Trade bore some relation to foreign policy. As William Appleman

Williams's work has shown, American involvement with the world was shaped by the quest for markets, first for agricultural and then for industrial products. Nonetheless, it is hard to argue that the international political system determined tariff policy. The United States had no need to worry about foreign control of resources or food supply, and in any case the foreign policy of the low-tariff coalition was not very different from the foreign policy of the high-tariff coalition.

SWEDEN

At the beginning of the 1870s Sweden was the least developed of the countries examined here. The economy was overwhelming agrarian and extractive, based on timber, grain products (which Sweden exported up until mid-century), and metals, both ores and partially finished products. Sweden was already quite involved in international trade, exporting these primary products to the United Kingdom, to Germany and Russia, and to other continental countries. During the prosperous years of the 1850s Sweden began its first growth spurt, chiefly in agriculture but also in forestry products and forestry processing, which had extensive forward linkages. The growth was rapid, faster even than in Germany and the United States, for Sweden began at a poorer base.[46]

In the 1870s Sweden's industrial development "took off." Using both foreign and domestic capital, Swedish entrepreneurs developed a range of fine engineering products for which the country was to become famous: cream separators and other products involved in the dairy industry; ball bearings; electrical equipment, from generators through motors to telephones; and the internal combustion engine. It was international trade that drove the economy. The home base remained relatively poor and could not possibly have provided enough demand for the range of high-technology goods that were being developed. Not until later in the period did prosperity spread sufficiently to encourage the formation of a home market.

The crisis of 1873 posed severe problems for Sweden as for other countries. The Swedes faced the same choices as everyone else: accept the new international division of labor by shifting resources to areas of comparative advantage, or slow the process of specialization and adjustment by setting up tariff barriers.

The battle between these conflicting economic policies was acute. It was not the only issue in Swedish political life—it had to share the stage with religion, democratization, constitutional issues, administrative reform, and foreign policy, workers', and property issues. But it was a bedrock issue, and at times the dominant cleavage of politics. On the protectionist side were the large estate owners, members of the aristocracy located in Skåne, a relatively flat, fertile, rich, grain-growing district, as well as numerous smaller farmers in that area. In the center and north, however, small farmers worked less fertile, rockier ground. They had never done well in relation to their southern brethren, and now they found opportunities in the new economic situation. With cheap foreign grain and rising demand for dairy, meat, and truck goods, it became possible for them to make a better living.

Textile and some iron manufacturers, and other sorts of industrialists, sought protection. In support of free trade were entrepreneurs in high-technology industries, shippers in port cities (who lived on exchanges that grew as specialization increased), and bankers involved with large industries. Workers tended to favor free trade, concerned, as in other countries, with food prices.

The alignment in Sweden thus bore a strong resemblance to that in the United Kingdom and in Germany. Export manufacturers of high-technology products concerned with expanding world markets, workers seeking to keep food and other living costs down, farmers seeking to carve a specialized niche in the new division of labor—these groups together fought for free trade. The coalescence of their economic interests spilled over into other issue areas. It helped to sustain collaboration on constitutional reform (establishing the principle of government accountability to elected representatives, not to the Crown), on democratization of the suffrage, on religious liberalism, on administrative reform: in sum, a familiar package of liberalism and individualism in society, economics, and politics.

The protectionist camp is equally familiar: large estate owners of aristocratic social origins, vulnerable manufacturers, groups with strong links to the Crown and the traditional establishment of Sweden. As in Germany and the United Kingdom, the politics of the protectionists were conservative—High Church, paternalistic, and authoritarian. For most of this period the protectionists won, and their victory is congruent with most of the explanatory approaches we are examining. The protectionists had the ample weight of the structure of interests on their side; they had all the advantages of special access and privileged information in the state; they had some organizational advantages; and they had the leverage provided by ideological resistance to market ideology.

Several things about the Swedish case are, however, distinctive.

Although Sweden had an aristocracy and a bureaucracy, its army did not have the same importance as its counterpart did in Germany because international considerations differed for the two countries. And, relatively small in population, Sweden could not pursue a strategy of growth by protecting a large domestic or imperial market. Sweden could grow only in the way it did, through specialization—though objective necessity hardly explains the Swedish choice, for many systems fail to fulfill their functional requisites. Ultimately, international factors (and especially World War I) played a large role in bringing about the realignment of domestic forces which reversed policy.

In the later nineteenth century, then, Sweden had its own iron-rye coalition. Compared to that of its German counterpart, the Swedish coalition's control was far less solid, mainly because the economic link was much weaker. All the dynamic, rapidly growing industries were on the free trade side; a large bloc of farmers were more clearly sympathetic to free trade; and the working-class parties, which also favored free trade, were less politically isolated. The consequences of these differences would become clear in the crisis of the 1930s.

ALTERNATIVE EXPLANATIONS OF THE CRISIS

The last third of the nineteenth century confronted countries everywhere with a rather dramatic change in the international economic environment. All had to respond. In four of our five cases there was a turn away from free trade; only the United Kingdom continued on the path that it had invented. In the quarrels within countries over foreign economic policy, proponents of alternatives required social support. In all countries evaluations of the tariff by economic actors turned largely on situation in the world economy. European farmers threatened by new sources and methods of production, iron and steel producers facing stiff international competition and immense amortization problems, textile manufacturers, nascent industries of all kinds facing competition from earlier industrializers—these supported tariffs. The leaders of new industries, including chemicals and electrical equipment, and manufacturers of finished goods, traders, together with shippers and commercial bankers, supported free trade.

What differs from one country to another is the particular mix of elements. In Britain the internationalists held a unique position in the country's production profile. The power of the City, the early lead in industrialization, and the earlier adaptation to commercialized farming provided the base of social support for free trade. In all the other cases the internationalist business elements were weaker and, except in the United States, the protectionist farmers stronger. This interpretation of policy outcomes in response to this first crisis demands that, to account for policy choices, we must specify the production profile of each country: the composition of its economy, what was made and by whom, sold to whom in what kind of markets, in competition with what sorts of producers, in what sort of relationship to other producers in the same country. This is a familiar argument, deployed by myriad analysts from the *Wall Street Journal* to *Pravda*.

Yet the production profile argument is not without its problems. Among the winners of the policy debate in each country were, of course, economic actors whose preferences had some relation to their position in the international economy. Unfortunately, the same is true of the losers; on the losing side there were also economic actors whose preferences were connected to trade relationships. To explain why one policy was adopted rather than another, therefore, we need to know why one set of economic actors defeated another.

Economic situation directs our attention to preferences, to *why* groups wanted one or another outcome. The argument is, however, less clear about *how* those preferences turned into policy. Obviously we need some notion of the connection between economic actors and political process, of the mechanisms whereby preferences acquired power. No single group, it will be recalled, was able to get all of its wishes. Some trading among actors occurred, and there had to be a process of aggregation by which coalitions were constructed. And when the coalition formed, it still had to acquire the power to win. It is not enough to say that the group which won did so because it had enough power, if the only proof of the sufficiency of power is the winning itself. That is circular reasoning. Rather, one must think about the links among preferences and interests, the aggregation of interests, and the getting of political power.[47]

A second problem with this sort of reasoning is the ambiguity of interests. The economic interest explanation presumes that the meaning of any given economic environment is clear to the groups within it, so that the "best" policy preferences and subsequent political behavior to get them are compelling. But this is frequently not the case. In 1873, as we have seen, it was not clear that British industrialists would do better with free trade, or that farmers in France and Germany might not have done better with free trade. Indeed, economic actors are often cross-pressured. Workers, for instance, sometimes have to choose between their concerns as producers (saving their jobs, higher wages) and their concerns as consumers (cheaper goods, even if imported and thus costing other domestic workers their jobs).

These two problems, translating preferences into power and the uncertainty of interests, lead many analyses of policy toward other types of argument. Economic ideology contributes information about the understanding of interests, intermediate associations tell us something about the representation of economic actors, state institutions reinforce the power of some groups over others, and the international state system favors some policy arguments over others.

Given the ambiguity of economic reality in the last quarter of the nineteenth century, actors may well have been guided in their behavior by their perceptions of the economic universe, by their theories of economic cause and effect, rather than by some objective, compelling reality. The clearest example is to be found in the contrast between German and British analyses of the economic situation after 1873. Germany adopted tariffs, Britain continued with free trade in relation to other industrial nations. The two countries had experienced the development of the industrial revolution quite differently, leaving them with different "cultures" about economics. In the first industrializing nation Britons fused general ideas about the free market with Britain's own pattern of development. To a later industrializer these ideas seemed linked to the self-advantage of another country, and nationalist economic ideas flourished instead. Thus the pattern of economic ideology in Britain and Germany is congruent with the pattern of policy outcomes in the late nineteenth century: the country with a liberal ideology pursued free-trade policies while the country with a strong interventionist tradition pursued protectionist ones.

Yet this line of reasoning has its own characteristic difficulties. At least one country without much of a statist tradition, the United States, turned to protection. And in every country one can find economic actors who switched policy positions rapidly under the influence of new economic conditions, most clearly the Junkers in Germany. Germany was not without elements of a free-trade tradition, and for centuries the Junkers had been staunch free traders. Yet in the nineteenth century, when prices plummeted, they embraced protectionism wholeheartedly. The ideological interpretation cannot account for this rapid change of policy position. Ideology, to have leverage as an explanation, must be relatively fixed in comparison to whatever it is used to explain. But if relatively permanent, it does badly in accounting for swift change, as with the Junkers.

A second problem has to do with the sociology of ideology. Germany had free-trade ideas and protectionist ones, and so did the United Kingdom. To understand why one set of views defeated another, we need to inquire into the identity of those who held each position and the power resources that they could use. The point is Weberian, not simply vulgar Marxist. In analyzing religion, ideology, culture, belief systems in general, Weber spoke of "idea bearing classes"—the social strata that learned, promoted, and transmitted ideas about the world and the social system.[48] Ideas and the power to spread them, we must recognize, are by no means equally distributed in any society.

Power, when one focuses on societal actors, derives from the functions that groups play in the economy. Investment, work, buying, and similarly critical functions can apply leverage directly. But many forms of activity require organization and institutions to represent them. Political parties and interest group organizations do this. In linking economic actors to the state, they affect outcomes, but not necessarily directly. Such organizations acquire the ability to mediate the preferences of societal actors on policy outcomes.

The systems of parties and interest groups varied widely in the late nineteenth century. Parties had developed gradually in the United Kingdom in tandem with the parliamentary system, while in Germany the national system was new, and so were national associations. But in all countries the systems of intermediate associations were relatively undeveloped in these years. Mass politics was only just coming into existence, and with it came the associations that sought to organize it. Parties and interest groups were permeable at the beginning of the period, tougher and more institutionalized at the end. They changed positions quickly as their constituents shifted preferences (the German case is particularly striking in this regard). The impact of associations lies in their influence on constituents at one end, the state at the other, but in the years in question that capacity had yet to be created.

The state—the system of rules and bureaucracies—favors some groups over others, hinders some coalitions and helps others.[49] In Germany it favored the protectionists; in Britain, the free traders. In Germany the free traders had to fight for institutional change in order to get their policy goals; in the United Kingdom, they could concentrate on policy alone. Policy outcomes in this period thus seem to conform quite well to the institutional line of argument. That line addresses a problem overlooked by the economic interest and economic ideology arguments, the issue of political power. Nonetheless, it has pitfalls of its own. When we look at each country separately, we find the role of institutions and the personalities who led them looming large. When we look at countries comparatively, however, the importance of state institutions washes out. Countries with different structures adopted similar policies: France, Sweden, and the United States all raised their tariffs in the late nineteenth century. Yet the most conspicuous features of the German case—the Junkers, the army, and Bismarck—have no equivalents elsewhere. Meline and McKinley were no Bismarcks. The United States is typically held to epitomize the weak state in most analyses that distinguish weak from strong states; France may have had a highly articulated bureaucracy, but it did not have a strong executive. A convergence of policy outcomes despite a divergence of institutions suggests that those idiosyncrasies of political system limited to one country are not crucial in explaining results.

The institutional argument has a second problem: in its criticism of the "reductionist" elements of societal arguments, it discounts those elements, leaving the group element theoretically unexamined and undeveloped. Yet institutions have effects that cannot be comprehended without an account of the societal actors who work through them and whom they affect. Rules and bureaucracies bias power relations in one direction or another. The state may even play a role in creating actors and defining their situation. But we cannot understand what the institutions do without some model of the society to which to relate these mechanisms.

In the case of Germany, the bias of the state machinery toward the protectionists derived from the social linkages between that machinery and segments of German society. The army was not automatically predisposed toward one side, but it did have a particular connection with the Junkers which reached back to the seventeenth century. In forming the Prussian state, moreover, the Crown had worked out a particular arrangement with the aristocracy. Its autonomy was intimately linked to Junkerdom, and the way that Bismarck and the kaiser used power would be closely connected to that historical relationship.

The ability of the state to shape society makes the state important in political struggle. But the purposes to which the state apparatus is put cannot be explained by looking solely at the capacity of the state or at its rules. The effects and strength of state action depend on the authority that the state is able to mobilize in relation to societal actors. Rules can be changed, bureaucracies created or dismantled, authority generated or demobilized. The ability of institutions to explain nineteenth-century tariff policy therefore requires some account for each country of the relationship of those institutions to societal forces.

The state system interpretation of divergent policy outcomes links the tariff debate to the varying positions of countries in the era's system of military and political rivalries. Otto Hintze, in particular, related the different political development of Britain and Germany to geography (island vs. continent), which affected the type of military (navy vs. army), which in turn gave the Prussian Army leverage in German political debates. For the nineteenth century, the same contrast may have affected differing national attitudes toward the costs and benefits of specializing in the international division of labor. By accepting specialization, Britain increased its dependence on the international economy. No longer self-sufficient, Britain had to import raw materials and food, and export finished products. The sea was its lifeline, the international economy its heart, and disturbances in either would have a catastrophic impact on the homeland. The British were willing to accept this vulnerability, it can be argued, because they had the world's most powerful navy. That navy secured the country's ability to protect trading routes and to intervene overseas in defense of an economic system that Britain dominated.

Germany, on the other hand, was strategically far more vulnerable. Specialization was riskier for a country surrounded by large powerful neighbors capable not only of disrupting trade but of invasion. War could threaten not only German military security but also its economic security. The navy facilitated British sympathy toward an internationalism based on trade; the German security situation induced a disposition toward autarchy and domination. Fearful of foreign enemies, Germany stressed military capability, which required economic capability, which meant self-sufficiency. The causal chain led to protection, which would guarantee self-sufficiency of food, iron and steel, military products, and, it was argued, a better crop of soldiers because peasants were thought to be more obedient than industrial workers, more disciplined, healthier, and more politically reliable for conservative purposes. As the empire and navy allowed Britain to become dependent on free trade, so the absence of empire compelled Germany toward autarchy.

This powerful argument has its difficulties, however. It presumes that the placement of a country in the international system is an objective matter, one whose necessities impose themselves on domestic decision making. But international politico-military situations cannot be taken for granted. They can be perceived differently, with varying implications for policy, and any country can experience disagreements about its situation and what to do about it. It is therefore necessary to provide some explanation of why a specific understanding of security imperatives prevails over other understandings. That in turn requires a consideration of domestic factors such as interest groups, institutions, and ideology. This has long been debated in social science and history, and Germany is the argument's locus classicus.[50]

The notion that Germany was vulnerable and hence required a powerful military and economic autarchy was embraced by some groups, opposed by others. There were Germans in the late nineteenth century, as there would be in the interwar years, who urged a foreign policy of cooperation and collaboration with other major powers, of specialization in the international division of labor, of strength through trade. Bismarck himself, some analysts have argued, sought some degree of restraint in the use of the very German power that he had forged through unification.

On the other side were far more aggressive and bellicose activists, seeking world empire and domination of Europe. Nationalist-imperialist sentiment was already growing under Bismarck, and after his departure it spread apace. It solved a domestic political problem for Bismarck and his successors, the problem of how to mobilize popular support for an authoritarian regime and how to prevent a liberal reformist coalition from coming together. Nationalism bound groups together in deference to authority, providing legitimacy for policies that helped win support for the regime—naval shipbuilding and defense contracts for industry, tariffs for Junkers and peasants, national glory for the insecure of many classes. Germany helped to develop a formula with which the political theorists of antiquity were familiar: foreign adventurism as a way of containing domestic conflicts.

The security problems of a country and its placement in the international state system are not to be taken for granted. Such problems are part of the domestic political struggle and need to be considered in relation to other policy debates. Those problems form a point of view whose acquisition of power requires analysis and understanding. On both economic and security issues there is much to be learned when we examine a country's situation in the international system, but often that situation leaves some degree of freedom to the country in question. Just how the country uses its freedom requires explanation, in terms of which group or groups with what views predominate politically.[51]

THE EXPLANATIONS COMPARED

For the tariff controversies of the late nineteenth century, all five modes of interpretation point in the same direction, as a pairing of

Britain and Germany makes clear. Britain's preference for free trade fits the production profile of the first industrializer, while the protectionism of Germany corresponds with its situation as a late industrializer. German economic thought was nationalist and statist, while British thinking was free trade and internationalist. The system of intermediate associations was weak in Germany, reflecting the nature of societal pressures; in Britain a stronger system was already attached to free trade and so hindered protectionist impulses. The state structure favored German protectionism, free trade in the United Kingdom. International state rivalries and security concerns induced different interpretations: for Britain, the navy made possible dependence on the world; for Germany, the absence of a world position strengthened inward-looking autarchy.

The various elements thus reinforce one another at each step of the argument. However, they are not simply equals in some grand equation of causation. The comparisons among countries show linkages, the places where each point comes into play, and something of the relations among them. The situation in the international economy of various domestic actors is the most important place at which to begin analyzing policy battles, at least those of this period. Other factors enter the analysis through their impact on the relationship among economic actors. They affect policy, that is to say, not independently but by mediating the coalitions that form. To comprehend the outcome, therefore, we require a mapping of the policy preferences of the coalitions, of the terms of trade among the groups, and of the ways in which they combined. Finally, we also need some consideration of how else the coalitions might have combined.

In this period the feature of the outcome that comparison makes strikingly clear is the similarity of winners across countries, regardless of all the characteristics that differentiate countries. Highly concentrated industrial producers with strong and intense preferences, who occupy strategic positions in the economy, seem to win out everywhere, whatever the institutions, parties, and ideology of the particular country. This suggests that political resources may indeed have been linked to economic resources, that political advantage was connected to economic placement. Whatever the system, these actors won. Opposite types of regimes (Republican France, Imperial Germany) chose protection. Similar types, the constitutional democracies of France, Britain, and the United States chose different policies. In fact, it is quite likely that different regimes in each country (a republican Germany, say, or an imperial France) would have produced the same policy result as the historical case did once the pressures of 1873 set to work.

Indeed, in these years the permeability of political systems to the policy demands of societal actors helped strengthen each of those systems. The ways in which the economic crisis of the 1870s was handled became deeply etched in the politics of each country. Tariff policy in Germany, for instance, helped reconcile a range of conflicts. It provided a hub into which the various spokes of empire could be securely fitted. Catholics, Liberals, Junkers, industrialists, and peasants would not have come so easily to an understanding without the fact of tariffs by which to orient themselves. The policy then generated its own lobby. Once grain was protected, all the smaller farmers who might have modernized instead became dependent on high tariffs and fought ferociously to keep them. Similarly, the country's naval building program helped produce a classic example of the military-industrial complex.

It is not clear how much low tariffs would have changed German society. A Germany dominated by the low-tariff coalition would have been a very different place, but only a different Germany could have been thus dominated in the first place. An anti-corn-law league triumph in Germany would have created cross-class alliances in constitutionalist forms, as in the United Kingdom; the contrasting victory of the Bülow bloc accentuated the actual tendencies within German society. Still, nationalism, militarism, and imperialism do occur in liberal systems, and it is conceivable that a Caprivi-type alliance might have used these instruments of legitimation as well.

In France protection strengthened the Republic. Conservatives, both landed and industrial, found that the Republic could be conservative and that they could protect their interests through it. Tariffs helped preserve conservatism on the land and in the shop, and limit radicalism in the city and the factory. As in Germany, protection acted in France as a solvent of other cleavages, especially over the constitution and the church. In the early 1890s, it is true, a party realignment around economic issues was conceivable. The Dreyfus affair became possible partly because the interests of property had been secured, and it was precisely to avoid a potential party realignment that men on both sides pushed the case.

In Great Britain the constitutional monarchy was solid even without new sources of support, but as on the Continent, the decision on tariffs accentuated existing tendencies. With the confirmation of repeal of the Corn Laws, the position of agriculture and the landed interest continued to fall. After 1880 the absolute number of people employed in farming declined sharply, and the United Kingdom became the first country in which a majority of the population earned its living from nonagricultural pursuits. Erosion of the aristocracy's privileges continued: the County Councils Act of 1888 (which ended control of local life by justices of the peace), the secret ballot, reform of the House of Lords, reorganization of education, and reform of the status of the church can all be linked to the waning influence of agriculture; so can British reluctance first to join and then to remain in the Common Market a century later. The shrinking of agriculture also facilitated the development of the modern British party system, which emerged in the 1890s characterized by two broad formations with contrasting positions along a single cleavage line, the organization of industrial life; the development preceded the supplanting of the Liberals by Labour.[52] Had agriculture been protected, it is plausible to think that other issues would have remained salient in British politics, as they did in France.

In the United States, too, the survival of the constitutional order was not at stake. The issues affected by the tariff controversy were the dominance of industry in American life and the nature of the party system. A party system built on Jacksonian vs. Whig lines would have been national rather than regional and sectoral, in that voters would have lined up with their sociological counterparts all over the country on the same set of issues. When the depression of the 1880s hit, Southern farmers could then have worked with Western ones through a Democratic party far more responsive to their concerns, in a modified version of what C. Vann Woodward calls the left fork of the South: alliance with the West on Jacksonian reformist principles extended to include the Eastern poor.[53]

Instead, the Civil War produced a North-West alliance extended de facto to the Southern upper crust, thus fragmenting the agrarian sector. The upshot was industrial domination of politics. All other groups were forced to adjust their conceptions of themselves and their interests to fit this domination, and the preindustrial elites that might have preserved a strain of Tory conservatism were swept away by the Social Darwinism of the parvenus. Large portions of the working class came to interpret the stakes of politics not in terms of a property/antiproperty cleavage but in sectoral terms, as industry vs. agriculture. Identifying with industry, they came to adopt its standard of success—the accumulation of wealth—within the system. The South, meanwhile, was encouraged to develop racism as the only way of keeping Bourbons and Crackers inside the same party. Industrialists emerged triumphant and remarkably unrestrained. In no other western country, not even Germany, did they (or do they) share power so little; in no other country was (or is) there such an absence of criticism of their vision, position, and policies. The Civil War set this up, and high tariffs and the election of 1896 confirmed it. The election of 1932 would modify things somewhat, but it would not really change the pattern.

Such observations on the political consequences of the tariff debate are clearly speculative. More immediately, I believe that it is important to think about the linkage between the broad struggle for domination in society and the more specific policy problem posed by a drop in prices. The two once seemed to me to be different sides of the same coin: the tariff levels and the coalitions that supported them would stand or fall together. If the coalition were defeated, the tariff levels would change; if the coalition could not defend its tariff level, it would collapse. After carefully comparing the cases, however, the two now seem to me much more nearly independent.

The character of the political system may have little impact on the content of various policies. Policy issues are to some extent neutral mediums, able to take on widely varying political tints. Regimes of quite different types may use the same policy as proof of their superiority, efficacy, or legitimacy.[54] The precise impact that policy has on regime type, then, depends on historical context, and its effects may last long after the policy itself has become obsolete or been abandoned. Some may see this as evidence of the derivative and dependent character of politics. To me, on the contrary, it suggests the originality and independence of politics, for the type of political system, the mode of decision making, is a value in itself whose impact on the content of policy may be less than on these other values. Issues are plastic in their political effects, less plastic in their content, and so the political use that politicians make of issues may be quite separate from the substantive effects.

The striking feature about policy in the late nineteenth century is the relatively large role of economic circumstance in shaping outcomes and the relatively small role of other factors. At the same time politicians used the objective pressures of the policy debate, over which they had limited control, to effect political objectives, over which they had more. It is not obvious that the causal relationships which hold for the late nineteenth-century crisis will also hold for later crises, however. The role of politics is, therefore, something to watch in the economic crisis to which we now turn, the Depression of the 1930s.

CHAPTER FOUR

Breaking with Orthodoxy: The Formation of the Mixed Economy, 1929–49

The Great Crash of 1929 was the greatest economic catastrophe since the industrial economy's beginnings in the mid-eighteenth century. In disaster the international division of labor, already becoming more intense in the crisis of the late nineteenth century, showed that it had deepened awesomely. The boom of the years before the Great War and World War I itself had spread productive capacity into new areas, deepened it in older ones, and brought into being a new generation of products and a new round of production techniques. The decade immediately after the war was spent trying to reconstruct the halcyon days of the Belle Epoque, but the crash showed how ineffective were those efforts. No country, whatever its domestic politics and policies, could escape the grip of collapsing trade, skyrocketing unemployment, and escalating value of real debt.

As the Depression rippled around the world, most countries responded with the same economic policy—deflation, the response prescribed by orthodox analysis of the market economy. It did not work. After some two to four years of failure most countries abandoned deflation and broke with orthodoxy. Initially, most of them turned to familiar deviations from the classical rules: tariffs, devaluation of the currency, leaving the gold standard, and some corporatistic regulation of domestic markets. Some countries broke more drastically, either immediately or after a few years of "neo-orthodoxy," to try more unusual departures from standard views. They experimented with demand stimulus through deficit spending (known after the war as Keynesianism), social welfare systems, extensive regulation of and subsidies for markets, and some degree of public ownership of production.[1]

During the thirties these departures from orthodoxy were experimental and uneven both within and across countries. In that decade what was striking was the divergence in economic policy and the even greater divergence in political form. Germany tried extensive demand stimulus, as to a lesser degree did Sweden and the United States, while Britain rejected the same course. Some countries created extensive social security systems, while others were more restrained; some countries institutionalized trade-union rights, while Germany destroyed them. Constitutional government survived in Britain, Sweden, and the United States, collapsed into the nightmare of Nazism in Germany, and ran aground in France.

In a political environment already torn asunder by the Depression, the transforming impact of World War II pushed change even further. The divergence among countries was reversed; in effect the war created new opportunities to resume a debate begun in the thirties over how to accommodate new changes in the international division of labor and the international business cycles that are part of that division. Some countries, among them Sweden, evolved a policy pattern in the thirties which they would continue after the war. In other cases, most notably Germany but also France and the United Kingdom, the war altered the trajectory of policy and politics.

In all four European countries, as well as in the United States, the postwar years saw the construction of an accommodation. It was not "automatic." It required action to structure both the economy and politics.[2] By mid-century, in policy terms, the innovations of the thirties had become the established and institutionalized norms for the constitutionalist capitalist economy. The Western economies functioned not through free-market orthodoxy but through regulation and intervention aimed at ensuring market stabilization and political peace both within and between countries.

The two periods 1929–39 and 1945–49 are generally treated separately, with World War II as the great divide. In terms of economic policy, however, they can be seen as parts of a single historical development that culminated in the construction of a mixed economy located in a constitutionalist political framework. The policy debates of the postwar reconstruction years rotated around conceptions of politics and policy options defined by the interwar years. Capitalism and socialism, the market and the welfare state, protectionism and free trade—understanding of these alternatives, their vices and virtues, came from the searing experiences of the Depression. The goal of policy debates in the late forties was to prevent the economic catastrophes of the interwar years from ever happening again.

The war was certainly an important event for the policy debate. In

Germany it brought down the Nazi dictatorship, allowing the reopening of policy discussion there. In France it changed partisan alignments; in Britain it changed social understandings. Continuity was clearest in Sweden and the United States. But in all five countries the impact of the war was to add new dimensions to a framework of debate shaped by the interwar years. The war emphasized the catastrophe of social conflict brought on by the Depression, and in this way it contributed to the accommodation worked out in the late forties.

It is this very accommodation which is under attack today, in the 1980s. The third crisis of the international division of labor, which began in the early seventies, has reopened policy debates muted during the consensus era of the fifties and sixties. The politics of the current period are strongly affected by the attack on incumbency, for the hegemony of stabilization ideas during those decades made them politically vulnerable when the situation changed. The crisis of today involves linkages forged half a century ago. Looking at those crucial years thus provides not only another case study of crisis response but also an opportunity to continue tracing trajectories from the earlier period and to prepare the canvas for a portrait of the system that has become subject to strain since the early 1970s.

The policy debate opened by the Crash of 1929 reaches a settlement in 1949, and within this period are distinctive sequences. The endpoint is reached only after a number of important events and shifts. To draw out the whole, it is thus useful to employ the more conventional periodization of pre- and postwar years, within which there are particular subphases. This chapter is thus blocked out in two parts. First, in the divergences of the thirties, the interesting questions have to do with the various ways in which countries broke with orthodoxy. Second, in the convergences of the late forties, the interesting questions concern the construction of an accommodation or partial consensus. I examine the policy sequences in each country, focusing on evidence most useful for a continuation of the explanatory debate begun earlier: the policy demands expressed by various societal actors, the role of institutional arrangements in shaping the distribution of power, the linkage between state and society provided by intermediate associations, the influence of economic ideology, and the impact of strategic considerations arising out of conflicts in the international state system. As in the previous chapter, my interest is the ways that these variables shaped the environment in which politicians operated it. In each case politicians sought a mixture of power and substantive goals, and to attain both they sought policies that suited their politics. They had to construct coalitions of interests and ideas, that is to say, in specific institutional frameworks and in response to specific international pressures.

The policy debate of the thirties and forties marked a decisive break with earlier political patterns—it constitutes another "critical realignment" of societal actors. Some older alignments, such as that between export business and labor, crumbled, at least for a time; some new alignments emerged, among them one between farmers and workers. New institutions were formed to articulate policy shifts; economic thinking changed; and efforts were made to recast the international system.

THE CRISIS OF THE THIRTIES, 1929–39

In this second crisis the range of policy alternatives seriously considered and attempted was much wider than in the first. Dealing with the first crisis had itself expanded the instruments of response: countries had learned how to regulate markets, sustain industries through government procurement, interfere with trade through the use of tariff and nontariff barriers, take over failing enterprises, promote certain products, devalue currencies, and inflate demand. Private actors had learned how to merge, cartelize, and obtain contracts. World War I dramatically increased both the types and the instruments of intervention. All of the belligerents created some sort of war production board, which combined centralized economic decision making with private ownership, extensive regulation, and taxation. Peace brought new economic hardships in the attempt to replace the wartime economy by reviving the old order. By the mid-twenties pretty nearly everything had been tried, deliberately or unconsciously, in one place or another.

Although the range of choices had expanded, the range of politically plausible choices remained limited. Countries tried to restore the capitalist order as it had been before the cataclysm, and at the beginning of the Depression policy debate pitted two orthodoxies against each other. The classicists, arguing that the problems of the market could be fixed only by the market, advocated *deflation*. They wanted to defend currency values and to cut wages and prices in order to reduce costs. The Marxists, arguing that private investment could not sustain a full-employment economy or avoid the frightful costs of the business cycle, advocated *socialization of investment*. They wanted public ownership and state planning.

These two options were seen, as far as economics was concerned, as zero-sum, because each required sacrifice from one major component of society and benefited another. The deflation school insisted that high wages and taxes discouraged investment and production; hence labor had to cede income share to profits. Conversely, the socialization school advocated what would lead to the elimination of the owners of capital. Each position had dramatic political implications as well. To attain the desired economic end, each might find it necessary to destroy the constitutional system. The deflationists would need somehow to block labor's ability to resist wage and welfare cuts through strikes and the ballot box; the socializers, on the other hand, would have to break capital's ability to engage in a "capital strike" or to use state power against labor organizations.

The policy debate deadlocked around these two options. Then mixed-game alternatives came forward, able to blur both the effects of policy across different categories of the population and the nature of the sacrifices demanded of each. Two such alternatives are particularly noteworthy.

The first was protectionism mixed with a type of mercantilism. This package of policies involved devaluation of the currency, which allowed a relaxation of deflation because spending no longer had to be curbed in order to reduce pressure on exchange rates; tariffs, which protected local industry from imports; and market regulation, which shared out production, controlled prices, and provided subsidies, either officially through government-sponsored agreements or unofficially through private arrangements. This combination of policies can be called neo-orthodox in that it was derived from remedies to disorder suggested by classic economic theory and it preserved private property. Nonetheless, it remained both intellectually and politically controversial.

The second was demand stimulus. This meant boosting demand through deficit spending for public works, transfer payments, and other targets. Demand stimulus was the new scheme of the thirties. It may actually have occurred earlier, through unintended budget deficits, but it was not tried deliberately until the Depression. It entailed a more substantial break, intellectually and politically, with existing orthodoxies.

Modified protectionism and demand stimulus changed the political struggle because they made it possible to attract people across the boundary lines defined by the two orthodox schools. The protectionist-mercantilist mixture helped to draw together producers of different sorts, from business and agriculture and labor. Demand stimulus altered the game entirely by arguing that wages and profits could rise together rather than moving always in opposite directions.[3]

An important caveat is needed here: reality was more confusing than this simplification suggests. In fact, countries did a mixture of things, and some even said they were doing one thing while actually doing another. Interpretative boundaries blur easily: recent interpretations of Sweden, for example, argue that the actual effect of the country's supposed demand stimulus policy was far less significant than commonly imagined. The United States did not really try demand stimulus until late in the decade, in 1938. Nazi Germany was the most extensive experimenter in the thirties and had the most success with it. Demand stimulus would come of age only after the war. Nonetheless, reflation through public spending was proposed in many countries even before Keynes; attempts were made, experiments tried, doctrines developed, and alliances forged. The postwar pattern took form in the 1930s.

To comprehend the emergence of this pattern, we must analyze the controversy over economic policy between the wars, probing the connections between the struggle over policy choice and the struggle over political system and political coalitions which occurred at the same time. The controversy over orthodoxy is particularly fascinating because it may tell us something about the political preconditions for policy innovation. We need to ask why some countries stopped the policy sequence with neo-orthodoxy while others went on to demand stimulus.

In descriptive terms this question asks what Nazi Germany, Social Democratic Sweden, and New Deal America have in common. (These are the countries that experimented with the most extensive breaks from orthodoxy.) What makes them different from the United Kingdom, which in the thirties followed more conventional policies? In what ways do coalitions that supported dramatic breaks with orthodoxy differ from those which opposed it or which chose only the cautious move of neo-orthodoxy?

At first it may appear that national policy coalitions have nothing in common and that there is no connection between politics and economic policy. What, after all, could be further apart than Social Democratic Sweden and Nazi Germany, or the Third Reich and the United States of the New Deal? The very question recognizes that demand stimulus policies, though they may in the long run have strengthened democracy by helping constitutional regimes deal more effectively with economic crisis, were by no means a monopoly of constitutional regimes. Indeed, Nazi Germany used demand stimulus techniques more extensively and brought the rates of unemployment and underutilized capacity down faster than any other country.

Because different political systems pursued the same policies, and

Table 4. Economic policies, coalitions, and regimes in the 1930s

Policy Sequence for Crisis	Regimes and Support Coalitions	
	Constitutionalist	Authoritarian
1. Orthodox Deflation (defend currency; cut spending; push down wages) Procyclical.	UK to 1931 (PLP, business liberals)[a] Germany to 1933 (mixed; e.g., SDP, Catholics, etc.)[b] Sweden to 1931 (business, agriculture) U.S.A. to 1933 (business, agriculture)[c] France to 1936 (business, agriculture) and post-1937	
2. Socialist Orthodoxy (socialize investment through nationalization, plus planning) Not pursued.	Supported only by Communists at times; unions and Socialist parties use it rhetorically, but actually endorse deflation combined with resistance to wage and welfare cuts, 1930–32	
3. Neo-orthodoxy (devalue currency; use tariffs and official or private cartels)	UK post-1931 (all but unions, PLP) U.S.A. 1930–31, 1933–35/7 (business, agriculture) Sweden 1931–32 France post-1937	
4. Demand Stimulus (deficit spending through public works, transfer payments, etc.) Countercyclical.	Sweden post-1936 (farmer-labor, part business)[d] U.S.A. post-1936 (farmer-labor, part business)[d] France 1936–37 (farmer-labor, part business)	Germany post-1933 (agriculture, domestic business, nonunion labor)

a. Parliamentary Labour Party. b. German Social-Democratic Party. c. Except for tariffs. d. Partial moves only.

similar political systems pursued different ones, we might think that therefore there is no connection and that economic policies are polyvalent. I am unsatisfied by such a conclusion, however. Economic policies are not completely polyvalent; not just anyone supported one or another policy. Farmers were very critical of the market everywhere, while business interests uniformly denounced socialism. In the crisis of 1873, as we have seen, the preferences of various groups played a considerable role in explaining the choice that different countries made among alternative policies. And so it seems appropriate to proceed now along the same lines—to examine each country's response by beginning with the behavior of groups and then looking at other factors.

In its simplest form, the observation that I wish to make about the demand stimulus coalitions of Sweden, the United States, and Germany is that they were *cross-sector, cross-class* alliances of groups whose patience with market solutions had run out. Farmers everywhere were fed up with the operation of markets that favored creditors and middlemen and denied them assistance in the name of market principles. Certain kinds of labor unions in each country also protested the effects of the market. In Sweden and the United States, the labor component of this alliance was provided by labor organizations themselves, and linkages were constructed through the constitutional system; in Germany, by contrast, labor organizations were crushed, and linkages were extraconstitutional. Finally, some business sectors also sought to free themselves from the economic orthodoxy of their brethren.

Sweden

At the worst of the Depression, in the tense year of 1932 when the Weimar Republic was crumbling, a dramatic *renversement des alliances* took place in Sweden. The Agrarian party, traditionally allied with center and conservative parties, entered into an agreement with a traditional enemy, the Social Democrats. The economic terms of this cow trade, as it was called at the time, were Social Democratic acceptance of higher food costs through various price-support plans in exchange for Agrarian backing of high unemployment insurance, the rights of labor organizations, and a declared policy (though a more complex reality) of using fiscal stimulus to promote full employment. The political terms of the deal involved a coalition cabinet dominated by the Social Democrats. The policies and politics of Sweden were the most durable of any forged in this period; they lasted forty-four years, until the Social Democrats lost the election of 1976 by a narrow margin. Other Scandinavian countries developed similar alignments: Norway in 1935, Denmark in 1932–33. In Denmark the major policy shift took place on January 30, 1933; the leading Danish newspaper gave it more prominence than Hitler's takeover in Germany, which occurred the same day.

During the crisis of the late nineteenth century Swedish politics and policy quarrels had borne a strong family resemblance to those of other industrial countries. Politics and politics had been split sharply by the issue of protection vs. free trade. Economic policy had interacted in familiar ways with other political issues—religion, the constitution, institutional development, and foreign policy.[4] Although these issue areas each had a certain amount of autonomy, they tended to cluster around two poles. At one pole were free trade, democratization of the suffrage, an accountable executive, freedom of worship, secular education, union rights, and a pro-British internationalism, all issues supported by labor and the Liberal party. Protectionism, preservation of royal and elite predominance in politics, religious orthodoxy and education, control of labor, and a pro-German foreign policy formed the other pole, supported by the Conservative party and most of the Agrarian party formations.

In 1914, when war broke out, the conservative pole predominated and led Sweden to pro-German neutrality. Britain blockaded the country, causing considerable privation: food became scarce, exports fell, unemployment rose, hunger spread. In 1917 the Liberals, urged on by export-oriented businessmen, combined with the Social Democrats to overthrow the conservative government of Hjalmar Hammarskjöld; the terms of this "anti-corn-law" type of alliance were free trade, universal suffrage, and subordination of the executive to Parliament. What would become the Swedish model in the late 1930s was thus foreshadowed in these years.

With the war and postwar readjustments over, labor's utility to the Liberals in fighting conservative policies declined, and the Social Democrats went back into relative isolation (though they did participate in some governing coalitions). As in Britain, to which Sweden's economy was tightly linked, economic elites sought to restore the national currency to prewar exchange levels, and as elsewhere, high valuation produced strong pressure against industrial wages. On issues of wages, union rights, social insurance, and overall management of the economy, the Social Democrats found themselves faced with a heterogeneous but solid bloc of opposition which included the Liberals and the Agrarians. From this isolation, however, would come one very large advantage: when the Depression began, the Swedish Social Democrats, unlike their British and German counterparts, had been out of power for a number of years. They were thus not tainted by the need to impose austerity measures.

Sweden's first response to the Depression was, of course, the economic orthodoxy of deflation and defense of the currency. When Britain devalued in 1931, the run against the krona forced Sweden to leave the gold standard. As the world economy deteriorated, however, the competitive advantage of devaluation proved to be of limited advantage, and domestic dissatisfaction with market solutions heightened. Labor organizations, party and union, fought to preserve unemployment compensation and began to propound explicitly the idea of deficit-financed public works. Farmers, meanwhile, sought aid through marketing boards and price supports, but though they made some progress in getting policy concessions from nonlabor groups, that support seemed unstable and piecemeal. Business interests seemed reluctant to support higher food costs and government intervention in markets, and the bourgeois parties were all reluctant to accept labor's demands.

The cow trade between the Swedish Workers party (SAP—the Social Democrats) and the Agrarian party overcame the political obstacles that each faced. The surprise at the time was that workers would accept higher food costs and that farmers would agree to higher wages for workers. That particular trade had never occurred before. After the fact, however, it seems clear, and not at all surprising, that these two groups would be the least committed to economic orthodoxy and the most willing to try experiments in times of stress. The striking point is not the terms of trade but the fact of agreement.[5]

Business historiography for the period is not sufficiently detailed to allow careful exploration of differential capacity to accept the costs of participating in such a coalition, but it does appear that Swedish business behavior went through a sequence. Before the Depression the high-technology export industries and their banking allies, the Wallenbergs, had shown a willingness at various times to work out accommodations with labor. With the onset of the Depression, though, the two came into conflict. Export businesses wanted to lower wage costs in order to improve their international competitiveness. The various aspects of economic nationalism, such as domestic reflation, the boosting of internal demand, the protectionism, would do little good for big Swedish companies, because the home market was so small. Imperialism was beyond Sweden's military capabilities. If the cow trade partners were to find business allies, therefore, these would have to come from domestic-oriented companies, which in Sweden were smaller and at a relatively lower level of technology.[6]

Before 1936 the big internationalist firms were "rejectionist"; they hoped to break up the cow coalition. After 1936 they became accommodating. The change came about because of the election of 1936, which strengthened the Social Democrats (an attempt by the Agrarians to rule alone having failed) and confirmed that they were there to stay; simultaneously an improvement in the world economy eased the conflict over how to right the Depression, opening the way for a compromise. The accommodation in Sweden was the most explicit piece of social bargaining among social forces in any of our five countries for any of our three periods. In the small resort town of Saltsjöbaden representatives of labor, business, farming, and the government met to hammer out the accord of 1938, a model for what all of Western Europe would do after 1945. The terms of the agreement were business acceptance of Social Democratic government, high labor costs (high wages and the benefits of the welfare state), full-employment fiscal policy, and government activism for social services, in exchange for labor peace in labor markets (i.e., no strikes), continued private control over property and capital markets, and openness in relation to the world economy. This pattern has prevailed in Sweden, and even the bourgeois coalition that held office from 1976 to 1981 was not able to alter the power relationships that lie beneath the overall policy pattern.

Although the Social Democrats were successful in using the Depression to bring about a critical realignment in Swedish politics, their own policies did not play a large role in bringing Sweden out of the Depression. The rhetoric of demand-stimulated employment aroused considerable attention at the time, but it would not have much effect on economic life until after the war. Indeed, the Swedish recovery after 1933 derived less from the cow trade of that year than from the revival of the international economy, for reasons completely beyond Swedish control (policies pursued in the major markets of Germany, the United States, and the United Kingdom), and to Swedish policy decisions that helped take advantage of that revival—the devaluation of 1931 (in fact beyond Swedish control as well), low interest rates that stimulated building and investment, and considerable private restructuration of industry. Even in Sweden, however, improvement in conditions remained limited until stimulus of war wiped out unemployment.[7]

Demand stimulus and economic intervention by government became politically and intellectually respectable in the thirties, even if their real effects were limited then to agriculture, insurance schemes, and some leadership of direct investment (in the case of rural electrification). British and German social democrats paid dearly for incumbency at the time of the economic disaster; the Swedes got the benefits. Not only was the coalition more firmly implanted in Sweden, but so too were the ideas that the political leadership was able to associate with the revival. The Swedish policy sequence shows the importance of farmer and labor discontent in creating the conditions for policy and political realignment, of skilled party leadership in taking advantage of that opportunity, and of the capacity of historic antagonists to overcome their differences in a constitutional framework.

The United Kingdom

In response to the Depression, Sweden forged a new political coalition, made a partial break with deflationist orthodoxy through its monetary policy and corporatist market arrangements in agriculture, and began experimenting with countercyclical fiscal policies and an extended welfare state. Britain's was a contrasting path. In politics there was no social democratic breakthrough, but instead division in the Labour party and renewed dominance by the Conservatives. In economic policy there were breaks with the orthodox past—devaluation, tariffs, and corporatistic market arrangements—but no experimentation with demand stimulus. Britain shows that it was possible to limit moves away from the old ways to neo-orthodoxy without driving labor to rebellion or crushing it with police terror.

In terms of performance the results of this approach were not bad. The image of a Britain continuing to stagnate because it rejected economic experiment is clearly exaggerated. The product cycle moved new industries eastward across the Atlantic; autos, road building, and electrification stimulated a building boom, fueled by lower interest rates. After the trough of the Depression was reached in 1932–33, all countries did better, no matter what policies they pursued. Economic historians quarrel over whether the United Kingdom could have done even more: the unemployment rate never did go below 10 percent in the decade, and some historians think that fiscal stimulus could have made things better.[8] The interesting point here, however, is not whether some improvement occurred in Britain but why some efforts tried elsewhere made no headway in the United Kingdom, and what effects the political conflict of the period had on the development of British politics. In particular, the Labour party missed its opportunity to establish a political hegemony like that of its Swedish counterpart.

Why was there less policy experimentation in the United Kingdom during these years? The Liberal party adopted the ideas of John Maynard Keynes; so did many elements in the trade unions and a few scattered business and political leaders. But the Conservative party rejected those ideas, and so did leading Labour ministers in the government. Efforts to construct a Lib-Lab coalition around fiscal stimulus failed to take place.

Britain's production profile differed from that of Sweden and the other countries examined here in two striking ways: one is the importance and character of the finance-trading complex identified with the City, the other the relatively small and modernized agricultural sector. The strength of the City reinforced British attachment to orthodoxy and British resistance to the inward-looking ideas of Keynes in the early thirties. The weakness of agriculture deprived labor and dissident business elements of smallholding property owners as political allies with whom to challenge that orthodoxy.

Images of British consensus to the contrary, there was disagreement about British economic policy in the 1930s as there had been for many years. Before World War I, Joseph Chamberlain had led Birmingham-centered steel and other threatened industries to clamor for tariffs. Despite some agricultural and labor support, he failed, but the conflict continued into the 1920s. The international banks and their allies, shipping and insurance, pressed for a rapid return to convertibility and at a high rate; industry feared that a high rate would price them out of foreign markets and force deflationary policies that would cut into domestic markets. The banking view prevailed, and the subsequent sharp deflationary pressure led to the General Strike of 1926 and a major defeat for organized labor. It is in this context that Ramsay MacDonald came to power in 1929. The defeat of 1926 had undermined Labour's willingness to challenge the internationalist orthodoxy, and it contributed to that immense concern for the approval of the City which seems characteristic of Labour party politicians, though not of British union leaders, from MacDonald to Harold Wilson and James Callaghan.

The trade unions did press for public works and deficit spending. While serving on the Macmillan Committee, whose mandate was to explore the country's economic plight, Ernest Bevin had been deeply impressed by the failure of the banking-Treasury world to consider the implications of exchange and interest rate policy for industry and unemployment. Fighting employment by getting factories to produce again appealed to his pragmatic mind, and he led the acceptance of the new idea by the Trade Union Congress (TUC). Some figures in the Labour party supported such ideas in the late 1920s as well, most notably Oswald Mosley (who subsequently left the party). The two top party officials, Ramsay MacDonald and Philip Snowden, remained resolutely orthodox.[9]

As the Depression deepened, so criticism rose, not only in labor ranks but in the opposition as well. The Conservatives became advocates of tariffs, though not of devaluation. It was the Liberals who pressed hardest on behalf of public works and deficit budgets, which they wanted in tandem with tariffs or devaluation or both. Almost a decade before the publication of *The General Theory*, Keynes and other economists helped work out for the Liberals a broad program of expansion to fight unemployment. In pamphlets Keynes criticized the stress placed on the pound, arguing that the currency should serve productivity and employment, not the reverse. Though historically the Liberals were free traders and continued to criticize the Conservative push for tariffs, Keynes and the Liberals were willing to contemplate devaluation, which has a protectionist effect.

It is by no means easy to determine why it should have been the Liberals who in the late twenties took up this Chamberlainian theme in the new intellectual guise fashioned by Keynes. The Liberal social base seems still to have consisted of free-trade-oriented elements of industry and agriculture. The industries that had sustained critiques of banking and free-trade orthodoxy, and complained constantly during the twenties to various investigative committees and commissions, had Conservative party ties, not Liberal ones, and they could be pulled toward the more cautious, tariff-cartel version of policy change which the Tories preferred.

The solution to the puzzle may lie in the dynamics of party rivalry and leadership. The Liberals were, after all, in political trouble, having sunk to third place in the party system. They needed political "product differentiation" and their own arguments with mass appeal. Unemployment was certainly a great issue, one of immense political significance. Attacking both Labour and the Conservatives as wrong-headed made political sense, and the policy that the Liberals proposed had the political virtue of being neither clearly protectionist (so as not to offend the powerful "cheap loaf" stance of working-class voters) nor orthodoxy socialist (so as not to offend the middle-class electorate). Leadership also mattered. Lloyd George was a risk taker looking for arguments for a comeback, and he was smart enough to be convinced by the reasoning of smart men such as Keynes. His behavior contrasts sharply with the intellectual rigidity of Snowden, MacDonald, and Stanley Baldwin.[10]

Hitching Keynesian ideas to the Liberal party base aggravated an already strained situation. As Labour resisted the proffered Lib-Lab alliance, the Liberal party crumbled under the pull of competing policy programs. By 1931 so many had defected that the Liberal faction might no longer have been large enough to construct a working majority even if MacDonald had finally opted to try for one.

Because the Liberals were the third party, the interpretation of policy debates in the period cannot end with speculation about why they took up with Keynes. Breaking with deflationist orthodoxy required help from other societal actors and party formations. Elements of the Conservative party, for example, were sensitive to the needs of manufacturing industry as distinct from the banking-shipping wing. Such elements provided support for some sort of break from the old orthodoxy, but not enough to go the next step. As in America, the major debate in business circles was between classical orthodoxy (free trade, deflation, defense of the pound) and minor deviations (protectionism, cartelization). The elements interested in more activist, government-led schemes could not persuade their business brethren to go along. This is not surprising. As we have seen elsewhere, businesses got demand stimulus not by convincing their business brethren of its merits but by allying with other groups, such as labor and agriculture, intensely dissatisfied with market mechanisms.[11]

In the United Kingdom, the bloc of businesses under extreme pressure had some "positional" disadvantages compared to their counterparts in other countries. First, in no other country did industry face such a large group of interests tied to international trade and payments. As I have suggested, demand stimulus first appealed primarily to domestically oriented elements of the economy. No other country at the time had so many interests living off remittances, loans, shipping, and the like; the United States, Germany, Sweden, and France had fewer foreign investments and did not manage a reserve currency. To some degree this internationalism inhibited militarism: autarchy could not be appealing to those who lived off international trade, and hence militarism lacked an important legitimizing force. Second, agriculture as a sector was smaller in the United Kingdom than anywhere else, another consequence of the country's having been the first industrializer. As a result, fewer allies were available for the attack on money, banks, and internationalism. Third, British labor was very deeply wedded to the cheap loaf, making the construction of a protectionist alliance that included labor much harder. (As the experience of Joseph Chamberlain suggested, however, workers as electors could be won over to protectionism more easily than the organizations that represented them.)

The most puzzling question of all is why the Labour party did not take up demand stimulus. There is every likelihood that had Labour done so, it could have concluded an alliance with the Liberals. Credit for the post-1932 recovery (which was probable whatever the government actually did) would have gone to them, not the Conservatives. British politics might have looked more like that of Sweden, dominated by labor for a couple of generations. The interpretative problems are quite similar to those raised when one applies the same question to the German Social Democrats. Snowden, like Rudolph Hilferding, did not believe in the demand stimulus arguments; he was operating a market economy with orthodox rules. MacDonald seems to have been very much influenced by "good elite opinion," which excluded Keynes and Lloyd George. Thus the top party leaders seem to have been socialized into the British "orthodoxy." As in Germany, trade-union leaders may have been more open to new arguments because of a greater pragmatism, born of their closeness to labor-market conditions. But Bevin could not persuade MacDonald. MacDonald talked endlessly with the Liberals but failed to make the agreement. In 1931 the Labour party unified against Snowden and MacDonald, though the issue was cutting employment benefits not a program of public works, and it seems highly likely that had the party leadership then formed the Lib-Lab alliance around a demand stimulus scheme, both the TUC and the parliamentary Labour party would have supported it. Such a move at such a moment would have made the subsequent evolution of British policy and politics appear quite different.

What actually happened is well-known and needs no lengthy discussion. MacDonald tried to save the pound through further deflation, by cutting unemployment insurance, was expelled from the Labour party, and formed a new government that excluded most of the party. The pound quickly proved impossible to defend. When the financial circles most deeply wedded to a strong currency finally realized this, MacDonald devalued. Soon afterward, Britain adopted the first significant peacetime tariffs since the Corn Laws. The Conservatives quickly came to dominate the National Government and were swept into power at the next election. Under the impact of tariffs, very low interest rates, product innovations, and the revival of demand in other countries, the British economy did improve. Low interest rates plus automobiles and electrification helped spur shifts in residence patterns and a housing boom. The government helped with electrification, and eventually through military purchases, but demand stimulus as public policy would not be adopted until after the war.

The British case shows well the interaction between political choice and sectoral constraint. The contours of alternative coalitions supporting different policy options can be detected and appear plausible. The obstacles to such alternatives, while not insurmountable, appear large; they include the unique role of the City, the smallness of the agricultural sector, the orientation of labor toward the cheap loaf, and the cultural hegemony of economic orthodoxy in the first industrializing nation. In the absence of political imagination in the right place— it was with the Liberals instead of with Labour—and with the historical accident of a Labour government in office at the onset of the Depression, these obstacles proved insurmountable.

Germany

Sweden and the United Kingdom may have diverged in their economic policy choices and in the political experiments that their parties and social forces conducted, but both confronted the Depression within their constitutionalist systems. In Germany the experimentation was considerably more drastic in both policy and politics. Germany deliberately used strong fiscal stimulus earlier and more extensively than other countries, and it constructed a system of economic corporatism, protection, and state enterprise far more sweeping than other countries had done in peacetime. Meanwhile, its political experiment was spawning one of the most monstrous regimes in all of world history.

Despite the horror of the Nazi period, or rather because of it, the parallels between the German experience and those of other countries are important. The economic policy experimentation of the early years of the Nazi period is an enhanced form of what Sweden, the United States, and France were groping toward in the 1930s and what most of Western Europe and North America pursued after World War II: a mixed economy, with fiscal stimulus, regulated markets, and some public ownership of production. In its early years the political experiment combined elements of mass support, including nonunionized labor, agriculture, and anti-internationalist elements of business, into a coalition quite different from the more orthodox Cabinet of Barons, which held office in 1932, or the center-right coalitions of the late Weimar period. Tragically, the innovative capacity of this new coalition permitted disaster. Innovations in economic policy were inextricably linked to extreme nationalism and savage repression. It took the catastrophe of World War II, occupation, and partition to put Germany on a track that Sweden and other countries had discovered at rather less cost to themselves and to the world.

Military defeat played, of course, its own considerable role in the economic policy debates of the interwar period. The hegemony of the iron-rye bloc endured until 1918. The hardship of the war years and the suddenness of the defeat loosed an explosion of discontent, and what emerged was a grouping of forces first seen as backers of Caprivi; now, in the interwar years, they supported the Weimar coalition.[12]

For a few years the progressive elements of German society managed, fitfully and facing many obstacles, to form some loose, de facto accommodation. The constitution of 1919 survived the many challenges it faced during the first five years—the polarization and revolutionary conflict of December 1918 and January 1919, settled only at the high price of the Groener-Ebert agreement; then the Versailles treaty, the Kapp Putsch, the occupation of the Ruhr, and hyperinflation. For the next five years, from 1924 to 1929, the Weimar coalition of Social Democrats and progressive elements of business formed a policy entente with some family resemblance to the partnership formed at Saltsjöbaden.

In foreign economic policy, and in foreign relations generally, the Weimar coalition acquiesced in the settlement of 1919. Although critical of Versailles, as were all Germans, the coalition partners neither renounced German obligations formally nor attacked them militarily. Instead, they worked within the treaty to revise the reparations schedule and win foreign (largely American) loans with which to stabilize the Deutsche mark and finance the revival of production and exports.

For high-technology, internationally competitive firms, revival of a stable international economic order was essential. Autarchy would be too confining, too costly in resources lost to support the domestically weak. Integration into an open world economy, access to foreign capital, mass civilian purchasing power, restraint on the drain of inefficient sectors, modernization and rationalization at home—these were the goals of the electrotechnical and chemical industries, symbolized by Siemens and I. G. Farben and by prominent heads of the biggest firms, such individuals as Carl Duisberg and Walter Rathenau. Labor and capital were, in Germany as everywhere, in conflict on some issues; on others, however, under the right circumstances, collaboration was possible. Foreign economic policy issues drove some elements of German industry to manage relations with labor in order to promote a particular international position.

Labor's side of the bargain involved its acceptance as a coalition partner in politics, recognition as a legitimate actor in the labor market, and acquiescence in high wages and social insurance measures. On the Social Democratic side, Fritz Ebert, party leader and first president of the Weimar Republic, symbolizes the Weimar coalition's exchanges: control of the radical elements on the left in 1919, a constitutionalist polity, trade-union rights in collective bargaining and a ministry for the arbitration of labor disputes, full employment as a policy goal, and social insurance programs.

Agriculture was not integrated into this accommodation. Business elites and labor continued to see agriculture as part of the opposing bloc and demanding too high a price in subsidies. The failure to woo agriculture would cost the Weimar coalition dearly.

The Weimar coalition thus sought to integrate Germany into an intensified international division of labor. A stable and open world economy would allow Germany's high-technology, competitive industries to generate through exports the income needed to pay off reparations, pay back loans, pay high wages, and absorb resources being shifted out of less competitive sectors. The opposition in Germany resisted this course. It preferred revision of Versailles to restore an older pattern, one that provided shelter from the world economy and help for industries in trouble. The social core of this conservative opposition was heavy industry. The war had seen a considerable worldwide expansion of industrial capacity, and iron and steel were now in worse shape than before; though German heavy industry remained comparatively efficient, it could not cope with worldwide overproduction. In agriculture there had also been considerable expansion, and a fall of prices marked an agricultural crisis several years before the Great Crash of 1929. All sorts of nationalists supported revision of Versailles, but heavy industry and agriculture remained more protectionist, more autarchic in policy preferences, more resistant to accommodation with the international trading community, more resistant to accommodation with labor at home.

Although economic policy was not the only issue on the German political agenda, there was some clustering of issues. Foreign policy internationalists tended also to be progressive on questions concerning the constitution, civil rights, and labor; economic nationalists were also foreign policy revisionists, and hostile to the constitution and to labor. So many issues made a variety of combinations of policy and political formulas possible.[13]

As long as the world economy remained healthy, the pressures for autarchy could be resisted. When the world economy collapsed, however, the costs and benefits of domestic coalitional behavior changed considerably. Electoral studies have documented these shifts at the level of the mass electorate, in the abandonment of the system parties for more extremist formations.[14] The context in which these electoral shifts occurred, the conflict over economic and other policies, a conflict shaped strongly by interest groups and the structural situation in which they operated, has, however, been less explored. The flight from the system parties was a response to the deadlock among them and among the interest groups struggling over different conceptions of policy.

As exports plummeted, so industry's ability to pay the costs of the labor alliance dropped. The assertions of the heavy industry groups now sounded more plausible to export industry: a revival of sales required lower prices, which required lower costs, which required lower wages and taxes. In business associations the export group was weakened, and heavy industry leaders replaced exporters as spokesmen. Export and heavy industry both initially supported deflation, as a way of cutting costs. Elements of both sectors were soon to turn toward other policies, such as reflation, armaments and exchange controls, corporatism and structured markets. But in both branches the Depression led immediately to sharp conflict with labor.

Labor found itself squeezed ever more tightly between its economic policy preferences and its desire to preserve a constitution whose political features helped guarantee labor's economic and political power. The trade unions and the Social Democrats opposed the deflationary content of Heinrich Brüning's policy, but they sustained the government in office in order to preserve the republic and bar the way to the far right. As defenders of labor in the market, party and union opposed the reduction of unemployment benefits, the pressure against wages, and the rollback of state expenditures. In the last matter they were particularly constrained as the representatives of large numbers of civil servants. To defend labor rights won in the political arena, the Social Democrats felt compelled to support a prosystem government even when that government pursued economic policies contrary to their goals in the labor market.

Socialist leaders, particularly Rudolf Hilferding, the finance minister and leading party intellectual in matters of economic theory, allowed their economic ideas to constrain sharply Social Democratic politics. These leaders saw no alternative between full socialization of the economy, for which they had no electoral majority, and operation of the capitalist economy by its own logic, which Hilferding understood by means of the same orthodoxy accepted by the economists who favored deflation. Hilferding rejected completely the demand stimulus ideas that were circulating in Europe at the time. The trade-union movement had been persuaded to adopt such a program: the WTB plan (so called for Wladimir Woytinski, a Russian émigré social democratic economist, Fritz Tarnow, a trade-union official, and Fritz Baade, an agriculture expert), which called for deficit-financed public works. In a showdown between union and party leaders, Woytinski and his colleagues were unable to overcome Hilferding's commitment to an orthodox capitalist interpretation of capitalism.[15]

The SPD thus lost an opportunity as much political as economic. By 1932, when this debate inside the SPD took place, all circles of German society, including the various wings of industry, were exhibiting considerable dissatisfaction with economic orthodoxy. Heavy industrialists had always had misgivings about the deflationist line. Market mechanisms had not worked well for the steel and iron producers in the twenties, and in crisis the producers turned readily and rapidly back to such familiar policy instruments as tariffs and other forms of autarchy, and government spending, particularly on capital goods for the military. Although demand stimulus per se had no particular intellectual basis in heavy industrial circles, the notion of government assistance was thoroughly familiar there.[16] Military and infrastructure spending was an old and well-understood pattern, and thus domestic business found demand stimulus thinking more acceptable than export did when the world economy went sour. Previous relations between labor and business were reversed: the traditional labor enemies, domestic and heavy industry, were drawn together with labor toward domestic reflation and found themselves in conflict with labor's traditional ally, exporters for whom the home market was too small.

International crisis may also move an industry or a company from one bloc to another. I. G. Farben, as James Kurth points out, had invested heavily in coal gasification. When oil prices dropped sharply in 1931 after the Texas oil fields came in, the chemical giant quickly gave up its internationalist stance and desperately sought aid. In the maneuverings of late 1932 I. G. Farben preferred Kurt von Schleicher's variant of intervention (demand stimulus corporatism with labor participation) to Adolph Hitler's (which excluded labor). So

Farben leaders did not play an active role in bringing Hitler to power; once Hitler took power, however, they did rally to his policies and in the end played a greater role than any other company or industry in the Nazi regime, down to building synthetic rubber plants at Auschwitz.[17]

In the conflict over economic policy the behavior of agricultural interests (voters, interest groups, and parties) was vital. German agriculture rebelled against bourgeois economic orthodoxy most thoroughly and rapidly. None of the system parties showed much responsiveness to the countryside's plight. The bourgeois parties defended the market against rural landholders' pleas; the left saw no reason to help private property, in particular a property-owning segment that never gave any evidence of willingness to cooperate with labor. So, though there were individuals among the Social Democrats, the bourgeois parties, and the farmers' parties who sought to promote alliances, they made no headway. The sort of collaboration seen in the United States and Sweden did not occur in Germany.

By 1932 political support for waiting for results from Brüning's economic orthodoxy had dissipated. Most of the alternatives were considered, and some were tried. Devaluation fared poorly, because it evoked the horror of hyperinflation. Nationalization, at least as propounded by the left, lacked political strength. Several mixtures of the remaining elements—corporatism, fiscal stimulus, protectionism—were tried before Hitler's won out.

Schleicher tried to organize a quasi-parliamentary version of demand stimulus, but unlike American and Swedish experimenters, he omitted agriculture. He thus failed to draw in the mass of small farmers but threatened the special advantages of the Junkers, thereby angering the camarilla around Paul von Hindenburg. Labor and business could not agree on a package, because labor would not shoulder the costs as business demanded. In the United States and Sweden, where business came to accept demand stimulus, it did so only when the labor-farmer alliance showed sufficient political strength; then some sectors of business became more accommodating. In Germany, however, the attempt was quite different: agriculture was excluded from Schleicher's discussions, which tried to effect a direct bargain between labor and heavy industry, the two actors with the historically deepest antagonism.[18]

Instead of Schleicher's explicit social bargaining among major social groups within a modified constitutionalism, Hitler's politics mixed explicit bargaining among actors in business and agriculture with direct mobilization of individuals and the exclusion of their institutionalized representatives (particularly unionists and Social Democrats, but some elements of agriculture, white-collar workers, and business as well). Direct accommodation among agriculture and business elites (as attempted with the Cabinet of Barons in 1932) could not work because it lacked mass support. Hitler could provide that support from unemployed workers who were not unionized, farmers, salaried personnel, and property owners small, medium, and large.

The social diversity of the Nazi vote was more complex than the traditional explanatory stress on the "middlestand" warrants. Hitler combined rejection of the dominant economic alternatives, socialization and the market, with nationalism, which appealed to many different elements of society. It did worst with those strongly integrated into alternative interpretations of the world—unions, the Marxist parties, and the Catholic Center party. But settling the question of who voted for the Nazis will not in the end explain either the *Machtergreifung* or the content of policy. In the last normal election, November 1932, Hitler did not exceed 34 percent of the vote. To take power required help from other sources; he got it from the conservatives in agriculture and business, who sought a deal; the chancellery for control of labor.

This political bargaining for economic policy is important. By themselves, the economic elites would not have undertaken what Hitler did in economic policy after January 1933, however much they liked the economic results and (at least until the late thirties) the political ones as well. Neither the economic results not the political outcomes matched the desires of any single group. Rather, they emerged from an interaction. Everyone had reasons to prefer some other, "purer" policy and political choice, and here lies the weakness of many social explanations of fascism, the notion that fascism derived from big business, or from the Junkers, or from the petty bourgeoisie. Big business preferred the Cabinet of Barons, as did the Junkers; the petty bourgeoisie sought a kind of regulatory capitalism which put it in conflict with other social groups. Nonetheless, the interaction that brought Hitler to power did have social bases—which is what is wrong with purely institutional, individualist, culturalist, or psychological explanations. The heavy industrialists may have *preferred* the Cabinet of Barons, but they accepted Hitler rather than other alternatives. And though they may have preferred the Cabinet of Barons politically, in economic terms that group had become too orthodox for them.[19]

The break from economic orthodoxy was difficult without political help. Property owners everywhere found it difficult to reconcile contradictions in their attitudes, preferences, and political comportment.

They wanted defense of property, restraint of labor pressures, and limits on state interference in "appropriate" ways. Many wanted state aid for an emergency but were reluctant to pay the price of social insurance and state aid for employment. Ordinary "bourgeois" politicians had trouble integrating these various goals in politically effective ways, and they ended by appearing to defend capital at the expense of the masses. Hitler had mass support. An accommodation between Nazis and certain social forces thus gave the government the autonomy it needed to try a blend of policies.

The Nazis proved better able than policy makers in other countries to bring down unemployment, and they did so even *before* the upswing in military spending. With extensive public works and government purchasing, they ran deficits that infused the economy with new purchasing power. Exchange controls and trade restrictions curtailed imports and effectively devalued the mark while maintaining its nominal value. By the end of 1934 unemployment had dropped; indeed, it was a sharper drop than anywhere else. In Sweden and the United States, the other countries that attempted some job-creating activities in this period, demand stimulus was far less ample than in Germany and had lesser effects. Revival in these countries had far more to do with the boost to exports from devaluation, the boost to investment from cheap interest rates, and an upturn in worldwide demand. Thus the first country to try demand stimulus and make it work was, sad to say, Germany under the Nazis. (Japan experimented with demand stimulus as well, also as the regime was becoming increasingly fascist; but that case is outside the framework of this book.)[20]

What we see in the German case is the impact of international economic crisis on the way that societal actors aligned themselves domestically around economic policies and politics. The crash of 1929 undermined the accommodations among societal actors which sustained Weimar. As the Depression worsened, demands for policy shifts grew. Situation in the international economy helps us predict the direction of these policy shifts. The structure of policy preferences in turn helps us define the situation within which other variables—political leadership, circumstance, ideology—play a role. In Germany the pattern of group support for breaking with orthodoxy had some remarkable similarities with patterns in other countries; the sharp difference was the political formula.

The United States

The American pattern most resembles that of Sweden. The classical policy of deflation crumbled early in the Depression, giving way to the political and policy experimentation of the New Deal in its several phases. Issues of foreign economic policy played a large role in the complex movement of social forces and politicians, producing a result less formal than Saltsjöbaden, less extensive in its welfare state provisions, and weaker in labor's power—but nonetheless a result roughly similar to what emerged from Sweden's efforts to strike a new balance among business, labor, and agriculture.

The Depression weakened the grip that Republican business leadership had exerted over American economic policy for more than half a century. In all the years between Lincoln and Hoover the Democrats had broken through to the White House only twice, with Grover Cleveland, a Gold Democrat, and Woodrow Wilson, who benefited from the Bull Moose split among Republicans. For most of those years, a nationalist approach dominated economic policy. Concern with domestic markets over foreign ones, control of labor, containment of populist agrarian protest, sound money—these were the goals of the business leadership that worked through the Republican party.

The internationalists continued to dissent. They sought an intensification of the insertion of the United States into the world division of labor, and for that, they advocated low tariffs, trade treaties, and active American involvement in collective discussions about international economic and security arrangements. The nationalists, or isolationists as they were called at the time, saw little need for "foreign entanglements" and little need to promote trade through accommodation with the needs of other countries. Core support for the internationalist position came from trade-oriented bankers, largely from the Northeast, from shippers, from high-technology industry at the export phase of the product cycle, from commodity crop–exporting agriculture, and, increasingly, from oil. Core support for the nationalists came from the large, smokestack industries of the Midwest, typically steel.[21]

In the 1920s prosperity helped the Republicans continue to manage a system that integrated working-class ethnic groups into a coalition led by their employers. The dynamism of the American economy muted potential conflicts among various segments of capital and between capital and other elements of society. Some role in international affairs could coexist with the isolationism of the victorious opponents of the League of Nations; witness, for example, American involvement through the Dawes and Young plans to deal with the payments problems of the postwar years. But there were many fault lines in the American political economy. The shock of the Depression burst them open.[22]

When the Depression hit the United States with a vengeance, in late 1929, Herbert Hoover's responses mixed two forms of orthodoxy: the neoclassical one of deflation, and the habitual Republican one of high tariffs. As the Hawley-Smoot Tariff Act swept into law over the opposition of one thousand economists, Hoover began the cycle of cutting spending and taxes. The Federal Reserve kept money tight. But the Depression got worse, and Hoover sensed the need for unusual action. He apparently believed in some sort of business corporatism as a way of correcting the ills of the market, but he wanted it to be entirely voluntary, without any involvement of the state. Because he also believed in a balanced budget and stable currency values, he effectively eliminated all remedies except the orthodox ones.[23]

As the Depression worsened, discontent with orthodoxy rose in labor, agriculture, and business. Franklin D. Roosevelt brought all three together in one type of coalition, leading to the policies of the first New Deal. As that failed, and economic conditions changed, another coalition was assembled, leading to the second New Deal.

Agriculture's problems preceded the Great Crash of 1929. International production had expanded in response to World War I, pressing prices downward in the twenties; when industrial demand collapsed, things got even worse. Farmers in the United States, as in Europe, clamored loud and hard for help, any kind of help.[24] As unemployment climbed to 25 percent (and probably even higher than the counting system specified), discontent rose among workers as well. Large chunks of the ethnic working class electorate which had voted Republican left the GOP and linked up with those workers who had always voted for the Democrats. And many elements of business turned against economic orthodoxy as well, seeking a more activist role for government. In the early days of the New Deal, support for change came from domestic-oriented business interests; in the second New Deal it came from internationalists. Involvement of domestic business in a coalition with labor through the Democratic party was unusual and, as it turned out, short-lived.

FDR came to be seen by many businessmen as a "class enemy" for having broken with orthodox market liberalism. Nonetheless the first New Deal, at least, expressed the thinking of a very large portion of American business at the time. Many in the business elite no longer believed that the workings of the market corrected themselves automatically, in time, and at acceptable costs. Rather, they came to believe in the need for deliberate acts of coordination, order, stabilization, market sharing, and administration. Hoover also believed in these things but thought they should be done voluntarily; FDR took the same ideas and linked them to the state. The National Industrial

Recovery Act (NIRA) called for the National Recovery Administration to set up committees of businessmen which would set standards of price and quality for every product and allocate production shares to each producer. The principle of corporatist representation would be extended to labor through section 7b of the NIRA, which gave labor rights to organize.

This corporatism was a domestic solution, and generally the first New Deal marked a strong defeat for internationalists. Roosevelt ignored the free-trade traditions of the Democratic party in favor of the protectionist sentiments of its working-class elements and the business allies with whom he sought to work. The United States went off the gold standard, broke up the London Conference on the monetary system, and showed no signs of altering Hawley-Smoot.

Farmers got the Agricultural Adjustment Act, which replaced the market with a system of government-backed price, production, and marketing arrangements—every form of subsidy except direct cash payments, which farmers regarded as welfare and hence unacceptable. Prices would be kept up by government purchasing, by curtailing production, and by regulating the sale of products. Consumers would pay for the subsidies both out of general tax revenues and in higher prices at the stores. Farmers were also given a variety of development programs, including rural electrification, and large public works such as the Tennessee Valley Authority.

Labor and agriculture provided much of the energy for the first New Deal, but the New Deal was also what a very large portion of American industry thought had to be done.[25] Demand stimulus suggestions did exist in the Washington of 1933, but they were marginal to policy discussions. Various plans showed a lot of imagination, political skill, and human sensitivity—the Civilian Conservation Corps, for example, and the Work Projects Administration—but not a considerable amount of economic impact.

Yet the coalition behind the first New Deal was itself riddled with fault lines. The economic situation improved but only slowly, indeed painfully so. Continuing hardships increased the stress on the coalition, until the partnership cracked. Within business, the corporatist ideology of conflict-free self-regulation proved illusory. As business committees came together to discuss the codes for each product, differently situated firms proposed different codes. When a committee majority did manage to reach some sort of conclusion, their decision would face enough opposition so that enforcement required coercion by means of the courts and the federal bureaucracy. The United States lacked a coercive bureaucracy, and there was no support for creating one even among the most unorthodox elements of business.

By the time the Supreme Court declared the National Industrial Recovery Act unconstitutional in 1935, business had already abandoned the first New Deal, thereby bringing into the open conflict over what economic policy to follow. The partial revival of the world economy exacerbated disagreements over foreign economic policy. Internationalists wanted to wriggle out of the Hawley-Smoot tariff and to restore a stable international payments and trading system. Nationalists and domestically oriented producers wanted to retain these features of the first New Deal's policies. At the same time labor militancy was growing, producing ever sharper conflicts with some business elements concerning the labor clauses in the NIRA.

These tensions burst open the coalition of the first New Deal, reopening the door for possible policies and politics. Policy could have gone back to an orthodoxy in the Hoover mold, or to cautious forms of neo-corporatism such as the British Conservatives were trying, or to further experimentation toward what became the social democratic model. These options, and the ingredients of the support coalitions for each, were profoundly shaped by the economic situation of various actors. But as in any complex crisis, leadership played a role: FDR chose the third route, and his choice had significant consequences.

Faced with eroding business interest in the economic experimentation of the NRA and with growing business hostility to labor demands, FDR facilitated an American *renversement des alliances*. Economically nationalist business interests left his administration's coalition, and internationally oriented business came back in. Some consumer-oriented producers concerned about maintaining stability of demand and mass consumer purchasing power also stayed in. The new element of the bargain, in contrast with the populist and progressive reformism of the days before World War I, was the willingness of these types of business groups to accept concessions to labor and agriculture in order to block their more orthodox brethren.

On international questions the administration reversed its behavior of 1933. It entered the Tripartite Monetary Agreement of 1936, designed to stabilize the international payments system, and it began to use the authority given to it at the end of 1934 to erode Hawley-Smoot through reciprocal trade treaties. Some forms of corporatistic market arrangements were rescued from NRA wreckage and renamed regulation: the oil industry kept price and production fixing, as did the airlines; banking kept the changes of the Glass-Steagall Act, which weakened some banking circles with traditional Republican links on behalf of others linked to the Democrats, and the Securities and Exchange Commission regulated that market. In agriculture the principle of state intervention for the stabilization of markets and the guarantee of price floors were restored after the Agricultural Adjustment Administration was found unconstitutional. Labor obtained social security, in the Wagner Act of 1935, and rights to participate as organizations in a system of collective bargaining, in the National Labor Relations Act of 1936.

These different elements can be characterized loosely as an effort to introduce some degree of corporatism into a liberal political economy. Agriculture, labor, and some elements of business were allowed to organize their markets, providing some shelter from unrestrained market forces.

In fiscal policy the new coalition showed, albeit fitfully, more flexibility than its predecessors. In campaigning for the presidency, FDR had shared orthodox views about balancing the budget. In an emergency he and his advisers were somewhat more willing to essay greater spending, on some more public works and some more explicit job creation programs. But they remained averse to large deficits. At the first opportunity, as the economy continued to revive after the election of 1936, the administration moved quickly to balance the budget by raising taxes. The result was the very steep slump of 1937–38, one of the worst downturns in American history. It was this experience which persuaded FDR's entourage that deficit stimulus had some validity, and it led to the first deliberate attempt by the United States government to try it.[26]

The combination of policies which developed during the Second New Deal mark the de facto American equivalent of the Saltsjöbaden Accord. Societal actors worked out rather similar accommodations, exchanging concessions for gains. Labor reversed its historic antipathy to higher food costs, accepting them in exchange for agrarian backing for the new industrial relations system, social security, and more active government pursuit of full employment. Agriculture, meanwhile, overcame its traditional hostility to labor, ethnics, and the city, paying that price for stabilization of the countryside. Internationally oriented business elites acceded to the demands of labor and agriculture in exchange for help to restore the international trading system, regulate certain industries, and stabilize the domestic economy through macroeconomic management. Some business elites came to see virtue in the programs of labor and agriculture as stabilizers, providing a floor to demand as well as discipline and peace in labor markets. The business elements most willing to think in these macroeconomic terms and to accept the accommodation with labor were, it appears, those whose location in the international product cycle made them at once interested in foreign trade and large consumer markets and able to bear higher labor costs.

The creative energy in the second New Deal came from the triangle of its social base—business progressives, labor, and agriculture. These businessmen were willing to make concessions for mass support, albeit reluctantly. Social security, institutionalization of labor markets, macroeconomic policies, and other forms of intervention provided effects useful to manufacturers, but they were also costly. Even progressive businessmen sought limits to reformism. Agriculture proved to be the swing group, for having gotten its program and economic revival, it moved away from labor. The pattern of the next few decades was already clear in the late thirties. Hard times made farmers available for reformism with labor in the Democratic party; better times led them into the cross-party coalition of southern Democrats and conservative Republicans.

In policy terms we observe a shift in the political location of experimentation with demand stimulus. Such experiments began life as part of an inward-looking, nationalist impulse, an attempt to rescue domestic economies from the ruin of the international one, and so was demand stimulus proposed in Europe and America in the early thirties. Where constitutional politics ended during the nationalist phase of the Depression, as in Germany, demand stimulus remained wedded to nationalist-imperialist uses. Where constitutionalist politics survived however, demand stimulus was free to seek other sponsors. It took a certain amount of learning—economic, intellectual, and political—to produce acceptance of Keynesianism. That learning involved sequences of trial and error, policy attempts and policy failures. Demand stimulus would not be fully used until after World War II. In the second New Deal, however, we see the pragmatic working out of the postwar social democratic model: an open foreign economic policy, full-employment fiscal policy, social insurance transfer payments, trade-union rights in collective bargaining, high wages, and stable monetary policy.

France

France tried a wide range of policies to fight the Depression, and a wide range of political formulas also. None of them worked well. Although the Republic survived, it was badly weakened and left vulnerable to the Nazi juggernaut. The Popular Front was able to break with orthodoxy in ways similar to those of other countries—social insurance, union rights, wage increases, demand stimulus, and agrarian price supports. But the governing coalition was deeply divided, and when it crumbled after a year in office, France shifted to somewhat more conventional policy moves boosted by military spending.

The supporters and opponents of economic experimentation in
France fitted into patterns found elsewhere.[27]

World War I modified the balance of forces in French politics,
though not dramatically. Labor groups gained considerably in importance there, as in other countries; the Socialists became part of governing coalitions. They were not, however, able to alter economic
policy in major ways. Economic orthodoxy prevailed in France: after
some considerable inflation Raymond Poincaré stabilized the franc
and restored French politics and policy to prewar patterns.[28]

The Poincaré franc turned out to be somewhat undervalued. For
several years, the cheaper franc sustained exports and gold inflows,
shielding France from the Depression. The currency devaluations of
1931 in Britain and elsewhere broke the shield and brought the Depression to France. Conservative governments tried the classic deflationary remedy of cutting the budget and pressing down wages. The
conservative cabinets drew for support on agriculture, business, and
Catholics of all kinds, including workers, to the exclusion of labor
unions and labor-connected parties.

These policies did not work in France any better than they did in
other countries. Discontent mounted rapidly on all sides. Right-wing
groups marched on the Palais Bourbon in 1934, seeking a mixture of
fascist politics and somewhat more active, and authoritarian, economics. This incident, together with the example of catastrophe in Germany, helped to set in motion the political shifts that led to the Popular Front. On the left the Communists, *téléguidé* by Stalin, switched
from attacking the Republic as a version of social fascism to defending
it as a bulwark against German revanchism. On the center and right,
French bourgeois republicans and nationalists rallied to defend the
Republic. Socialists, Communists, and Radicals formed an electoral
coalition that won a majority, though not a massive one, in the election of 1936. The tension among these coalition partners was considerable, for economic policy was only one of a range of policy issues
that divided them. Only republicanism and the German threat kept
them together, and then only for a short time.

Although the coalition was formed for political defense, it also created the political capabilities to alter economic policy. The constituencies that supported the coalition parties were also those most dissatisfied with the deflationary policies of preceding governments. Labor
union members and farmers, in particular, had grown increasingly
unhappy but were unable to do anything about it. The electoral victory touched off a wave of strikes as workers sought through direct
action to get what had hitherto seemed unattainable.

The political pressure of the sit-down strikes allowed the new premier, Léon Blum, to do things that might otherwise have been harder to achieve, but it also pushed the government farther and faster than it wished to go. The Socialists and the Communists benefited from having been out of power when the Depression hit France; they could mobilize discontent without having to be clear about what compromises they would accept if in power. In general terms they interpreted the Depression as a crisis of capitalism, which could be solved only by socialization of the economy. But the political realities of France in the mid-thirties, they understood, made this impossible. By 1936 both parties were giving pride of place to the defense of the Republic, and they would accept whatever economic policies it took to keep a republican coalition together. Thus their programs expressed the effort to anticipate and to accommodate themselves to the demands of other groups (agriculture and business) and other parties (particularly the Radicals).

Left-wing thought contained ideas congruent with demand stimulus, particularly underconsumption theory, which argued that by squeezing wages, capitalism deprived workers of sufficient income to buy capitalism's output. These ideas, however, were not an explicit part of the Popular Front program in 1936. The policies actually pursued, which included some elements of demand stimulus, arose from a complex political progress of responding to the diverse and conflicting pressures of various societal actors—agriculture, labor, and different business groups.

In France, as in other countries, a major source of discontent with orthodox deflation was agriculture. Bourgeois governments generally did rather little to help the countryside to deal with plunging prices. Whatever their partisan attachments, farmers agitated for some sort of assistance, be it price supports, government purchases, or marketing agreements. But in their discontent with deflation, farmers moved in different political directions; some were drawn to the right, others to the left, particularly to the Communists who gained the most votes among the three parties of the Popular Front coalition. What farmers moved in which direction? Available electoral sociology on this question focuses on demographic characteristics of farmers (size of farm, location, religion) but not on situational features such as the product raised, the nature of the farm's relationship to markets, and recent experience with government policies. Something was done for wine growers in the early thirties: did that make wheat producers easier to mobilize for dissent? Does religion explain more of the behavior of subsistence farmers (a large proportion in France) than of market-oriented ones? In short, rural discontent with orthodox deflation appears clearer than the mechanisms whereby that discontent was translated into political action. Large blocs of farmers were, it appears, available to support programs of state intervention in the rural economy—not socialization but some kind of market regulation.[29] But the politics to which that support could be linked seem to have been somewhat plastic.

Agricultural support for a farmer-labor alliance did exist, then, through the mechanisms of party politics, but as elsewhere it was not enough. Support from at least some elements of the bourgeoisie was vital, but where might it come from? To a considerable degree, in fact, such support materialized either not at all or only to a very limited extent. Bourgeois support for the Popular Front was strong enough to win the election of 1936, to sustain defense of the Republic for a few years, and to work out and ratify the Matignon Accords as a solution to the sit-down strikes. But it was not strong enough to sustain the Blum government in office, to continue the economic program begun in 1936, or in the long run to generate a cross-class program of national self-defense. As one of the leading historians of the Popular Front, Georges Dupeux, has argued, the moderate social democratic policy stance of Léon Blum failed because it lacked a necessary partner—a moderate business bourgeoisie.[30] Why that lack?

A production profile interpretation would stress the relative weakness in the French economy of industries and firms that were strong, internationally competitive, and high-technology, and that had a low labor component. Unorthodox ideas about the economy did circulate in France during the interwar years, and in precisely the same places as in other countries. Ernst Mercier and Auguste Detoeuf are perhaps the best known of the French equivalents to Carl Duisberg, but they were tempted more by a kind of technocratic business elite solution than by cooperation with labor. Their industry was electrical equipment. These figures and industries, however, are strikingly atypical of French economic history from 1870 to 1940, which is full of the destruction of economic pioneers, not of their success. The men who represented business in the Matignon Accords came from the largest companies, particularly metallurgy. Bitterly attacked by smaller, more backward companies, they were forced out of office in the employers' association.[31] Most French industry was small, labor-intensive, and overwhelmingly protectionist, and relatively few companies were looking for allies to create an open, internationalist strategy.

Small property owners were, however, by no means unanimous

defenders of orthodox deflation. In France as elsewhere smallholders were cross-pressured, fearful of labor radicalism but also fearful of big business and untrammeled competition. Attacks against *les gros*, the *deux cent familles*, and the *mur d'argent* resonated loudly and were by no means the monopoly of the left. The Radical party electorate had little sympathy for nationalization and deep hostility to devaluation, but it did have some sympathy for an effort to break free of deflation.

These conflicting pressures from diverse constituencies put the Blum government in a situation from which demand stimulus experimentation was actually an easier next move than neo-orthodoxy would have been. Despite the prior experience of other countries that had sought to defend their currencies without success, virtually all segments of the French public remained attached to defense of the franc Poincaré. Only one politician of any significance, Paul Reynaud, pleaded for devaluation; he was scorned for his efforts. The parties of the left proposed exchange controls instead of devaluation, but the idea was unacceptable to the Radicals. In the campaign of 1936 Blum had stated that he would accept neither deflation nor devaluation, but if the latter were excluded and the former found wanting, then what other course was there?[32]

The reflation of the economy through some sort of demand stimulus became central to government policy, though not intentionally. To handle the strike wave of May and June 1936, the government negotiated the Matignon Accords. This sweeping program of change included increased wages, a national retirement system, a limited work week, paid vacations, and trade-union rights. The agreements would have long-run structural effects, but their more immediate impact was to increase the purchasing power of workers.

The effort to resist devaluation failed. Blum refused to devalue upon taking office, but by September the runs on the franc proved unstoppable. As in the United Kingdom, a labor government finally abandoned monetary orthodoxy, but only when the guardians of that orthodoxy, the bankers and elite economic opinion makers, said it had to be done.[33] For agriculture, the Popular Front extended corporatistic marketing arrangements through the Office du Blé.

French efforts to break with orthodoxy did not work well. The stimulus of higher wages and the cheapening of exports through devaluation were to no avail; capital fled the country, inflation was sharp, and production did not increase. Divergence on economic policy merged with disagreements about many other questions, and within a year the government had disintegrated and fell. New coalitions swung rightward and undid many of the Popular Front's reforms. The work week was lengthened, real wages sank, and unions were ignored or brushed aside.

The coalition of interests that supported the Popular Front looked a lot like the crisis coalition in Sweden (agriculture, labor, and some elements of business). Swedish solidarity, however, proved far greater than that of the French. France is thus the case where the demand stimulus coalition within a parliamentary system was weakest and least successful.

I should note that in exploring the social correlates of the Popular Front, I do not mean to brush away the other forces that shaped voting and alliances. A republican, revolutionary, and anticlerical tradition in France, strong among farmers, businessmen, teachers, professionals, and civil servants, certainly affected Popular Front politics; so did the example of the collapse of Weimar, which galvanized republican defense and helped get the Communists to switch positions, from critics of "bourgeois republics" in the Germany of 1932 to supporters of constitutionalist liberties in the France of 1936. The Popular Front coalition may have come into being to save the Republic. But the coalition formed for that purpose had political capabilities different from those of its predecessors. For a time, for as long as it cohered, the coalition shifted the course of French economic policy considerably. When the coalition collapsed, however, the older political pattern of center-right governments returned the country to traditional economic policies. Military spending provided some stimulus effect, and the economy experienced improvement. Politically, the country lurched on toward the disaster of 1940.

Policy Formation in the 1930s

The politics surrounding economic policy choices in the 1930s were very varied, much more so than in the crisis period of the late nineteenth century. Nazi Germany, Social Democratic Sweden, the France of Laval and the France of Blum, the United Kingdom under Baldwin, the United States under Hoover and the United States under FDR—the range of political forms is considerable. In terms of economic policy, different regimes used similar techniques, among them demand stimulus, corporatist market structuration, devaluation, military spending, protection; and similar regimes diverged considerably, as some experimented while others stuck to the orthodoxies.

Nevertheless, underlying the diversity of political forms here, as in the first crisis period, there seems to be some consistency across countries in the political sociology of efforts to break with economic orthodoxy and to experiment with demand stimulus. That consistency is to be found in two patterns. One is the "marginal propensity" of various groups to support or fail to support sharp breaks with market principles in the 1930s. The other is the "alliance valence" of groups, that is, their propensity to form alliances with other groups to support particular policies. The patience of various actors with orthodoxy and neo-orthodoxy does not appear to have been uniform.

Trade unions, agricultural associations, industries concerned with the stability of demand and the home market—these were the first groups to find a general appeal in policies that went beyond the market mechanism and more specifically in policies that involved government pump priming, the creation of jobs and demand, and the concluding of production and marketing arrangements. At the height of the Depression, in 1932–33, these were the groups most likely either to press for or to support state-led solutions to the crisis. On many points these groups had traditionally been, and continued to be, in intense conflict over food costs and industrial prices, wages and property rights, welfare and services, urban and rural values, and authority relations. As conditions worsened, however, the policy preferences of these groups evolved rapidly: they wanted help and would accept help of almost any kind. Ideological commitments toward the "proper" role of government disintegrated, and so did political commitments of long standing. Traditional hostilities were overcome, at least for economic policy purposes; historic enemies supported policy innovation and the political experimentation needed to get it. At the same time links were collapsing between historic allies. International banking, export industries, labor, and export farming fought among themselves as the first two resisted the market interventions that the latter two supported.

After 1935, as economies revived, we see a second phase of both political and economic experimentation, with some important shifts in the political sociology of policy choices. Recovery allowed suppressed conflicts to reemerge and older forms of cooperation to reform. The initial reflation coalition waged increasing internal battles over wages, industrial relations, welfare, regulation and market structuration, and foreign economic policy. In the United States and Sweden the coalitions were refashioned. Internationally oriented industry sought to restore an open, stable international economy. As before, the aim brought such interests into conflict with their more isolationist, inward-looking brethren and made them more willing to collaborate with labor for support. The big contrast between the 1930s and the late nineteenth century was the ability of labor and some business elements in the thirties to work out understandings and policy exchanges.

In Germany the collapse of constitutional government shut off the open operation of political processes, and so coalitions could not be refashioned with an internationalist-labor-farmer orientation until after the war and occupation. Within the authoritarian framework, however, some change did occur. Some of the larger export-oriented industries that had had doubts about Hitler before 1933 became leaders, helping promote both policies for internal modernization and stabilization and foreign economic policy toward eastern Europe.

The policy sequence is quite clear. Deflation began as an expression of faith in the market and as an internationalist strategy, designed to beat down domestic costs of production to lower prices in order to revive foreign and domestic sales. Neo-orthodoxy marked a step toward a nationalist strategy, designed to satisfy domestic demand with homemade products and share the market among existing domestic producers. Demand stimulus entered the policy sequence as an accentuation of economic nationalism, but it then shifted quite rapidly to association with internationalism. It would retain that association until economic strains in the 1970s pushed it back toward more nationalistic proclivities. Sweden and the United States went through the sequence in this order; France and Germany jumped steps; and the United Kingdom stopped at the second step.

In its ability to disrupt existing political alignments, the Depression rivaled war. Coalitions formed in the first international trade crisis were strongly shaken by World War I and then "recast," as Charles Maier aptly labels the postwar readjustment. The Great Crash of 1929 shook the members loose from these coalitions. Rather quickly Europe and North America came to resemble a building site without an architectural plan—chunks of material lay around, available to be assembled in any number of different ways. New patterns and formulas were tried, and some succeeded.

Farmers and workers were the two groups most clearly open for new alignments. Both groups reacted strongly against the orthodoxies to which they had been attached and to which their leaders remained attached. It is difficult to find in the years before World War I labor-farmer coalitions in power at the national level (though not at the local level) anywhere in Europe or North America. Some governing coalitions had managed to integrate elements of labor and agriculture into a de facto majority, but the relationships were indirect and strongly mediated by noneconomic issues: religion and nationalism in Europe, the Civil War legacy and ethnicity in the United States. After 1929, however, farmers and workers were drawn together in support of new politics.

They were not alone. Some businessmen revolted as well from bourgeois economic orthodoxies. Businesses with a heavy dependence on the stability of demand, businesses with large debt, businesses concerned with the purchasing of abilities of consumers, businesses able to get government purchasing—the leaders of many such enterprises turned away from classical thinking about economics and toward extensive intervention in the market. Business thus split, into the orthodox who could not wrest free of their attachment to traditional solutions and the heterodox, interventionists who were willing to pay various costs to get state help.

By themselves the interventionists could not have prevailed. The orthodox, whether deflationist or protectionist, could not or would not pull free of their attachment to traditional solutions. Most businessmen continued to support their traditional representatives and the traditional medicines for economic ills. As a result, business activists could not accomplish much without support from other societal actors, even those who were in various ways in conflict with capitalism.

Here lies the vital role of mass discontent. In masses of voters desperate for some sort of change, in large political parties and important interest group organizations that gave voice to that discontent, in massive strikes by workers and by investors, and paramilitary organizations and mobs in the streets, the business activists found possible allies for change. Where the interventionists were willing to rely on mass support, they could find the political support needed for significant departures from orthodoxy. Complicated cross-class, cross-sector coalitions could liberate politicians from the conventional wisdom in many policy arenas, economic policy among them. If the various sides were willing to make concessions, they could exchange them for benefits. In a game as complex as that of the thirties, the possible combinations were numerous. Economic policy was merely one of many counters in the bargaining process, and it could be traded for other goals.

The big policy and political shifts in the thirties came where "deals" or bargains were made—where diverse societal actors were willing to make major trades that took them away from their traditional political as well as policy attachments. Where in Europe labor was willing to give up the rhetoric of socialization of the economy and to pay for higher food bills, it could get demand stimulus, reforms in labor relations, social insurance plans, some planning, and some regulation

of markets. Where agriculture was willing to accept the goals of industrialists and labor, and to stomach its distaste for state interference, it
could get extensive assistance of many kinds. Where business was
willing to pay costs for agriculture and labor, to give up market dog-
mas, to accept the state's extension into economic life and the coer-
cions that that involves, it was able to get measures that ranged from
institutionalization of cartel-like arrangements to pump priming, government contracts, and government buyouts.

Where concessions were not forthcoming, however, orthodoxy prevailed or was revived. In the United Kingdom the elements for a
trade were present, but the trade did not occur. The failure of Lib-
Lab negotiations left more conventional business elements in control.
The Conservatives went some way toward tariffs, agricultural corporatism, and government action. But their moves were far more limited and cautious than those that would have been tried in a coalition
ministry under Lloyd George or some Labour politician with more
political imagination than MacDonald and Snowden. In France the
weakness of the alliance among societal actors put a rapid end to the
Blum experiments.

What the combination of businessmen, farmers, and workers produced, then, was a political autonomy that permitted escape from the
economic orthodoxies of left and right. Each member of the new
coalition got something, but it also made concessions. Crisis induced
societal actors to bargain, to make trades that in "normal" times they
might have found unacceptable. It created a political capacity to take
actions that hitherto had seemed politically impossible.

The Social Democrats in Sweden, the Nazis in Germany, and the
Democrats in the United States had in common the great political
capacity that arises out of the forging of new linkages among societal
actors. In Sweden the Socialists and the Agrarians stunned other
groups by their cow trade. In the United States, one complicated
cross-class, cross-ethnic, cross-sectoral, cross-regional coalition was
shattered and replaced by another. Both countries were able to mobilize the support of the "masses," thereby acquiring the legitimacy,
vital in constitutional systems, of mass support expressed both
through the ballot box and through interest groups. And both were
able to persuade sections of the bourgeoisie to cooperate in a program
of reforms through constitutional government. The source of Nazi
power in Germany had some similarities: enough mass support to
give a plausible appearance of democratic legitimacy, despite the authoritarian features of the party, and enough elite support to take
power without a clear majority.

To the economic policy similarities of these countries there is thus some explanatory logic: all three went farther than Britain and France in policy experimentation. The crisis did, however, help create the political capacity for the United Kingdom to do things seemingly impossible in normal times, such as cutting back unemployment insurance, setting tariffs, and intervening in agricultural markets. And the reforms of the Popular Front drew on sources of support in France which echo those found in Sweden and the United States.

Crisis made it possible to change policy by creating political capacities. But the potential in both policy and political terms varied, as my placing of Nazi Germany, Social Democratic Sweden, and Democratic America in the same category suggests. These were shockingly different regimes. Whatever the neglects of the regimes of the 1930s in the United States (blacks, the rural poor) and Sweden (also the rural poor), the horrors of the Nazi barbarism transcend them. The connection between political support and policy outcome was obviously very different in these regimes.

Across societies, dissatisfaction with traditional conservative economics and support for new policy moves tapped similar social categories. Several other elements of the outcomes also require examination. The politics of coalition formation and the political context of policy, for example, differed in ways that shaped both politics and policy—agriculture and labor fought in Germany, allied in Sweden. In part this and other capacities for bargaining have to do with differences in the economic situation of the comparable categories. But they also have to do with differences in intermediate associations, state structures, ideology, and international strategic issues.

Intermediate associations. In the crisis of the late nineteenth century associations were relatively weak, as political parties and interest groups were in the process of being created. By 1929 these organizations had attained major importance, filling in the space formed by mass politics. Elites had to bargain on a terrain dense with associations, but across countries there were major differences in the formal features of those associations (how many organizations, size of membership, internal rules) and in substantive ones (ideological outlook, experience, legitimacy).

The contrasts between Germany and Sweden are particularly striking. In Germany labor was weakened considerably by political fragmentation; Communists, Socialists, and Catholics competed for organized labor. In Sweden, however, the Social Democrats operated from a broader base in their party's core constituency; party and union leaders converged in a highly pragmatic attitude toward economic theory and political alignments. In Germany the SPD leadership fought with unions over strategy, and the party's policy officials subordinated theory to politics. Moreover, German agricultural groups were highly resistant to bargaining with labor, but their Swedish counterparts proved willing to collaborate.

Party systems proved relatively stable in France, Sweden, the United Kingdom, and the United States. They managed to channel discontent as well as adapt themselves to it. There were shifts in strength among parties, of course, but the framework itself remained secure. The contrast with Germany is sharp. There many of the existing parties collapsed, and the Nazis rapidly formed an enormous organization. They did so by pulling individuals away from party and interest group memberships.

To achieve their policy goals, economic actors operate in an organizational universe that has some plasticity but also some resilience. The organizational materials available at the time that an economic crisis is beginning thus affect the opportunities and constraints that these actors face. At the same time, many new organizations will be created during the crisis, thereby changing the structure of possibilities.

State institutions. Several important differences among state institutions affected the policy struggles of the period. The Weimar Constitution left the German cabinet vulnerable to paralyzing negative majorities. The absence of institutional reform after World War I left intact antirepublican control of the army and influence in the civil service, judiciary, and teaching corps. Centralization in Sweden, by contrast, facilitated the concentration of power in a small number of parties and interest groups capable of bargaining for social accommodations. In the United States, political fragmentation, limited powers of intervention, and the absence of a well-developed civil service put limits on the capacity of governments to intervene in various policy areas, strengthening the influence of those who opposed such interventions.

Although institutional arrangements affected coalitional politics in the 1930s, it does not seem possible to demonstrate that the form of institutions shaped policy independently of other factors. France was centralized but did not produce a Swedish outcome; Sweden had a multiparty system with the potential for negative majorities but did not produce the German outcome. When political support was available, the United States created institutions capable of extensive intervention: during both world wars the wartime production boards directed the American economy more extensively than the National Recovery Administration wanted in the early thirties. The impact of institutions must thus be gauged by observing what happens to the groups that seek to use state power.

Economic Ideology. Although the hurts of the Depression were certainly clear and acute, enough confusion existed in reality to support quite different views about causes and solutions. Countries differed considerably in the values they gave to inflation and unemployment, nationalization and the market, international interdependence and national autonomy. Theoretical arguments among specialists seem to have been less important than the "practical religion" of policy-making elites and publics. Ideology surely affected political calculation, but its effects, like those of institutions, cannot be observed independently. To shape policy, economic ideologies had to find believers with power, and so they were linked to society, associations, and state institutions.

International state system. Nationalism and economic policy shaped each other in the 1930s, and trade questions became mixed up with military ones. Military insecurity could be used to justify economic action when other goals were unable to find political support. The most obvious case is the German one, where the Nazis linked support for revision in foreign policy with support for economic intervention at home: the fight against unemployment was linked politically to remilitarization and quite soon shaped the implementation of policy as well. As before 1914, so it was in the 1930s—the evaluation of the national interest in the international system was inextricably linked to the struggle for control at home.

The same linkage occurred in other countries, but the connection between economic interventionism and military-political "toughness" was the reverse of that in Germany. Economic nationalism, the fight against the Depression, and the break with market orthodoxy were outside Germany parts of an accommodationist foreign policy, one loath to prepare for war. In the final analysis it was military spending that ended the Depression. For four of our five countries, however, such spending was pressed upon them rather by the international state system than by domestic political alignments, which, if anything, sought to avoid the linkage through appeasement and neutrality.

The Role of Politics

In a political game as complex as the thirties several outcomes were plausible. Actors had interests and demands; parties and organizations articulated and shaped those desires; institutions structured incentives and resources; international military rivalries provided opportunities and constraints. But in all these commonplaces actors could have played their hands differently. Under such conditions politics, the specific struggle among leaders and organizations fighting with myriad resources for advantage, plays a great role. In the search for generalizations the contingent can never be ignored, and in the thirties, it loomed large.

The important generalization that overrode the contingencies of the specific was, I believe, the linkage between economic experiments and political ones. Left to themselves, most business elites would have tried the regular way out of the Depression, letting the business cycle do its job. Those among them who wanted a different solution could not do without support from other sources. Some kind of mass support was indispensable to them, but as the Greeks noted long ago and the 1930s confirmed, mass support can come in more than one form, with or without the rule of law.

What connection was there between the political formula and the policy chosen? We can explore the capacity of different political formulas to accommodate various policies by testing out alternative combinations of support. In some cases the obstacles seem only moderate, as for a Lib-Lab coalition in Britain. In others the obstacles seem formidable though not totally impossible, as in Germany for a neo-orthodox policy shift under a moderate constitutionalist (Hermann Müller of the Center party) or a military dictator (Kurt von Schleicher) or a demand stimulus break under a moderate constitutionalist (Gustav Stresseman) or a military dictator (Schleicher again). Nor was anything inevitable about the cow coalition in Sweden or in the United States a Republican incumbency in 1929 helping a Democratic counterattack. Impossibility is, however, too strong a test for alternative outcomes. We can be sure that the success of alternative political coalitions was affected by their handling of economic issues, and therefore we can be confident that the struggle over economic policy must of necessity have affected the political outcome.

ANOTHER CHANCE, 1944–49

In the 1930s the countries of Europe and North America had diverged sharply from one another in their construction of political economies. Rather different formulas arose in each country as the chemistry of international depression interacted with different domestic situations. Then came the cataclysm of World War II, which shook these formulas to their roots. Arrangements were reconsidered, and another round of debate and resolution became possible. In some cases a drastically new social compound emerged—Germany went from the most virulent of all fascisms to the Federal Republic. Elsewhere the pattern worked out in the thirties survived, being merely defined and delimited more clearly—Sweden is the obvious example. From these heterogeneous parts emerged some common elements of policy and politics: a historical compromise took hold in most of Western Europe and North America based on a system of market stabilization in economics and constitutional democracy in politics.

In substantive policy terms this stabilization model sought to contain the chaos to which capitalism was vulnerable. It flattened the amplitude of business-cycle swings by combining market forces with demand management, built-in regulators, and an extensive social security system. Despite considerable nationalization, the economy remained fundamentally capitalist, and private, decentralized managers and owners continued to control the allocation of investment and the organization of work. Even nationalized firms were run according to principles of market profitability, and in general it was market rhythms that sent out information, allocated rewards, and inflicted punishments.[34]

At the same time a wide range of measures served to channel the explosive force of the market, to increase the range of predictability, and to limit the amount of oscillation. The labor market saw wage determination institutionalized through unions, the labor relations system, taxation, and social welfare. In industry, competition became organized through systems of regulation. Agriculture mixed private ownership with regulation in the most obvious way, but the same approach also permeated banking, currency, retailing, aircraft manufacture, energy, health, and a whole range of other industries and products, even in the extreme version of a free-enterprise country, the United States. Welfare programs helped not only recipients but producers, providing a floor to demand and a stabilizer for the swings of the open market.

These domestic programs were inserted into an international order that was to be both open and institutionalized. To combat the economic nationalism of the 1930s, countries subscribed to the General Agreement on Tariffs and Trade, committing themselves to free trade. To create predictability and order, countries committed themselves at Bretton Woods to a regime of stable exchange rates, with the International Monetary Fund as the system manager.

The key operating principle of this model of political economy was "managed stabilization." Its key political principles gave it the label "social democratic" or "Scandinavian," after the parties and countries that expressed it most fully. The model was, in Antonio Gramsci's term, a "historical compromise," an accommodation among major social forces in society aimed at preventing the economic, political, and military disasters of the previous two decades. The policy-political compromise expressed interactive learning for important segments of each society interpreted those years in a particular way. Major segments of business, labor, and agriculture reacted strongly against the harsh punishments of the unbridled market. Left to itself the market did, it is true, bring about adjustment, but with too much suffering and at too great a cost.

In the first part of this chapter we have already seen the universality of the revolt of labor and agriculture against the market. At the same time a large bloc of capitalists also thought that efficiency required some degree of stability greater than what the market could provide. Those who made mass-produced, standardized items wanted some evening out of the flow of demand. Exporters, often high-technology producers, wanted a stable, open international environment. Large elements of both groups were willing to collaborate, at least to some degree, with labor and agriculture to realize these goals.

It was that willingness to collaborate, that capacity of groups to make compromises, which produced the historical compromise. Labor movements in all five countries abandoned, or least put on hold, their aspirations for extensive socialization of the economy. In exchange they got the welfare state, collective bargaining, and acceptance into the political system. Business abandoned, or least put on hold, desires for a passive labor force so atomized that workers could be treated as a pure commodity, and accepted much of the welfare state and considerable government participation in economic management. In return they got acceptance of private ownership, the primacy of profits and the market, rejection of planning and complete nationalization, and free trade and strong currencies. Agriculture preserved its corporatistic market regulation.

This led to two decades of relative social peace. One might be tempted to infer therefore that it arose out of cooperation and harmony, but this was by no means the case. In most countries the accommodation arose from conflict that was in many cases quite bitter and included violence and persecution. Consensus was not natural; rather, it was constructed. The right and the left had to be contained, emasculated, and repressed by being defined as extreme and thus without rights. McCarthyism in America, the strike wave in France, denazification and control of the Communists in Germany—these were the obvious expressions of this movement. Yet less dramatic processes were also at work. Republican moderates worked to contain the traditional right in the United States. In Britain the "wets" restrained the "drys" inside the Conservative party, while moderate Labourites worked to contain the left. Similar developments occurred on the Continent.

The late forties were full of tension and uncertainty. Exhaustion combined with hope, aspirations for the future ran up against diversity and disagreement. By 1949 the peace had given way to the Cold War, and out of the complex politics of those years arose an accommodation that continued the policy debate of the 1930s. The accommodation forged in those years would last over two decades and produce an epochal prosperity. It is that consensus which has come under attack in the 1970s and 1980s. So before we examine the current crisis, it is worth our while to understand the politics of the model that is now being challenged.

Germany

The most obvious shift from the thirties was, of course, in Germany. The war and its aftermath destroyed the foundations of the coalition that had dominated German politics since the days of Bismarck, and Germany changed or was changed for each the explanatory variables used in this book. In the Western zone the party system and the structure of interest groups were completely transformed. Partition, the new boundaries east of the Oder, and the Soviet occupation wiped out the Junkers as a class. Gone were the great estates; gone also was a very large chunk of Protestant Germany, where both fascism and bolshevism had been strongest, as well as many industrial areas where the Communists and left Social Democrats had been strong.

The occupation authorities promoted the development of certain political parties, particularly Konrad Adenauer's Christian Democrats but also the Social Democrats, while repressing or inhibiting others. The Nazis, already discredited by the complete devastation that their leadership had brought, were barred from political life. Although the record of denazification would be spotty, this organizational exclusion had lasting effects. The Allies also helped keep the Communists out of any effective role in postwar politics. The Federal Republic of Germany thus began its constitutional career with a dramatically simplified and centrist party system: Christian Democrats on one side,

Social Democrats on the other, with the small Free Democrats, expressing secular, constitutionalist market liberalism, as a swing coalition partner.

Another highly important change in organizational forms concerned trade unions. The Allies consolidated all unions into sixteen branches, organized by industry. German trade unions were thus very large with clear boundaries. Unlike in the British system, there would be no competition between unions for types of workers and no fragmentation of an industry across many unions. In their relative unity and organizational coherence, German unions thus came to resemble those of Sweden: well-positioned to think collectively and strategically, in macroeconomic terms, about the broader view. They would take account of how their behavior affected the overall trends of the economy, not limit themselves to purely parochial, particularistic concerns.[35]

Events left a deep imprint on ideological trends. The hyperinflation of the early twenties and the Crash of 1929 left bitter memories of what the market could do. The figure of Hitler discredited state-dominated corporatism, while the bolshevik regime, Stalin, and Soviet control of Eastern Europe provoked great fears of communism. The ideological and organizational space of Germany was thus temporarily open, allowing Allied influence a great role in shaping what would fill it. The leaders whom the Western Allies allowed to emerge all accepted constitutional democracy, the legitimacy of labor participation in economic and political life, and the welfare state.

In the international sphere Germany lost the freedom that had permitted attempts at conquest. The United States and the Soviet Union defined the spaces of postwar Europe. Neutralism or integration into the West were thus Germany's only options. The older, imperial controversies were pushed out of German political life.

It was from this sharply delineated set of conditions that the Federal Republic emerged. With Konrad Adenauer's defeat of Kurt Schumacher in 1949, power came to rest firmly in the hands of leaders who shared American preferences for the liberal market. Adenauer and Ludwig Erhard resisted nationalization, planning, and greater worker power. Although they accepted social security systems and power sharing far beyond anything the Americans had, the new chancellor and finance minister both believed in running an economy by rewarding private initiatives. Liberated from the heavy hand of the fascist state as well as the heavy hand of the occupation, the German economy, thought Erhard, would take off. General Lucius D. Clay, the American high commissioner, supported him.

The *Soziale Marktwirtschaft* expressed the balance between the liberal and the social democratic impulses in postwar Germany. Labor—protected by social insurance, formal recognition of its organizational rights, political freedom, and *Mitbestimmung,* or workers' comanagement—was willing to accept the linkage of wage gains to productivity. Germany entered a period of labor peace greater than that in any of the five countries save Sweden. German capitalists could thus count on a steady supply of highly skilled, hardworking labor. Government policies encouraged growth and support. Erhard's tax laws encouraged the reinvestment of profits and gave substantial benefits for investment in capital equipment, while a tight monetary policy kept inflation very low, which helped provide the necessary stability for foreign trade. Strong foreign demand for German goods pushed up the price of exports but helped justify wages restraint and, through a strong mark, keep down the substantial bill for imported raw materials, especially oil.

The economy boomed, led by a tremendous expansion in machine tools, chemicals, electrical equipment, and high-technology consumer items. These were the products which had propelled Germany into world eminence in the late nineteenth century. Policies favorable to those sectors had been blocked previously by the opposition of other social forces. Now this fragment of the old Germany, to paraphrase Louis Hartz,[36] could develop unhindered by the constraints, both feudal and industrial, of the old order. Export business and labor—the coalition that had tried for three-quarters of a century to escape the bondage of the autarchic and imperialistic bloc of iron and rye—was now able to shape Germany's political economy.

West Germany now sought wealth not through imperialism, by force and occupation, but through trade, as German internationalists had always wanted. The ideological flexibility of the exporters was great. The Soviet occupation of Eastern Europe did not deter exporters from seeking trade penetration in an old area of German interest.[37] Indeed, at a time when the Federal Republic was limited by the politics of the Atlantic alliance from making overtures to the east, German firms through trade quietly laid the groundwork for what would become the German strand of detente.

The German economic miracle reinforced the centrist tendencies of the Federal Republic's formative years. At a conference at Bad Godesberg in 1959 the SPD shed much of its Marxist past to become a more electorally appealing catchall for the center-left, and its new leader, Willy Brandt, was a much more appealing figure than Schumacher had been. The tight security provided by the integration of West Germany into NATO made possible the demand for easier relations with the east. Even conservative Germans wanted access to relatives in East Germany. Meanwhile, the labor and middle-class electorate of the SPD was more flexible in its attitudes than the Christian Democratic/Christian Socialist union of Adenauer and Franz-Josef Strauss, and the Free Democrats were eager to promote trade. A business-cycle slump in the mid-sixties weakened the Christian Democrats, preparing the way for a political shift.

The Grand Coalition, an all-party approach to the delicate shift in foreign relations, helped certify the SPD and Brandt as *regierungsfähig*, worthy of governing, and then the SPD, with the support of the Free Democrats, took over the chancellor's office directly. The accommodation of the late forties, seeking to reverse the disastrous course taken in 1933, here showed its strength. The reformist elements of the labor movement and the progressive elements of German business managed an understanding not so very different from the one that the Swedes had worked out in 1938.

France

Among our five countries France was least successful in working out a centrist accommodation, but nonetheless it experienced some very important shifts in policy and politics. Disaster, as in Germany, was the major agent of change. The Depression, the social disintegration leading to the "strange defeat" of 1940, the German occupation, and collaboration discredited elites, organizations, and ideas. Into their place stepped the coalition forged during the war among Socialists, Communists, Christian Democrats, and Nationalists (Gaullists), in terms of party, or workers, trade unions, farmers, civil servants, and some businessmen, in terms of social position. A diverse mixture, homogeneous neither by class nor by region, these groups disagreed on much, but they did believe in the need for drastic change. With the traditional right weakened by events, this broad interclass coalition provided just the kind of complex mixture of support that Léon Blum had never been able to mobilize. It was the French equivalent of the Weimar coalition, and it too got another chance after 1945.

The strength of this coalition came from political protection on either flank. Labor support gave it the legitimacy to worry about the needs of capitalists; business support enabled it to enact items of importance to the trade unions. It was France's first postwar modernizing coalition. Without it, the elites that commanded the levers of the state could not have used them as they did.[38]

The discrediting of the right gave the state the political leverage to change the direction of the economy; the exigencies of reconstruction gave the state the instruments to do so. Although most contemporary analysis sees the French state as strong, its capabilities of intervention in the economy were created only during and after World War II. For almost all of the Third Republic (1871–1940), French civil servants and politicians had favored cautious market conservatism behind tariff walls. The state had intervened remarkably little in the economy, indeed had had few capacities for doing so. So poor was French performance in the economic area, in fact, that Marshall Plan authorities threatened in the late forties to cut off aid unless France organized itself better. With political leverage, the early postwar governments created institutional framework of the modern French state for economic intervention.

Postwar economic conditions gave the government various tools. With so much rebuilding, capital was scarce, and in these circumstances the control of credit meant substantial power. The elites given the task of planning reconstruction were a markedly different type from those who had dominated the French economy before the war. The new group, a mixture of civil servants, economists, and businessmen, sought to recast the incentive structure of the economy in ways that would promote dynamic growth. Along with their nationalization of utilities, the Renault company, and much of banking, the modernizers reshaped much of the organization of the economy by grouping together, merging, and consolidating. Through a set of planning commissions, these modernizers promoted expansion. Through coordination among the various ministries, they guided public investment in infrastructure. Through the Coal and Steel Community, they integrated the basics of the French economy into a wider free-trade area, sending France down the path of openness to international market forces. Although, as before, the French economy remained shaped by the market, it was recast, and the difference was in what was being rewarded. Those in control of the state set France on a course for growth and expansion. They were in control long enough to make this course permanent, even when later political shifts changed personnel at the top.[39]

When the euphoria of Liberation dissolved into bitter fighting, first that of de Gaulle against the political parties, then that of the Cold War, the political foundation of government behavior shifted considerably. With the Communists excluded from politics on the divided left and the Gaullists holding aloof on the divided center and right, "third force" governments had to turn those elements of French society which had been excluded from power—the Radicals, the independents, conservatives of various stripes interested in preservation and self-defense, not modernization and reform. The apparatus of the state was no longer at the service of a modernizing coalition but in the hands of a static one. Regarding these years from the late forties to the collapse of the Fourth Republic in 1958, scholars discuss the state's ability to provide some stability and continuity despite the change of cabinets, to keep the country going despite *l'immobilisme;* rarely do they write about changes of government.[40]

Economic policy became a matter of restoring the confidence of investors. Big structural changes stopped and the Pinay loan of 1952 stabilized capital markets. With the old elites drawn back into political life, the conservatives were strong enough to stop the changes. They were not strong enough to reverse them, however, and the big changes of the first Liberation years continued to work their effects. The economy grew strongly and steadily. France's economic policies, like the other countries' under consideration here, were a begrudging accommodation—the mixed-market economy, with all enterprises (including the nationalized ones) run along market principles, demand management to promote growth and employment, freedom for parties and labor unions (though for the latter a rather weak role in labor markets and restricted powers in the plants), and social services and welfare.

With the structural reforms of the late forties, the state allowed the economy to push millions off inefficient farms, to consolidate firms, to modernize infrastructure and factories, and to create out of France a modern industrial economy and what would be one of the most successful of postwar economic records. To replace the cautious protectionism of the Third Republic, the Fourth moved toward openness by accepting the GATT and thorough European economic integration. The European Coal and Steel Community (1952) and then the Treaty of Rome (1957) reinforced the power of market forces to shape French society.

Indicative planning, to which the world looked as the explanation of French growth, became increasingly what it said it was: a system of indication, of information exchanges, not a system of command. As the economy grew, credit became more available. The state lost the stick and the carrot of inducement, and had only the power of words. Even in France, that meant progressively less. And the information exchange bore little resemblance to the democratic corporatism that spread through the smaller countries of Western Europe. Political conflict prevented the translation of the planning mechanism into a system of regularized bargaining and decision making among French social forces. The institutional mechanism existed, but it could not fulfill its potential because of political limitations.

While the economy was growing, however, the political system was seizing up. Party fragmentation, fragile coalitions, and negative majorities made the Fourth Republic look increasingly like the Third or like Weimar. In 1954 the disaster of Dien Bien Phu made possible the six months of reform government under Pierre Mendès-France, but he held power only temporarily. Centrism triumphed in France as in the other countries, then, but far more than elsewhere centrism in France meant paralysis.

The United Kingdom

Social democratic reformism had failed to attain power in the United Kingdom during the 1930s, but the war gave it another chance. Winston Churchill's electoral defeat by Clement Attlee and the Labour party while the war against Japan was still being fought expressed the country's tremendous desire for social change, to which the wartime experience had contributed. In the Conservative party the "Tory Reds" had gained influence, and many supported the quest for social cohesion expressed in the Beveridge Plan. The Labour government enacted much of that plan, developing an extensive welfare state, reforming education, and nationalizing several industries.

But more extensive demands from within the labor movement for a transformation of society and the economy were quickly contained. Within a few short years of the war's end economic planning was rejected: neither labor nor business was willing to accept the restrictions on its autonomy of action which planning implied.[41] Many nationalizations were of industries already in bankruptcy or at least disorganized, and support for more takeovers dried up quickly.

In foreign economic matters the policy was a traditional one of free trade, strong currency, and Empire. Britain rejected overtures to join the European Economic Community and continued to give special preference to the Empire-turned-Commonwealth. The European Community represented expensive food, and so this move expressed the legacy of the "cheap loaf" tradition of urban industry within the production profile of the United Kingdom, in contrast with the far more agrarian profile common on the Continent. The United Kingdom accepted American leadership and the GATT–Bretton Woods arrangements for the world economy, and within that framework sought to continue as before: an importer of food and other raw materials, an exporter of manufactured products, and the manager of an important financial-trading system whose profits would make up the deficit on current accounts. Britain, it appeared, would continue to accept the pressures of the international division of labor, importing whatever was cheapest and using the market to push resources into more competitive areas.

By the early fifties the British historical compromise seemed deeply rooted. The left had been largely defeated within the Labour party. The classical right was largely contained by the Tory Wets within the Conservative party. Both parties bid for mass support by proposing social programs, defending the welfare safety net, and managing the economy for full employment. That Britain was not structurally well-positioned to pursue this course—having consumed in the fighting of two world wars much of the investment from which the income on "invisibles" offset weakness in export manufacturing—was not immediately apparent.

The United States

The war did not radicalize American politics as it had that of the European combatants, but it did nonetheless reopen the quarrels of the thirties. As the war ended, there was certainly some support for continuing New Deal reforms. Full employment, medical insurance, a universal cradle-to-grave social security system, greater union involvement in economic management, racial equality, and urban renewal were some of the items on the agenda of unfinished business. In comparison with what happened in Europe, however, the American reformist impulse after the war was weaker and the counterattack by conservatives considerably more successful. Some such measures were being enacted in Europe, but in the United States, little got through; indeed, some earlier changes were rolled back.

Even in the thirties the political limits on the reformist capacities of the progressives had been evident. As the New Deal coalition developed, so did its conservative counterpart, the understanding among Republicans and conservative Democrats drawn largely from farm areas and the South who, once the state had taken care of agriculture, became less willing to help other social categories. After the war the conservative counterattack intensified. The witch-hunt led most notoriously by Sen. Joseph McCarthy did far more than turn up a few spies and some Communists. It purged from American organizations, especially unions, thousands of individuals interested in continuing the reforms of the thirties, and it struck fear into countless thousands more. The Taft-Hartley Labor Act of 1947 clipped union power by allowing each state to decide on open and closed shops; states where unions were weak declared open shops, which encouraged the flight of industry from unionized to nonunionized states. The negotiations of 1946 between Ford Motor Co. and the United Auto Workers also bounded the aspirations of some labor leaders to play an important role in managerial decisions. Union, those negotiations made clear, could bargain over hours, wages, and working conditions, but the rest was up to management.[42]

Labor and reformists were contained, even pushed back to some degree, and on that a wide range of propertied elites could agree. But on other serious matters of policy they disagreed, splitting the Republican party as it had been split earlier in the century. Many elements of business were willing to accept portions of the second New Deal and more generally an American version of the historical compromise. These business elements wanted things that more orthodox, conservative business groups had difficulty accepting. Exporters and traders wanted to continue the internationalist leanings of the late thirties, not revert to the economic nationalism of the earlier part of that decade. They wanted what they had failed to achieve after 1918—American leadership of an open international trading system, Bretton Woods, the GATT, and the Marshall Plan. Isolationists and nationalists threatened these goals.

At the same time many producers saw real benefits in some of the programs developed during the New Deal. Many large-scale American businesses had come to understand the very great importance of macroeconomic stability for long-term planning and the amortization of massive investments. Social security and unemployment insurance, crop supports, and banking insurance all gave the economy a firm demand floor. Regulations, from oil to airlines, from trucking to broadcasting, from banks to securities, from safety and health to prices and market shares, all interfered with the pure market and in doing so rendered it more predictable. Meanwhile, high wages not only helped elicit peace in labor markets but also contributed to demand.

Much of American business thus supported a view of the postwar years which the traditional Republican right had trouble accepting. If conservatives would not accept it, then there would be some understanding with the Democrats. Postwar American politics revolved around the rhetoric of consensus and bipartisanship, a language that allowed both Democrats and Republicans to pick their secretaries of the treasury and state from the same sources and pursue more or less the same policies. Neither would rock the boat of consensus. When Barry Goldwater tried to do so as presidential candidate in 1964, the Republican moderates rejected him and he was buried in an electoral landslide.

With Europe and Japan in ruins, American manufacturing faced little competition, and an open international economy would favor American producers. The country's situation was now like that of the United Kingdom a century earlier. For three-quarters of a century big manufacturing companies and labor unions had formed a producers' coalition for tariffs and an inward-looking economy. Now, with a different set of incentives in the international division of labor, they formed a producers' coalition that favored free trade and internationalism combined with domestic full employment and policies for stabilization. If anything, this new coalition was stronger than the old, for it included two elements that the first had excluded: commodity crop agriculture, based in the South and the trans-Mississippi West, and internationally oriented banking and shipping.

Sweden

Sweden is the most obvious case of the class accommodation that spread through Europe after World War II. The pattern that Germany attained only through total devastation, partition, and occupation, Sweden generated out of its internal politics, as a way of handling the changing pressures of the international economy. From the cow trade of 1932–33 between the Social Democrats and the Agrarians to the decisive election of 1936 and the explicit bargain between labor and business at Saltsjöbaden in 1938, social forces in Sweden reached an understanding of how a small country could find constitutional democracy and prosperity by specializing in the international division of labor.[43]

In comparative terms the Saltsjöbaden was a political and policy success for Swedish labor, especially in contrast with the situation of labor's German, French, and British counterparts; meanwhile American labor shared power but got fewer policy rewards. At the same time the agreement of 1938 also showed the limits of labor's power. As in the United States, the politics was coalitional, and as in the United States, agriculture set limits on labor's attainments. This remained true in the postwar years, for the Social Democrats never acquired the strength to legislate their full agenda. Instead, the party accepted the reality of having to manage a capitalist economy, of balancing the often conflicting claims of the electoral and union constituency, on the one side, against those of private investors, on the other. It did so, as we shall see in the next chapter, more successfully than any other social democratic organization.

Conclusion

The late forties, as we have observed, saw the construction of a particular political economy, a mixture of capitalist market with stabilizing mechanisms guided increasingly by a theoretical model of demand management imbricating an open international economy. This pattern arose from the combined influences of wartime experience, memories of interwar Depression, and emerging Cold War. The specific historical mixture combined political goals with economic ones, and its aim was to recast capitalism: politically, in the development of a mass politics after the tolerance for complete subordination to the "long-run" discipline of the market had vanished; economically, in a situation where many capitalists no longer believed that the market could function properly without a considerable degree of institutionalization and management.

The pressures of war and depression pushed for extensive change in the proper mix between structuration and market. After a few years, however, the momentum of change slowed; reformers divided and conservatives regrouped. The Cold War contributed significantly to this process, for it split the left and, by shifting the terms of debate from domestic restructuring to foreign policy, made the left vulnerable to the force of nationalism in each country.

By the early fifties the pattern was set, albeit to different degrees in each country. An agreement most clearly articulated at Saltsjöbaden became generally accepted in many countries. Labor gave up demands for socialization of the economy in exchange for a welfare system, high wages, employment-oriented macroeconomic policy, union rights in shaping wage levels, and political rights to engage fully in constitutional politics. In Sweden this bargain had also included peace in labor markets. Business accepted this greater role for labor and a greater degree of state involvement in the economy, in exchange for labor's acceptance of the status of private property and private control of the economy. Agriculture's demands for state stabilization of its markets were accepted by all parties. Although the specific terms of the bargain differed from country to country, and not inconsiderably, and although the degree of political integration and stabilization also differed, in comparative historical terms the degree of convergence was perhaps greater than at any other point in the common histories of these countries.

Every causal factor we have examined contributed to this result: the economic situation of the various societal actors, intermediate associations, state organization, economic ideology, and the international state system. It is this consensus, this particular historical compromise, which has come partially unraveled in the third crisis of the international divison of labor, to which we now turn.

CHAPTER FIVE

Reopening the Debate:
The Crisis of the 1970s and 1980s

Since the early 1970s the historical compromise forged in the aftermath of World War II has been in trouble. The serial disasters of depression and fascism, Stalinism and war, together contributed to a consensus on policy and politics which held for over two decades. Then things started to unravel. Where policy debate had narrowed in the fifties and sixties, argument in the past fifteen years has widened. Where countries earlier had seemed to be converging in policy efforts, more recently differences have grown in policy experiment, political rhetoric, and actual policy. At the same time the deepening interconnections of the world economy have tightened constraints on politics and policy, limiting and even reversing experiments of various kinds.

The prosperity of the fifties and sixties appeared to have suppressed, perhaps for good, a whole range of policy alternatives. The mixed economy, with its package of demand management, institutionalized industrial relations, extensive regulation of markets, freer international trade, and a large welfare state, seemed to drive dissidents of left and of right into historical oblivion. But like any formula, the package was strong as long as it worked—"Pourvu que ça dure," in the famous words of Mme Mère, Napoleon's mother. When economic difficulties developed, however, with an overvalued dollar leading to the end of fixed exchange rates, the sudden rise in the price of oil, growing protectionism, inflation, recession, depression, and unemployment, the consensus gave way to renewed debate.[1]

Old arguments returned, often in new language. Neoliberals seek to roll back extensions of state power in the mixed economy. Neo-Marxists seek to develop that power into more nationalizations, while other elements of the left call for democratization of the workplace. Protectionism is rampant, and mercantilist-style industrial policy, or selective intervention for specific industries, is discussed everywhere.

As policy debate appears to have broadened, so has the range of political shifts. The victory of François Mitterrand and the French Socialists in 1981 marked the first absolute majority for a left party in French history and the first election of a leftist to the strong presidency of the Fifth Republic. Victories by Margaret Thatcher in 1979 and Ronald Reagan in 1980 expressed a strong tilt to the right in the United Kingdom and the United States. In West Germany two decades of collaboration between Free and Social Democrats crumbled in the early 1980s. In Sweden the Social Democrats were defeated for the first time in forty years (1976), then came back to power in 1982 seeking an extension of labor power in management.

If we include the other countries of Western Europe, we can see in the years since 1971 an even greater breadth of political change: in Portugal, Spain, and Greece the end of dictatorship and the development of parliamentary government was followed in all three cases by the election of socialist prime ministers. Meanwhile in northern Europe, for example, Denmark and Norway saw the weakening of social democratic majorities.

These political shifts coincide with significant changes in the international economy. Two decades of strong growth had substantially deepened the division of labor in Western Europe and North America. Masses of people left the countryside for the cities, industrial capacity grew tremendously, and older technologies were sloughed off as rationalization accompanied postwar rebuilding to lift living standards.

Success, as always, sowed the seeds of difficulty. The Euro-American boom triggered growth elsewhere. Through the open international regime of the General Agreement on Tariffs and Trade, the advanced industrial countries helped to fuel the expansion of countries that then became their competitors. Japan had started well before the war, and now new centers of production had grown in South Korea, Taiwan, and Singapore on one side of the Pacific; in Mexico, Brazil, and other parts of Latin America on the other; and in parts of Africa and continental Asia as well.

There was, then, tremendous productive capacity in the first and second worlds and tremendous growth in the third. As long as demand was strong, this specialization and the absorption it required would work. Developing countries could move from supplying raw materials and consuming industrial ones to producing products at the lower value end of the industrial spectrum, the products that advanced countries were willing to slough off, and then shift to products of even higher value. While the advanced countries could shift their own resources into new products as fast as imports wiped out the old, this was a happy, wealth-creating cycle. But when the boom sputtered in the early seventies, when an upward-moving cycle of expansion turned into a difficult, unstable one, the policy universe changed. The worst inflation was followed by the worst depression since the war with high rates of interest, business failure and unemployment, and high government deficits; an enormous destruction of jobs was followed, at least in the United States, by an enormous creation of new ones. No country seems to have been able to reconcile all three of the main goals of economic policy—growth, full employment, and price stability.

In response to these difficulties in the international arena, the range of policy attempts and debates has grown. It is much less clear, however, that the actual contents of policy have diverged as much, and many attempts at change have been turned back. Within a year of enacting a bold program of nationalization, equalization of incomes, and countercyclical spending, for example, the French Socialist government switched directions. In the spring of 1982 it adopted an austerity program, another in 1983, and in 1984 yet another, each time more severe, more accepting of the dictates of the market, and in short, more neoliberal and more similar to the policies of Giscard d'Estaing and other nonsocialist predecessors of Mitterrand.

In the United Kingdom, by contrast, the Thatcher government's neoliberal restoration program has not realized some of its more sweeping targets. Many "lame duck" industries have been kept aloft, social service and unemployment benefits kept high, government spending has been growing, and taxation levels are as high as ever. In the United States the Reagan revolution did slash taxes, but spending has reached record highs and coincided with the largest peacetime deficits in American history. With its enormous defense budget the Reagan government is more massively involved in state management of the economy than any in U.S. history. In Sweden the bourgeois coalition that took office in 1976 did very little to "reliberalize" the economy; if anything, levels of public investment and spending rose. Since coming back to office the Social Democrats there have not been able to embark on a course sharply different from the reality of what neoliberals are doing elsewhere, despite the differences in rhetoric. In West Germany the rhetoric and the reality of policy differences have been extremely mild despite the shift from a Social Democratic coalition to a Christian Democratic one.

The most striking change in economic policy common to all five countries since the early 1970s has been the growth of neoliberalism in rhetoric and to a lesser degree in reality. In the early seventies the challenge to consensus came largely from the left in demands for more democratization of the economy: workers' control, comanagement, union investment funds, equality of income. A decade later the focus had shifted to themes of productivity, renewal, job creation, rationalization, and restoring competitiveness. Market forces and market cues have replaced other values as guides to policy. In most countries the left is now fighting a defensive battle, seeking to preserve the wages, benefits, and institutionalization of power won in earlier conflicts.

All the countries examined here move within a universe of policy far more interventionist than that of the years before 1929. A mixture of social democratic collective benefits and particularistic corporatism remain powerful in all countries. At the same time, however, the policy consensus on how to run this mixture has weakened, and the neoliberal position has been strengthened.

Why has the debate widened, and what explains its trajectory in each country? What accounts for the content of policy and the limits on the exploration of alternative policies? These questions form the agenda for this chapter. The widening debate derives from pressures that changes in the international economy have exerted upon the social accommodations established in the late forties. Individual trajectories have to do with the particularities of that accommodation in each country, refracted by the group conflict, party incumbency, state organization, and other features specific to the country. The limits of policy come from the constraints that participation in an international market system puts on all countries; in none of the cases do governments have the political backing needed to resist what actors in the market indicate are the limits of acceptable behavior. From this stems the paradox of the current scene: political shifts, in terms of party and program, have been greater than policy shifts. The importance of coalitions in explanation lies in the ability of coalitions of societal actors to override partisan differences.

We can examine the politics of policy responses, here as earlier, by beginning with a paired comparison of the largest difference in policy as well as in politics. The two largest swings of recent years have been in France and the United Kingdom, and there the coincidence of political and policy shifts provides a neat set of contrasts for comparativists. In political outcomes one country has moved left, the other right. In policy attempts one has tried socialization, demand stimulus, and industrial policy, the other neoliberalism. In production profile one has traditionally sheltered industries unused to strong foreign competition, the other has a strongly internationalist industry-finance grouping. In institutional forms a centralized strong state in one contrasts with dispersed structures and a weak state in the other. They differ, finally, in traditions of economic ideology (statism vs. reformist market liberalism) and in international situation (European economic linkages vs. Commonwealth and American ties).

FRANCE

The election of François Mitterrand as president on May 10, 1981, followed by the first absolute majority in the National Assembly for the Socialists, marked a very sharp change in the political stance of those who controlled the French state and an equally sharp change in economic doctrine. The ending of over two decades of right-center rule occurred just as the international economy was entering the worst depression since 1929. The Socialists found quite soon that the realization of their ideas and ideals would have to confront the management of crisis in what remained a market economy firmly rooted in a capitalist international order.[2]

The Socialist party of France was the only one of its kind in the four European countries here considered which since the late forties had never had full responsibility for governing. It therefore had never confronted the need to manage the tension between the demands of its core constituencies (unions, schoolteachers, civil servants, and "cadres") and the constraints of capital flows and investment, profitability and modernization. French Socialists were thus forced to recapitulate the difficult history of their counterparts elsewhere in making choices, in balancing left-wing models of the economy, electoral pressures, and the marketplace, and they were forced to recapitulate that education in a period of deep economic distress.

The timing of the Socialists' victory is important to understanding the evolution of French policy debate. The French Socialists were the only national left group not in power during the difficult economic days of the late seventies, when recession was followed by inflation along with growing stagnation. They could blame the center-right and its ideas for France's economic ills. (In 1929 it had been the British and German socialists who had suffered from incumbency, the American Democrats, Swedish Socialists, and French Socialists who had benefited from being in the opposition.)

In France, moreover, the left drew together while the center-right split. This was in sharp contrast with the United Kingdom and the United States, where conservative parties rallied around a leader while social democratic parties divided along a number of lines. The fault lines for the French center-right gave evidence of the re-emergence of tensions that Guallism had covered over. These tensions were strongest between modernizers seeking industrial transformation and traditional conservatives defending old positions; between nationalists and Atlanticists or Europeanists; between state leadership of an activist industrial policy and market neoliberalism; between social reformism and social conservatism; between Catholic and secular views. They also involved several historic animosities regarding the fall of France in 1940 and Vichy, the war in Algeria, and decolonization. And personal rivalries also played their part, particularly the one between Jacques Chirac and Giscard. Having governed for over twenty years, the center-right was worn down by these divisions; the stresses and strains of compromise used up its ability to solve disagreements. While the left was working to overcome the costs of divisions, in particular the electoral failure of 1978, the French right was finding itself unable to work out a common stance for fighting the left.

In voting for the Socialists, the electorate was blaming the incumbents for economic troubles rather than choosing a specific new economic policy. The Socialists had a large but ambiguous mandate, which they could interpret in various ways. From the beginning there was disagreement about how this power should be used. The disagreement expressed both the conflict among various social constituencies within the party and the interaction of those constituencies with social forces outside the party.

Within the party's ranks, the left Socialists' analysis of what was wrong with the economy criticized the essential workings of French capitalism. Whatever the vitality of capitalism in other countries, such as the United States, French capitalism is, the left Socialists believe, deficient. It has always lacked the vigor needed to make a market system produce the cornucopia of goods and services which is capitalism's principal claim to legitimacy. And being weak in France, the market approach to the economy has been on the left morally suspect.

The left Socialists believe that to replace this enfeebled capitalism, the state must play a major role in guiding the economy: it must define targets, structure incentives, consolidate groups, and promote national champions. In the modern era of high technology the state must identify the complex chain of connections of each product family, the "filières," and spur its growth. To do so it must nationalize the major sectors of the economy. With this wider control of the economy, the state will then be able to mobilize national savings more effectively, shape demand to favor national products instead of imports, equalize incomes, and restructure industry.[3]

The policy position of the Socialist party left can be characterized as a mixture of Marxism (nationalization), mercantilism (industrial restructuration and selective targeting), and demand management (increased spending and income redistribution) with a strong protectionist overtones. Its principal exponent has been the CERES, an organization of party militants led by Jean-Pierre Chèvenement, and its political base has been elements of the union movement, the teachers' organizations, and, most important, the Communist party.

The alternative policy position in the Socialist party was a mixture of industrial reorganization, demand management, and a kind of socialized neoliberalism. For this wing of the party, strongly associated with Michel Rocard and the CFDT (formerly Church-affiliated, now reformist trade union), nationalization provides an inadequate solution to France's problems. It extends the state's formal authority without changing anything concerning efficiency, productivity, and competitiveness. The French economy needs considerable change in the allocation of resources, this wing believes; land, labor, and capital have to be moved around. Industries have to adapt to conditions in the real world and learn about markets, demand for goods, and real costs. A lot of painful readjustment will have to happen, and happen soon. To readjust in a humane and democratic way, the Rocardians argue, requires social compacts among the various elements of society, and with such agreements, resources can be allocated and costs and benefits shared. Public resources will be needed, and also some public ownership, but the heavy hand of the state and centrally determined decisions will not work.

This disagreement between Rocard and the CERES reflects a Europe-wide debate within the left on the definition of democratic socialism under contemporary economic conditions. All over Europe a participatory current has emerged in leftist thinking which stresses decentralized democracy and which accepts in a considerable degree the need to recognize market cues as sources of information. Critical of the stress placed by other leftist thought on state management through public ownership, it is also more internationalist and less protectionist. In France this Deuxième gauche has been strongest among those groups which flocked into the Socialist party during its rebuilding drive in the 1970s—young professionals, civil servants, cadres, and unions connected to French Christian democracy as well as nonunion progressive Catholics.[4]

In the first months of the Mitterrand government the Rocardians urged that the need for austerity and change be immediately confronted and opposed the emphasis given to nationalization. But Mitterrand decided against the Deuxième gauche and in favor of the Socialist party left. Industries were nationalized, wages equalized, and spending accelerated to stimulate domestic demand. Mitterrand's advisers thought the election of Reagan in the United States signaled the start of an economic boom, and they sought to position France to take advantage of it. Politically, Mitterrand sought to gratify the core demands of a major portion of the constituency that had brought him to power—the left unions, the CERES, the electorate of the Communist party—for whom nationalization was the touchstone of a serious commitment to a left program.

Within a year, however, it became clear that Mitterrand faced further difficult choices. The American economy continued to contract, and with it the world economy. The economic stimulus given by the French government in 1981 led to more inflation, pressure against the franc, and a flood of imports. The ills of recession hit France, and as businesses failed and unemployment rose, Mitterrand had to do something.

He could have continued the statist approach of the first year with restrictions on imports, exchange controls, state buying, price and wage controls, and credit control; in sum, a strong step away from France's liberal economic commitments to the Common Market and the GATT. Or he could reverse that approach by cutting government spending, balancing the budget, reducing obligations to save companies and jobs, and abandoning the inefficient. Such a policy would have been a long step toward the neoliberal posture of his predecessors in France and toward the policies being pursued in other countries at the time, from the United States to Sweden.

Mitterrand chose the latter course in 1982 and then a year later, in the spring of 1983, an even stronger version of it. Austerity became the key word. The discipline of austerity would modernize and restructure the French economy. Mitterrand chose this course after deciding that he lacked the support, even if he had the will, for another strong step toward the left.

There were strong sanctions that social groups could have employed had he tried. Despite extensive nationalizations, the French economy remains deeply integrated into the international market economy. That economy turns on investment and demand, and without capital to make products and consumers to buy products, the French economy cannot sustain its present income levels. If products are not competitive, no amount of state planning can force consumers to purchase them. If conditions of profitability are not fulfilled, no amount of state planning can oblige capital to enter the country. If coercive mechanisms are used to contain demand and capital, coercion quickly becomes the core of government policy lest capital flee the country.

It was clear to Mitterrand and his advisers that to take the left Socialists' route in 1982–83 would have wrenched France away from the track followed by the other countries to which France is linked, thereby provoking intense hostility from French and foreign capital alike. Capital would have left the country, trading partners would have imposed sanctions for treaty violations, domestic protest from all sorts of groups would have intensified. Before making his decision, it is reported, Mitterrand met with a number of company presidents, including those whom he had named to run the nationalized branches. All strongly opposed the left option, and apparently their opinion carried much weight.

Only vast internal support could have overcome this kind of pressure, support expressed through elections, opinion polls, and the cooperation of associations such as unions and professional groups. But when the decision was being made, Mitterrand did not have that kind of support. Indeed, dissent and disagreement was rising. The left did poorly in the local elections of 1982, and opinion polls had turned against it. Protests and demonstrations were constant, lobbying intense. Many unions continued to defer to the left government, and would likely have supported the left's programs, but other elements of the union movement would not. The CERES position in France was similar to that of Tony Benn in the United Kingdom: it had some strong support on the left and inside the left party, but it also provoked intense hostility, not only in the center and right but even among many of the left's constituencies. In particular, the elements whose new support for the French left had made possible the victory of 1981 would not back a further sharp turn to the left.

Mitterrand had gotten some acquiescence for the nationalization program. In many cases the program took over companies already heavily dependent on the state and in deep economic trouble and it was accepted partly as a "shareholders' bailout." It was also accepted for its political effects by many who in principle opposed it, for the program worked to obtain the complete neutralization of the Communists and in practice did indeed weaken them considerably.

But there was no support to go any farther, and having made moves for his left wing, Mitterrand chose not to lose the center and right wing of his support. He wished to be a popular president, not a sharply divisive one, and so Mitterrand chose austerity, the neoliberal approach to adjustment. Plant closings and unemployment rose; spending was slashed; and market pressures were allowed to operate. In 1984 the cabinet was charged, and appointed was a technocratically oriented prime minister of moderate economic policy views.

French policy thus converged with that of France's neighbors. Having taken the strongest steps of the postwar years toward the left and away from the historic compromise, France now moved back toward the center. But that center, as we shall see in looking at other countries, had itself moved toward more neoclassical lines. This change in French policy occurred without any clear change in electoral majority: the same president and the same National Assembly switched lines. But the social composition of the governing coalition did change. In the first year Mitterrand had tried to govern with a left strategy that would mobilize the constituencies that had elected him and bring them into a common program of change, modernization, and economic rejuvenation. When that strategy failed to produce the results needed to legitimize it, the government switched both its policy and its social appeal. From a line aimed largely at winning union support and obtaining passive acquiescence from the rest of society, the government now switched its emphasis to passive union acquiescence and more active work by other economic forces in restructuring the economy. Mitterrand set to work to recover his strength in the electoral center, and to that end he sought to recover the active commitment of business forces to reactivating the economy. Pursuing neoliberal market policies, or at least more of them, was vital to that end.

In many discussions of the role of the state in explaining policy and politics, France exemplifies the strong state—a highly articulated system of well-qualified civil servants organized into autonomous, and highly remunerative, career ladders; a tremendous institutional apparatus for intervention in all aspects of French life, especially the credit system and the powers of the Ministry of Finance and other bureaus; the high degree of centralization; and the concentration of power in the executive. France looms large in all efforts to explain policy as a function of state characteristics.[5] To the extent that such arguments rely solely on formal institutional features, however, recent French policy challenges such analysis quite strongly. The variation of policy efforts from de Gaulle to Giscard and Raymond Barre, then to the first year of Mitterrand, and then to the next few years, is not consistent with explanation that focuses on the apparatus of the state. What changed, through elections, was the identity of those in command of the levers of the state. These politicians were sharply constrained by social pressures between elections; various groups in society were able to exercise if not a veto at least the threat of strong sanctions upon governments, both through the ballot box and also through their performing those functions which make a modern economy run—buying, investing, working and managing.

In the early 1980s the French Socialists confronted for the first time something with which their counterparts in other countries were familiar. They had to balance the competing claims of core constituencies (both electoral and functional) and those of other groups whose support is vital not only to winning elections but to governing, to realize policy objectives whose effects shape the environment within which elections are fought. British Labour, Swedish and German Socialists, and the American Democrats have all had to deal with this problem. The Labour party has split and the Democrats have been weakened by it, and the Social Democrats lost power in West Germany over it. The Swedish Social Democrats have been the most successful in keeping political office, but even they have been experiencing the biggest challenge in four decades to holding together their support coalition.

The left's claims to power have been based on the ability to combine labor peace with productivity and growth. The economic success of the postwar accommodation thus served to reinforce a policy stance and a political accommodation worked out in response to depression and war. As economic conditions have deteriorated, however, it has become impossible to ease the frictions of economic adjustment. Without new jobs to soak up the unemployment caused by adjustment, hard choices have to be made about how much the market can be allowed to push workers and other resources around.[6]

In France the incumbents have suffered greatly from the costs of readjustment. Fearing strong reactions from labor, Giscard and Barre moderated their neoliberalism, and able to blame them, the Socialists won. When their alternative failed, they were obliged to turn to the policies against which they had campaigned. As in the thirties, societal actors were able to set limits on what politicians were likely to do. Labor, farmers, cadres, and business reformers rejected Giscard in 1981. International market pressures helped weaken this coalition by forcing difficult choices on the Mitterrand government, exposing the tensions within it. Some elements of the Mitterrand coalition may have sought to resist market cues about policy, but they have never been able to mobilize the electoral strength needed to do so. So far Mitterrand has been unable to provide a politically effective rival to neoliberal economic policies or a "progressive" version of them.

Here the "strong state" has been of limited help. It cannot solve political problems, nor is it able to create support for a government in the face of unemployment, plant closures, and the like. The strong state could not protect the Socialists from a defeat in the legislative elections of 1986 which forced Mitterrand to appoint a center-right cabinet, one of whose first announcements was its intention to undo the nationalizations of 1981. The intermediate associations of French politics continue to weaken the left. The right is less needful of collective action and hence less harmed by fragmentation, but the left needs unity badly and is rarely able to overcome the effects of long memories enshrined in organizations. Economic ideology has proved to be a constraint on Mitterrand's ability to find economic policies that suit political needs. Finally, France's role in the international state system has been a further constraint on "policy deviance."

THE UNITED KINGDOM

The British case, happily for comparison, provides a strong contrast with France in the policy orientation of its government. As France moved left, Britain moved right; where the French right split, it was the British left that fragmented. In Britain that space of opportunity was occupied by a revitalized conservatism strongly committed to ending the postwar consensus in favor of the neoclassical approach to economic policy.

In sharp contrast to the Mitterrand of the first year in office, the Thatcher government sought to cut back drastically on the role of the state in the economy. This change would reverse Britain's economic decline, it believed, by restoring the conditions needed for profitability. Private entrepreneurs had to be convinced that investing in Britain was worth their while, and so costs had to go down: lower wages, fewer social charges, fewer regulations, and lower taxes. Economic activity had to be returned to the private sector, as in the sale of public housing and previously nationalized enterprises such as British Airways. At the same time, however, the Tatcher government has been cautious about leaving much of the welfare state in place, has retained many public enterprises, has confronted considerable social unrest, and has had only limited success in effecting economic change. By 1986 there had been no policy reversal as obvious as Mitterrand's, but considerable constraints were obvious on what the government had been willing to try.

The politics that has pushed Britain in such a different direction from France's while imposing similarly strong limits stems from the interaction of two phenomena. One is changes in associations, particularly polarizing trends within the social constituencies of the major parties. The other is pressures deriving from Britain's production profile, particularly the sanctions that societal actors have been able to impose on governments with which they conflict. Labour governments have had to reconcile strong labor pressures concerning jobs and wages with demands from managers and investors for market rationality. Conservative governments have had to do exactly the same. Union strikes have played a major role in shaping the political and policy fortunes of British governments in the past two decades; business and consumer dissatisfaction has done exactly the same, albeit less visibly.

Strikes, at the extreme, have contributed to the defeat of governments. Edward Heath was blamed in 1974 for failing to deal adequately with a miners' strike. Labour successfully argued that it could handle labor relations better, and after electoral victory it did so until the winter of 1978–79, when a series of strikes in the public sector discredited the government and contributed to the Tory victory at the polls in 1979. In the late sixties Harold Wilson had not faced a strike wave, but he did provoke considerable union hostility when he proposed legislation on restructuring unions. This labor issue arises for governments because it inheres in the problems of economic adjustment and modernization. As foreign competition becomes acute, it requires some form of domestic accommodation, whether higher productivity or lower costs, and that accommodation may include lower wages or fewer jobs. Workers are likely to resist those policy responses which require unemployment or lower wages.

There are several ways in which governments can deal with this problem. Governments can deny responsibility for the unemployment caused by economic adjustment; this, the approach of neoliberal politicians, argues for lower expectations, but it flies in the face of public expectations about government responsibility for employment. Governments can use state powers to impose wage and price controls. They can appeal to workers to limit wage pressures in the interests of national solidarity, in order to improve the nation's performance. They can urge restructuring of the labor relations system in ways that either weaken unions or change the logic of union negotiations. British governments have tried all of these various tactics since the 1960s and have run into trouble with each and every one of them.[7]

In the mid-sixties Wilson faced a choice that has repeatedly confronted British governments since the emergence of strong industrial competitors in the late nineteenth century: should he defend the pound through "stop-go" policies or devalue in the interests of strengthening domestic industrial production. The pound in Britain continued to be the symbol of Britain's political economy. Maintaining its value was the test of trustworthy economic stewardship and concerned to show labour's ability to manage a capitalist economy, Wilson stuck with the pound. Like Ramsay MacDonald in 1931, he was forced to devalue anyway when holders of the pound around the world made it clear to the City that the old exchange rate could no longer be sustained. Wilson then had to confront the problem of modernizing the economy, and among other policies, he turned to restructuring British trade unions.[8]

By locating Britain's economic ills in the fragmentation of British trade unionism, the report of the 1968 Donovan Commission struck at the organizational base of union leadership. The consequent uproar produced terrible strains between the Labour government and its historic ally, the Trade Union Congress. The cautious policy of upholding financial orthodoxy during the first part of the Wilson administration, followed by this controversy over union organization and rights in the second, greatly weakened the bonds between the components of the Labour party, the unions, the constituency parties, and the parliamentary party. The management of an economy that needed considerable reorganization to become internationally competitive stressed the fault lines among societal actors and between those actors and the electorate.[9]

Those stresses contributed to Labour's defeat in 1970. With Labour in opposition, the party left no longer felt constrained to support the government, while fresh with anger at Wilson, the unions swung into alliance with the left of the constituency parties at party conferences. Together, these groups changed the party platform to encompass national planning, industrial democracy, nationalization, protectionism, and planning agreements at the level of firms. This program, associated with the figure of Tony Benn, grew.

At this juncture, polarization within the party was temporarily arrested by the behavior of Edward Heath and the Conservative government. Heath managed to redefine for the unions and for labor voters their understanding of enemies and friends. Through their own polarization the Tories were moving to the right. Seeking to hold down wages and to prune excess labor from the coal mining industry, Heath confronted the miners. The consequent miners' strike was followed by government concessions in one of the famous U-turns subsequently denounced by Margaret Thatcher. Labour, arguing that it would have managed industrial relations with the unions more sensibly, won the election of 1974.

The old alliance inside the Labour party was resumed rather quickly. Despite the shift in party platform, Benn and his supporters were ditched as the parliamentary party and the unions reformed their link. Under pressure from the International Monetary Fund and the commercial banks, Wilson and then James Callaghan sought to restore international competitiveness by restraining wages, prices, and government spending. The government appealed to union solidarity behind a collective national effort. Workers would have to settle for less to get things going again; the reward would be high wages down the road, when the economy was back in shape, and a Labour government in office. In policy terms, it should be noted, this was not so different from what moderate Conservatives were offering.

The trade unions cooperated, and the policy worked. Despite a very bad press for British labor from both academics and the general public, trade-union leaders proved willing to cooperate and to mobilize their rank-and-file members. Inflation abated, the economy began to pick up, and by 1978 the government could claim some real success. Then the whole arrangement unraveled. In the winter of 1978–79 a range of strikes, some of them wildcat, broke out in areas sure to enrage the public—hospitals, utilities, transportation. One of Labour's trump cards, its purportedly better management of the unions, proved to be worthless. Labour could not reconcile the conflicting pressures exerted by the managers of investment and savings on one side, by labor leaders and their rank and file on the other. The Conservatives swept into office.

This time the Tories were led not by a Harold Macmillan or even an Edward Heath, Tory "wets" or "centrists" willing to accept the postwar accommodation, but by Margaret Thatcher, leader of the "drys"—in European terms, the neoliberals seeking to roll back many recent features in British political economy. For the Conservatives had polarized in their own way and had tilted sharply to the right.

Like Labour, or any party that wishes to govern, the Conservative party must find ways of balancing the competing claims of its core constituency and of a broader social majority. With too narrow an appeal, the party risks being tagged as purely the servant of business, thereby alienating other groups. To build a broader movement requires that some groups pay costs. By seeking to cut back the role of the state in the economy, the theorists of the Thatcher program proposed to balance labor unemployment by cutting subsidies to business groups. This was a proposal quite different from the accommodationist strategy that ran from Churchill through Eden and Macmillan, which accepted the welfare state and the stabilization of the economy through various instruments of regulation and demand management.[10]

As the British economy deteriorated in the sixties and Heath failed in the U-turn of 1973–74, the Tory right critique grew in strength. It articulated the growing difficulty that British manufacturers faced from foreign competition. High social charges and labor rigidities may have helped the demand levels and stability of the postwar years, but they could no longer be afforded. One can, of course, question this interpretation of Britain's economic ills—some would blame the inefficiency of British management, derived from inappropriate education, poor socialization, bad organizational structures, and weak institutional links to British capital markets. But that was not an argument that the Conservatives were likely to make, particularly when an attack on labor, both labor unions and the Labour government, was so handy. The Thatcher remedy was to use the old-fashioned medicine of stronger incentives through lower costs, higher profits, pressure on wages, and the elimination of subsidies for and restrictions on business.

Because Labour governments had been in office for many years, and because Conservative prime ministers had shared their accommodationist rhetoric, Thatcher, like Reagan, was able to represent the classic arguments of the nineteenth-century market as something new. Indeed, both left and right in Britain now believe that there is a majority to be mobilized which cannot be tapped by centrist rhetoric, which requires that people be pulled away from their softer, interest-shaped, woolly, social democratic accommodation and toward an ideologically clearer new order, a new vision. Thatcher and Reagan skillfully mix a nostalgia for the old with a desire for something new.

Thatcher's victory, like Mitterrand's, was compatible with more than one interpretation of the policy content of the electoral mandate. Thatcher chose to test the limits of a neoliberal position but, like Reagan, blends pragmatism with rhetoric, guided by a careful evaluation of political as well as economic limits. She has tried to cut wages and spending, but the state budget has grown. Although critical of Heath's performance, Thatcher for a long time avoided confrontation with the unions and then focused on the weaker ones. (By the mid-eighties the miners' strike of 1984 had been the most strenuous confrontation.) Shares have been sold in some of the profitable nationalized businesses, but many of the large lame ducks have not been allowed to go bankrupt (which would menace jobs and cost the Treasury substantial sums in benefits, not only to workers but also to managers). In general, the Thatcher government has the neoliberal strategy of reshaping civil society to structure social relations in ways that promote individual mobilization rather than collective solidarities.

In policy the British government has been mixing the activism of tight money with a liberalism that lets the market then set the prices of everything else, including interest and exchange rates. As a result, the pound has fluctuated high and low, and interest rates have remained high. But many things that the British government has *not* done are also interesting. Unlike Reagan, Thatcher has avoided very large deficits. There has been little protectionism and no overt industrial policy, certainly no equivalent of the American defense budget. There has also been little interest in banking reform, even though some analysts have argued that the inability to link savings to industrial development is one of the structural deficiencies of the British economy.[11]

Some of the limits of Conservative policy have also appeared. There has been no great destruction of the welfare state, which was already far more developed than its American counterpart, and even right-wing Tories accept the electoral necessity for socialized health and welfare provisions to a degree that puts them to the left of many U.S. Democrats. Some neoclassicists in the United Kingdom may hope to restore the disciplines of before welfare state, but the politicians who manage the pragmatics of social accommodation and elections have not judged it wise to go far in that direction. In the mid-1980s Thatcher continues to face criticism from voters and from members of her own party.

Changes in the international economy have contributed to the crumbling of Britain's fabled consensus politics. The country's deteriorating ability to compete in world markets has put new pressure on society, generating a need for policies of adjustment. Several options are conceptually possible, each inflicting costs and benefits on different groups. The pressures have snapped certain historic arrangements: much of British labor, for example, has turned against free trade and now favors various forms of protection in defense of a nonmobile labor force. Much of the British business community has turned against the class accommodationism of the postwar year in terms of wage levels and welfare payments. The link between City, trade, and labor has weakened.

Thatcher articulates a Disraelian approach, but her Disraeli is the conservative nationalist rather than the Red Tory of legend. She blends the psychologically integrative gratifications of nationalism with the trickle-down incentives of the open market. Meanwhile, the centrists mix policies, wanting the market plus the welfare net, demand management as well as industrial restructuring. Organizationally, however, they are split among Social Democrats, Liberals, the Labour center-right, and Tory wets. The Labour left urges a blend of planning, nationalization, and protection; it remains strong among some unions and in segments of the Labour party. The Labour left appears isolated, with no potential allies, yet it is strong enough to prevent the formation of an antidry coalition. This fragmentation of the opposition has allowed the Thatcherite position to prevail in electoral terms.

The British case shows, like the French, the complex interaction between partisan political struggles for control of the state and the substantive issues that divide or unite societal actors. Labour and Tory governments alike are constrained by the behavior of trade unions, investors, and consumers. As the British economy has experienced the sharp competitive pressures of the 1970s and 1980s, so the tensions involved in accommodating these diverse forces have grown. Old understandings—free trade and capitalist management in a regulated context, in exchange for high wages, job security, and welfare—have eroded. In the early 1980s, it was on the center-left that attempts to work out a coalition encountered difficulties. Apparently a general trend in Western countries, that was in very sharp contrast to the 1930s, when difficulties seemed greatest on the center-right.

To realize their policy goals, societal actors require allies, and so in addition to the direct action of bargaining, managing, and investing they must work through party politics. All of the other factors connected to politics thereby enter the British system. The first is economic ideology. Although the role of the City may have declined, a particular attitude toward the government and economic policy survives: it is a weak tradition of industrial mercantilism in which state, business, and banking collaborate to promote industry.

The second is state structures and intermediate associations. The cabinet system allows the government (able as nowhere else to combine executive and legislative authority) the possibility of very extensive authority. In that sense the British state is the opposite of the American separation of powers and federalism, and we therefore cannot explain the convergence of British and American policy by reference to the distinction between strong and weak states. Other institutional features may also affect the policy debate: a financial system that tends to separate manufacturing from banking and thereby deprives the state of those mechanisms of intervention so well developed on the Continent; the fragmentation of the trade unions; and the way in which industry is organized and linked to social structure. Here, however, the boundary among explanatory categories fades, for these mediating associations shape outcomes by the impact they have on the alliances among social forces.

The third is Britain's place in the international system. The inability of the United Kingdom, like the countries on the Continent, to provide for its own security makes it dependent on a condominium of like-minded countries, particularly the United States. In the course of two world wars, Britain was forced to liquidate much of the overseas investment that had allowed it to shift from manufacturing to financial management. The liquidation foreclosed the opportunity, and the Commonwealth no longer offers an alternative to commerce with other industrial countries. Britain's choices have thus shifted. The international basis of the anti-corn-law tradition of policy, Britain as specialized workshop of the world, has declined. Britain has become a smaller country during this century, but it has not evolved the political understandings needed to sustain the policies that elsewhere many smaller countries pursue.[12]

SWEDEN

Sweden, like France, expresses both the possibilities and the limits of policy choices under current pressures in the international economy. In the elections of 1982 the political balance shifted back toward the Social Democrats, who had lost power in 1976 for the first time since the critical election of 1932. As in France, the new governing majority looked to extend the concept of social democracy into new areas, but, also as in France, it has been constrained from doing so. Similarly, after 1976 the bourgeois coalition, which is what the Swedes call the parties of the center and the right, had looked to use its electoral majority to move economic policy in a neoclassical direction. The center-right parties had failed. Thus whatever the outcome in partisan electoral terms, recent governments in Sweden have been sharply constrained by societal actors, international and domestic, in the formulation of actual policy.[13]

The bourgeois coalition consistently sought to challenge the accommodation formulated at Saltsjöbaden in 1938. Its constituent parties spoke of limiting the state, restoring the market, forcing modernization through the discipline of competition, cutting taxes, limiting social services, and pulling the state away from regulation and interven-

tion. When it took office in 1976, center-right government antici-
pated a strategy used quite effectively later by the Reagan administration—cut taxes before cutting spending and use the deficit to mobilize political pressure against government expenditure. (The program contrasted with that of Social Democrats, who used deficits to
legitimize taxes.)

In this effort to revive neoclassical economic policy in Sweden, the
parties of the bourgeois coalition sought to tap the considerable
changes in Swedish life since the 1930s. Rapid industrial growth had
altered society considerably. The farming population had fallen drastically, for example, as both smallholders and landless laborers left
agriculture for higher pay in industry. For the Agrarians, historic
allies of the Social Democrats, this demographic change meant the
decline of its core constituency. To survive, the party recast its appeal,
transforming itself from a party for farmers to a middle-of-the-road,
mildly reformist grouping that attracted a diverse social mixture
around a suitably anodyne name—the Center party. This shift
eventually led the party out of alliance with the Social Democrats and
toward the members of the bourgeois bloc, which formed a government under Torbjorn Falladin: the Center party, the Moderates (in
English usage, Conservatives), and the People's party (the Liberals),
which ruled in different combinations from 1976 to 1982.

This grouping was clearly heterogeneous, united only by a common
opposition to three decades of SAP rule. Like any coalition, it had to
link together diverse constituencies, each of which had its own internal conflicts. The large-scale, high-technology companies oriented
toward the world market had historically been partners in the compromise with the Socialists. Concerned about labor stability at home,
able to pass high wage costs on to consumers because of very high-
quality products, these companies differed in outlook from the smaller, less competitive firms that were less willing and able to accommodate labor. Farmers continued to have complex relations with the
suppliers of equipment and credit, because they were both buyers in
the distribution system and consumers of products. Industrial capitalists had learned the value of bargains with agriculture, but sources
of tension remained. Meanwhile professionals and white-collar and
blue-collar employees all had reasons for conflict with managers and
owners, not only over wages, powers, rights, and autonomy but over
consumer issues and environmental issues as well.

Although these various groups could come together to seek change,
they found it difficult to decide what should be changed and by how
much. Social services and the social welfare net quickly proved hard

to alter, because support for them remained strong. As for taxation levels, general resentment was not easily translated into specific spending reductions. Companies in trouble wanted and got state support and indeed nationalization actually increased under the bourgeois government. Farmers continued to demand subsidies and regulations that imposed considerable costs on consumers.

When economic pressure hit Sweden—first the inflation of the late seventies, then the deflation of the early eighties—the Falladin government faced the same problems as any other. A tight money policy to fight inflation would provoke business failures and unemployment, but government spending to the economic downturn would cause exchange rate and import pressures.

The only battle about which the bourgeois coalition partners could agree was the need to fight the power of organized labor. In the years after World War II the Social Democrats and their trade-union allies (the LO) had worked out a plan that linked together the various goals, a plan for economic growth through exports, labor peace, industrial democracy, and equality. Success for this plan required a capacity to adjust the economy constantly to shifting international markets. In the Swedish approach the state underwrote many of the costs of social adjustment while sharing the rewards of higher productivity in the leading sectors. In the Rehn Plan, formulated by a leading Social Democratic economist in the early 1950s, pay raises would be limited by the productivity gains in the strongest industries but applied to all; the less productive would have to adapt or go under. Labor would be helped to adapt through public funds being made available for job retraining.

This strategy thus relied heavily on the SAP's retaining office. Both economic plans and their political expression required state policies that would link the sharing of productivity gains with the sharing of transition costs. Political power meant labor peace, which promoted productivity and competitiveness, which provided the income to justify the retention of political power. Postwar Sweden had one of the lowest strike rates in Europe, which as Walter Korpi and others have shown, is neither accidental nor limited to Sweden. Generally, wherever political parties connected to the labor movement have held power, there strike rates have been low.[14]

The approach turned as well on the ability of the SAP and the LO to combine electoral strength with strong, comprehensive organizations. In sharp contrast with labor union organizations in the United Kingdom and France, the LO embraced most of the blue-collar group. Highly centralized yet extensive in coverage, it was capable of acting collectively and of imposing discipline on its constituents. That kind of comprehensive, general-purpose organization, as Mancur Olson has argued, is more likely than fragmented ones to be able to overcome those obstacles to collective action on the labor side which decrease labor's ability to realize its general aims. The LO leadership got deference from the SAP's policy success. The SAP could organize governing majorities, in the electorate and in parliament, by eliciting union deference to its larger political needs.

For both organizations, therefore, social change presented political problems. The reduction in numbers of rural allies and the growth of the white-collar and service sector made complex the problems of sustaining a broad appeal. A more complicated economy altered social solidarities. If the SAP were to restrict its appeal to its core constituency, it would stagnate and shrink. The SAP and the LO were aware of this problem. Their policies were devised to structure institutions in ways that created broader solidarities, binding blue- and white-collar workers together and linking them to other groups motivated by solidaristic appeals. The goal, then, was the opposite of what neo-conservatives such as Thatcher sought, policies that fragment and weaken solidarities in order to encourage "individualistic" (and conservative) mobilizations.

The Rehn Plan was to do this in the early fifties, the Meidner Plan of 1975 in the seventies. Faced with problems of adjustment and rationalization in the economy, problems that required individual sacrifice to achieve collective goals, the Meidner Plan proposed to elicit collective action by sharing power and rewards. It brought the issue of ownership back to the national agenda, but in a different guise. Instead of direct nationalization, the Meidner Plan proposed to divert a proportion of the profits of each company to purchase shares that would be owned by a union-managed fund. Slowly, over many years, ownership would pass into the hands of that fund. It is important to note that these shares would pass not to individual workers, which would privatize the effect, but to a union-controlled fund, which would use them collectively, holding them in trust for the work force. Through a market mechanism, unions would acquire an increasingly important voice in management. Firms would still function in the marketplace, still have to meet payrolls and generate profits, but the power of management would be shared, and so would the benefits of high investment.

The effects of the Meidner Plan were to be not only economic but also political. The political goal was to draw together the different elements of the workforce by creating an institution—the wage earners' fund—which would define their interests in a collective way. Participating in management and sharing the profits from investment would presumably make workers more ready to accept the need for adaptation. Moreover, the funds would help mobilize savings, creating pools of capital available for investment in the economy.

This plan, and the general assertion of union power that it represented, provoked antagonism from the forces within the bourgeois coalition. Its early version was one of the many elements that contributed to the Socialists' defeat of 1976, and in 1982 the SAP toned down its provisions quite substantially. What returned the Socialists to power was largely the effect of incumbency. In managing its internal tensions and its relations with labor, the bourgeois coalition stumbled in the way that Heath had done in the United Kingdom. Seeking to contain spending, it confronted the public-sector unions; the battle was over pay increases. The unions wanted to regain purchasing power lost to inflation, while the government wanted public-sector employees to absorb some of the costs of keeping down state spending. The result was Sweden's first large strike in over forty years. Among other things, this strike seemed to affirm the SAP's claim that it could manage relations with unions better than the bourgeois coalition, overcoming some of the political disadvantage that the party suffered from general anti-union sentiment.

Returned to office by a narrow margin, the SAP had to confront the same policy dilemmas as its European counterparts. Although some of the blame for the deflation of the early eighties could be laid on the bourgeois coalition, Sweden still had to deal with the problems of a difficult international economy—high interest rates, stiff competition, rapidly changing technologies, new products and productive processes, and a consequent need to create jobs and shift resources. The Meidner Plan offered no solution in the short run and did not command strong support. Historically, Sweden had responded to the international economy by being highly adaptive to market forces, an approach that Olof Palme's and his successor's government has had to continue. It continues to allow market cues to signal what can and cannot be produced at home, in part because the Swedish domestic market is too small to offer the temptations of autarchy. The SAP government allows the large, high-technology corporations and their banking allies to manage the industrial economy, using social legislation to share costs and benefits.

The Swedish Socialists, unlike their French counterparts, did not attempt extensive, direct nationalization of industry; they even sharply modified the indirect form of nationalization in the Meidner Plan, the wage earners' funds. Thus they have not tried to deal with the problems of economic adjustment through full-scale socialization. There has been some talk of industrial policy (basically mercantilism), but industrial planning remains in the hands of private managers. In sharp contrast with Mitterrand and various British Labour leaders, Palme devalued quickly and sharply, seeking to cheapen exports and stop imports. The Socialist government has stimulated the economy somewhat more than its predecessors and its counterparts elsewhere to keep employment rates high even at some cost in terms of inflation. It has certainly refused to revise the national tax system so as to favor investors, and in making policy it continues to stress equality and other social democratic values.

The SAP exemplifies the pragmatic exploration of policies that fit the party's politics. Having accepted the necessity of the market, more readily than many of its socialist counterparts in France, the United Kingdom, and West Germany, it seeks to infuse a neoclassical framework with socialist values. In the sharing of risks, costs, and benefits, its adherents believe, the economy can reconcile human values with efficiency, for workers who participate in governance become more likely to collaborate over change. So the SAP seeks to build the "third way," to move into another phase in historical sequence of gradual democratization and the sharing of power among the social classes of modern capitalist society.

Sweden, like France and the United Kingdom, illustrates the constraints that the international economy puts around policy choices. Politics tilts power toward one or another coalition, allowing it to form a government. But the difficulties of governing in a capitalist economy then push that government in certain directions, directions hemmed about by the sanctions of labor strikes, capital flows, and demand both domestic and foreign. The smaller the economy, the smaller is the leeway that remains. In the case of Sweden a degree of market pragmatism common to all sides, highly centralized associations and leadership skills all contribute to an outcome whose limits are shaped by Sweden's production profile: export-oriented, high-technology, market-sensitive corporations deeply involved in the international economy.

WEST GERMANY

In West Germany the pressures of the international economic situation contributed to shifts, albeit moderate ones, in both politics and policy. In politics the Free Democrats moved from a coalition with the Social Democrats to one with the Christian Democrats. Policy shifted from a cautious mixture of demand management with market discipline under Helmut Schmidt to a more neoclassical approach under Helmut Kohl. In comparative terms, though, the shifts in politics and policy have been small. The growth of new parties, notably the Greens, and new issues has not shifted the general contours of German economic policy. The nation most deviant in politics and policy during the interwar years, Germany has been among the most stable nations in the postwar decades.

The policy distance between Schmidt and Kohl has been relatively narrow in part because of the massive changes in all features of German society caused by war and reconstruction. Those changes allowed to emerge a coalition between export business and labor—the very coalition that for three-quarters of a century had tried without success to escape from the bondage of the autarchic-imperialist bloc of iron and rye. Indeed, the period of SPD rule from Brandt through Schmidt was Germany's fullest expression of the Weimar coalition, the type of accommodation which the Swedes had worked out in the thirties but which the alliance between conservatism and fascism had demolished in Germany.

The postwar coalition worked well as long as the economy worked well. As the international economy grew, so exports generated the income to lubricate the West German compromise. Adenauer's victory over Schumacher in the first national elections in 1949 marked the defeat of a statist approach to rebuilding. Instead Adenauer and Ludwig Erhard constructed an economy around the private control of investment and management: drastic currency reform and the elimination of controls set the market loose. Thereafter, cautious monetary and fiscal policies kept inflation low, prices flat, and exports high. At the same time labor was integrated into this new economy through an extensive welfare net and through worker representation in economic discourse (though not in actual management). Unions agreed to limit wage gains to productivity increases, management to share out the gains, and farmers got substantial side payments in the form of price supports. The economy was integrated into the open trading systems of the Common Market and the GATT. Profits from exports boomed and paid for dividends, new investment, and wage increases.

The world economy began to sag in the seventies, but at first West Germany did rather better than most of its neighbors. The linkage of wages and productivity kept inflation under control and also helped the country avoid stagflation. The high value of the Deutsche mark kept down spiraling oil bills. Schmidt pursued the centrist policies of market-oriented demand management, aiming to contain spending, monetary policy, and wage pressures through a mixture of market discipline and cautious policy regarding spending and taxes. There was even talk of German immunity from the international economic diseases of the day.[15]

The second oil shock of 1979 and deflation in the United States put an end to this illusion. West Germany's relation to the international division of labor began to show signs of stress. Not only was the country's oil bill extremely high, but the export goods that had paid the bill faced increasingly severe competition. Even machine tools, the high point of the export economy, had trouble. Foreign manufacturers were both undercutting the traditional technology of standardized production, through lower factor costs, and running ahead in the newer technology of computerized, highly flexible production.

As the world economy contracted, so Germany's ability to handle domestic pressures by sharing an expanding economic pie began to dissolve. Schmidt and the SPD found themselves in exactly the same bind as Callaghan and Labour, Carter and the Democrats, the bind also that Mitterrand and Palme would face after 1981. All the labor-supported governments had to make choices between their business and middle-class allies on one side and their labor constituencies on the other.

All costs to business became a problem when the economy started to contract. High taxes, high wages, high social security costs, all seemed plausible causes of the problem. Where previously employers had been divided about whether to accept the high wages of labor accommodation, now all employers could agree that wages and social costs were too high. Cutting those costs was an obvious remedy, one that fit easily with the market reasoning that had dominated West Germany since the war. Alternative explanations for economic problems were complicated, hard to demonstrate, and potentially divisive; they included weak entrepreneurship, managerial rigidities, inadequate research, and poor connections between research and marketing.

Although the Free Democrats had been willing to defer to the Social Democrats, paying some costs in exchange for access to power, industry's unity against labor costs increased the tensions between the two coalition partners. Schmidt's room for maneuver narrowed. The unions and the left in the SPD became increasingly hostile toward accommodation with the Free Democrats. The Free Democrats became increasingly split about the desirability of accommodation with the SPD, as the more conservative among them were tempted by the prospect of alliance with the CDU-CSU. If they could exclude the SPD from government, they believed, they would reduce the ability of labor to shape economic policy. The government would be freer to loosen the reins of the market.

The SPD, like other labor parties before and since, was caught between having to manage austerity (which could only bring dissatisfaction from the rank and file) and finding other solutions to the crisis which would not antagonize the German political center. As in the early days of the Depression the SPD found itself blamed for having caused the mess. Certainly the political context had dramatically changed in half a century; this time labor leaders lost control of public office, not their lives. Nonetheless, those leaders faced the common problem of labor parties in a time of economic downturn: how to devise programs that link the defense of wages and labor power to the broader need to increase productivity which concerns other social forces.[16]

The West German labor movement, both union and party, is much less deeply split than that of France or the United Kingdom. The union movement is broad, comprehensive, and centralized, and the party remains relatively broad as well. Nonetheless, there is disagreement about the future. Some wish to follow a German version of Benn and Chèvenement toward more state intervention and autarchy; others seek work power through industrial democracy; still others are attracted by the appeals of the Greens, their stress on ecology, defense policy, and the various issues that cut across traditional lines of social cleavage. Mostly, however, labor leaders would like to reorganize German industry in ways that make it both competitive and profitable but that do not require labor to shoulder the entire costs of transition. In the new international division of labor, however, they have not yet discovered a formula by which to transform their aims into practice.

The German policy path to date has kept closer to the postwar compromise than those of the other countries examined here. The CDU government is more moderate in rhetoric and policy than the government of Reagan and Thatcher; the SPD and the unions remain more moderate in rhetoric and policy than their French and British counterparts. Perhaps closest to West Germany in terms of continuity is Sweden, a country where shifts in policy have also been narrow. In a sense, the two countries are continuing the distinctively different versions of the postwar compromise which they evolved several decades ago. Yet even between West Germany and Sweden there is an interesting contrast: in the Federal Republic the mechanisms of democratic corporatism are relatively weaker than in the smaller countries of Western Europe.

THE UNITED STATES

The election of Ronald Reagan in 1980 marked a considerable shift in the U.S. rhetoric of political economy, and some important policy changes as well. Future historians will certainly locate some of those changes in the Carter years—deregulation, the revolution in monetary policy of Paul Volker's years at the Federal Reserve, increased military spending, pressure for wage restraint, and concern about corporate profitability. Nevertheless, the Reagan changes are both politically important and substantively significant; they include extensive tax cuts, the redistribution of the tax burden, spending cuts for social programs, looser enforcement of regulation, changes in the administration of industrial relations, substantial increases in military spending, and record-breaking peacetime deficits. The deflation begun under Jimmy Carter intensified in Reagan's early years, with record-breaking unemployment levels. But the subsequent boom was strong. High interest rates and opportunities for appreciation have drawn in substantial sums of foreign capital; indeed, the value of foreign debt has swelled to equal the value of foreign holdings by Americans. By mid-decade job creation in the United States was the envy of Europeans, and inflation had plummeted. At the same time, unemployment is still high compared to that of the postwar years; the deficit remains tremendous; the high value of the dollar hurts exports and punishes certain domestic industries; and the debt crisis potential in the holdings of vast sums of paper by American banks hovers over any hope of re-forming those years of stable growth, the fifties and sixties.

The Reagan policy moves, away from centrist demand management and stabilization and toward a neoclassical approach, have been accompanied by considerable political changes as well. The New Deal coalition has come apart at the level of presidential politics, though no deep realignment has taken hold at the level of Congress or the localities. Nonetheless, there has been both a decided shift to the right in American discussion of economic policy and a considerable weakening of the postwar accommodation.

Many factors, of course, were involved in Reagan's success. Even the most summary list would include the rejection of the incumbent during a period of inflation and rising unemployment, the foreign policy reverses of Iran, the divisive legacy of Vietnam inside the Democratic party, the issues of race and women, and the political skills of Reagan. But these various particular features occurred in a wider context, a profound change in the situation of American businesses in the international economy. Strong competition, shifts in prices, new technologies, and monetary flows have all exacerbated tensions within the coalitions that dominated American political economy in the postwar years.

The postwar accommodation in the United States rested on a consensus for stabilization within a growing free-trade economy. Both domestic industry seeking stability of markets and export-oriented industry seeking stabilized international arrangements were willing to deviate from the neoclassical rejection of nonintervention in the economy. Progressive elements of the Republican party and business elements of the Democratic party collaborated with labor to preserve and extend the charges of the New Deal. High wages to unionized workers, social security benefits, and unionized industrial relations were traded for union support on behalf of the GATT, the IMF, the Marshall Plan, the EEC, and other elements of American internationalism. Domestic prosperity and American hegemony in the world reinforced the policies and their supporting coalition.

Several changes in the international economy have served to undermine this arrangement. The rise of foreign competition undermines the ability of American companies to pass on the costs of high American wages and other stabilization arrangements. Foreign competition and the sharp swings of the international economy also weaken the bases of Fordist production arrangements (i.e., mass manufacture of standardized elements). As American companies have internationalized their manufacturing, so their commitment to domestic production has weakened. New forms of wealth have emerged in oil, real estate, aerospace, and defense; they relate differently to labor with regard to production and consumption, as well as having different regional bases in American politics. Finance has grown tremendously in importance as the United States has supplanted the United Kingdom as the center of the international payments system and the major force in international investing.

The groups involved in these various changes have their own internal conflicts as we shall see, but in the seventies, they converged on a general attitude toward labor and the state. They wanted to cut them back. There may be other reasons for America's competitive problems, but wages, taxes, and regulations make highly visible targets to attack. Where business had previously split about whether to accommodate labor arrangements, in the seventies and eighties it has united against them. Business interests of all kinds have been able to agree on a broadly neoclassical program to restore profit rates, to shift the balance of gains from labor back to capital, to encourage capital accumulation through tax cuts, to redistribute taxes toward savings, to deregulate, to limit wage increases, and so on. Whatever its other disagreements, business in the United States has supported efforts to curtail welfare and social services, to avoid wage-price controls and other such interventions, to avoid any deliberate industrial policy, certainly to reject nationalization or collective investment, and to reject claims for industrial democracy. There has also been considerable support for weakening the power of labor unions, whether it be by appointments to the relevant commissions or by the application of judicial power in, for example, the bankruptcy law.

The timing of policy shifts brings out the importance of structural changes in the international economy compared to purely electoral partisan shifts.[17] Major shifts have occurred within administrations as much as between administrations of different parties. Republican Richard Nixon broke with two decades of policy in freezing dollar convertibility, in devaluing the dollar, in imposing an excise tax on foreign cars and wage-price controls—all these measures from a presumably internationalist, conservative president. Within a few years, by the time of the OPEC cartel, the Bretton Woods arrangement of fixed exchange rates was in ruins. Carter continued this mixture of demand management, jawboning, and growing protectionism. Welfare and social services, which had expanded under Lyndon Johnson, continued to grow under Nixon, Ford, and Carter impartially, and so did efforts to deal with environmental problems and other forms of regulation.

But the downturn of 1974 and the strong inflation of the late seventies produced pressures for change. Important steps were taken under Carter. The most important was the policy of Volker's Federal Reserve to contain inflationary pressures by allowing the market to drive up interest rates, forcing a depression. This was a major departure for the Fed, which previously had accommodated inflationary pressures and made a priority of keeping interest rates steady. Some major steps in deregulation were also taken, most notably in the airlines industry. The Democrats and the labor unions were thus facing the same question as their European counterparts: What policies were they to pursue in difficult economic times? With the labor allies of the Democrats shifting to favor more neoclassical policies, Carter, in the best tradition of the Gold Democrats of the previous century, accommodated. But the combination of rising prices and rising unemployment produced too much tension within the Democratic coalition. Neither business nor large chunks of labor could see how Carter's policy was working.

Reagan thus took office as the country rejected the incumbent, and as in all such cases, the victor had some leeway in interpreting his mandate. Reagan's moves have been unconventional in the sense that they have gone beyond limits that traditional business conservatives would have observed. The most striking element of his policy has been the budget deficit that resulted from his cutting taxes before cutting spending. Reagan has combined tight money policy with loose fiscal policy, where the traditional neoclassicist would have prescribed the opposite. The greatest beneficiary of his spending has been the military, which has received the largest peacetime budget increases in American history. The effect has been a tremendous fiscal stimulus, leading many economists to call the growth of the mid-eighties a Keynesian boom. The effect has also been that of a de facto industrial policy, whatever the rhetoric might claim.

Reagan's unconventional approach stems from the political dynamics of a coalition that works both at the level of the electorate and at the level of the societal actors within the economy. Reagan and his advisers, like the Swedish Social Democratic leaders of the early thirties, were politicians in search of policies that would suit their political needs. What they wanted was a program that would link traditional Republican business concerns for profits, lower taxes, deregulation, and market discipline of labor with a mass populist appeal among voters, union members, and investors. Traditional Republican neoclassicism was too austere, too emphatic about the need to press down on wage levels and services. Supply-side analysis suited much better with its calls to cut taxes, make savings more profitable to the rich, spend for defense (which was politically far more acceptable than spending for the poor, for cities, or for social programs), keep money tight to defend the dollar, kill inflation, and draw in foreign loans to finance the debt. The rhetoric of the policy called for cutting taxes and cutting the fat from the budget (i.e., spending on the poor), and growth would automatically take care of the deficits. One might choose to call such a policy right-wing military Keynesianism, but whatever the label, the last decade it has been politically stronger than the alternatives of no-deficit conservatism and left-wing keynesianism.

Reagan's political role has been to find an electoral formula that works better than the traditional conservative one. Since 1929 the

Republicans have had a difficult time finding an approach that is not identified with the interests of business and the rich. The European solution has been Christian Democracy and the Red Toryism of the Beveridge approach; Eisenhower Republicans blended acceptance of the New Deal with internationalism. Reagan, however, has recast the formula, extending the neoclassical approach beyond its usual political bounds. Because of the timing of the situation, Reagan was able to present demand management and corporatism as the incumbent policy approach, and hence "old" and the cause of problems, market ideas as "new" and innovative.

His formula, like any other, is not without its own internal conflicts. Most business groups have strongly supported Reaganomics as providing the most probusiness administration in fifty years. They see costs to the policy package, but at least through the mid-eighties they were willing to view those costs as the price to be paid to the political expert, the president, in order to get the rewards. But conflicts over the policy package do exist, and with them the possibility of new shifts in alignments over both policy and politics.

Business groups sharply disagree about the deficit. Many argue that it is causing severe difficulties now and has the potential to cause more difficulties in the future. In the short term the deficit keeps interest rates high, discouraging investment in domestic production and (because it keeps the dollar high on currency markets) damaging exports and inducing imports. By drawing in foreign capital, moreover, the U.S. deficit harms economies around the world, making export markets yet weaker. By pushing up interest rates it menaces the ability of foreign governments to make payments on the massive debt that they owe American banks. Such debts cannot be paid until ability to pay is linked to ability of debtors to export, but the latter is being hampered by protectionism. Supply siders, on the other hand, argue that the deficit is not the cause of high interest rates. Rather, they claim, foreign money comes to the United States in response to profit opportunities. That foreign indebtedness can be useful if the money goes into productive investment.

A tension has developed between banking-finance and production similar to the tension that has obtained in the United Kingdom for many decades. As the American banking sector has grown, it has acquired its own prespectives that clash with those of domestic producers. Fighting inflation through tight money may preserve monetary values, but the policy takes its toll on funds for investment and in falling exports. Conversely, getting developing debtors to pay back their debts requires that they be helped to export. But such help

would encourage the international division of labor, moving production of some goods from the United States to those countries, which
would hurt U.S. domestic producers. Banks heavily involved in overseas lending therefore come to conclusions about the U.S. economy
which differ from those of domestic producers and of banks that
invest in domestic industrial development. As U.S. companies inter-
nationalize, they too become less interested in domestic production,
and so they may clash with the so-called Rustbelt industries, the factories of the Midwest and East which are organized around standardized production with a strong home market.

In foreign economic policy there is tension among different ways of
managing U.S. relations with other countries. A nationalist perspective asserts U.S. interests aggressively and is disinclined to worry
about collaborative arrangements, negotiation, or shouldering the
costs of economic leadership. A more internationalist view seeks
greater collective discussion among countries and is more willing to
have the United States bear the cost of providing international public
goods. Such divergences come to public notice in disagreements over
domestic economic policy and its international implications.

At home there is disagreement over the role of government. Although most in business are eager to see reductions in costs and
government interference, many also see that vital services may need
growth, among them transportation, research, education, energy
planning, agriculture, health standards, and environmental issues. All
of these areas provoke controversies that strain the business coalition.
Deregulation is popular, but poses risks as well. Bankruptcies, as at
Braniff Airlines, Continental Illinois Bank, and the close call at
Chrysler Corporation, lead some to urge intervention, others to oppose it. Military spending, whatever its foreign policy implications,
poses risks of distorting the economy and wasting productive resources.

Some business leaders believe that modernization of the economy
requires a government to play a more active role in a kind of industrial policy. They urge tripartite negotiations among government,
business, and labor to devise plans for the shifting of resources. Public
funds, channeled through a public bank, would help pay the costs.
Felix Rohatyn is one of the leading proponents of this approach,[18]
which applies to the United States the principles he used in handling
the fiscal crisis of New York City—a sharing of costs and benefits
through bargaining among societal actors, and collaboration from the
government in providing tax funds for economic modernization.[19]

Rohatyn's proposals would remake the coalition that emerged out of the New Deal: business, labor, and the government would collaborate directly rather than in an adversarial way through the market. Such an alliance would not be easy to organize, of course, for the parties have many conflicts between them, over wages, taxes, trade, and other issues. Before World War I protectionism helped link U.S. labor and business, and from the late 1930s to the 1970s internationalism did so. Today, however, labor has become quite protectionist while business largely favors free trade. And business groups have shown little inclination to collaborate with labor around Rohatyn's policy package.

American policy has certainly shifted rightward in response to the crisis of the seventies and eighties. Under pressure from strong international competition, business groups have rallied around a policy package that combines neoclassical principles with very strong fiscal stimulus. American labor has lost many of its allies from the New Deal days: agriculture receives support from even the most anti-interventionist of conservatives and no longer requires labor's help, and business groups have converged on a program that also excludes labor. In the past business conflicts created opportunities for populist pressures to exert an influence. At times that populism has been channeled through organized labor, at times through groups hostile to labor. But labor's influence has weakened, and unless issues arise to fragment U.S. business, the particular balance between intervention and neoclassicism devised by the Reagan forces will endure.

CONCLUSION

Recent changes in the international economy have put severe strains on the historical compromise that was fashioned in response to the great crisis of the interwar years. The policy approach of that compromise was the mixed economy: market capitalism embedded in structures that promoted stability, predictability, and social peace. International trade was located in an analogous "embedded liberalism," a model of stabilization and absorption where the market directed the shift of resources and social programs shared the costs of absorption into new activities. The politics that sustained this economic approach involved collaboration between elements of business and labor and the subordination of those who disagreed.

The policy formulas varied from country to country according to the balance of power among social forces, the organizational strength of different points of view, the particularities of national relationships to the international economy, and other features specific to the political life of nations. Most of the literature on postwar Western Europe and North America stresses the differences among countries, rehearsing the distance between Sweden and the United States. The differences are certainly real. But in wider historical comparison, all of these countries are more nearly similar, in economic policy and in its social-institutional manifestations, than any one of them is to the world that preceded the Great Crash of 1929. This is still true today. Despite their differences in policy, all of these countries have retained large parts of the arrangements made in the thirties. Even the most cursory analysis notes the retention of, for example, social security, unemployment insurance, health care systems, institutionalized industrial relations, macroeconomic analysis, national financial institutions and management, and agricultural corporatism.

Nonetheless, the new crisis of the international economy has led to a reformulation of both policy and political terms. Neoclassical market ideas have been revived, recast, and reintegrated into the 1930s' pattern of social insurance and stabilization. Policy makers have allowed market forces to push readjustment, cut back on spending, reduce taxes, and lift regulations to a degree that no observer had thought possible in the early 1970s. Then most analysts would have expected crisis to deepen a trend established in the thirties toward more intervention.

The shift rightward occurred despite the variation in political outcomes across countries. The victories of Mitterrand and Palme belie any general interpretation of partisan politics across countries, as indeed do election results in Portugal, Spain, and Greece. But outcomes in partisan politics do not coincide with or capture adequately the changes in policy. There have been shifts within the lifespan of individual governments, and governments of quite different partisan colorations have adopted similar policies.

It is possible to interpret policy's independence from partisanship from the standpoint of societal actors. All of the governments examined here must fight their partisan battles in the context of market economies integrated into an international production system. If we assume that politicians seek to win votes, then we can assume that all of them seek to create conditions of prosperity. Prosperity depends on forces other than votes, however; it depends on demand, investment, initiative, and work, which express themselves in various ways, only one of which is the act of voting. Worldwide competitive pressures have given leverage to investors and managers, who under present conditions particularly want a reduction in costs. When a busi-

ness-cycle downturn exacerbates general conditions, therefore, it
leads governments toward an austerity that will permit adjustment in
the allocation of resources—in short, toward a neoclassical approach.

Alternatives to this approach have been proposed by various forces
on the left and by some in the center and on the right; they include
nationalization, protectionism, and mercantilism. But in the 1980s
labor has been weakened. It has lost historical allies, and its arguments appear particularistic rather than general. Moreover, trade
issues have emphasized tensions between consumer interests and producer concerns. Labor in dynamic sectors sees no reason to sustain
those in declining ones. The increasing complexity of the economy
thus weakens collective solidarities in favor of what Alessandro
Pizzorno labeled "individualistic mobilization."[20]

In the late nineteenth century, it seems, general trends overrode
national differences, pushing policy makers to adopt protection. In
our period something similar has pushed policy toward neoclassical
approaches—though, as I have already noted, policy has not yet
moved far in comparison to the world before 1929. And so two main
changes require explanation. One is diachronic, between periods, between the mixed economic response to the interwar crisis and the
general neoliberal response of the present one. The other is syn-
chronic, the policy variance in the current period among countries
that have different mixtures of welfare, corporatism, and the market.

The first, diachronic shift, the tilt away from the postwar compromise, seems best captured by the production profile approach.
Changing relationships among economic actors, influenced by shifting conditions of competition in the international economy, have altered policy preferences and balances of power. The lines of cleavage
among workers, farmers, and business groups, more or less papered
over for many years, have reemerged. Coalitions have come unraveled without any clear sense of how the strands might be knitted
up again. These broad shifts in what we might term the plate tech-
tonics of coalitions shape the context in which other factors operate.
They have more importance than the particular feature of each country's state structure, intermediate associations, national ideology, or
international rivalries. Countries will differ on these dimensions, but
such differences do not capture the broad, epochal shift that can be
found everywhere.

In the present period countries differ conspicuously in the way they
choose to respond to these broader changes. Sweden and the United
States continue to differ greatly in levels of social welfare and in
strength of organized labor; the United States continues to differ

greatly from its Continental counterparts with regard to nonmilitary mercantilist policies, public ownership, and corporatist mechanisms. These specific policy variations are closely linked to the ways in which countries differ in institutions, associations, ideology, and so on. The weight of economic argument in each country is deeply affected by patterns of organizational commitment, by ideology, and by institutions that mediate the relationship between societal pressures and policy choices.

Each country is affected by these twin factors: the force of epochs, which cuts across the particularities of circumstance, and the force of national trajectories, which expresses the features specific to each nation's history. The relationships change over time, because the role that each factor plays is the product of specific historical circumstances. Nevertheless, some patterns become clear when we look, as we shall in the concluding chapter, at the crisis together.

Part III

COMPARATIVE RESPONSES TO INTERNATIONAL ECONOMIC CRISES

CHAPTER SIX

The Social Bases of
the Autonomous State

International economic crises are to countries what reagents are to compounds in chemistry: they provoke changes that reveal the connections between particularities and the general. If the comparativist can find countries subject to the same stresses, it then becomes possible to see how countries differ or converge and thereby to learn something about cause and effect.

My comparison of the responses of five countries to three crises has rested on one large assumption: that the three crises and the five countries are sufficiently alike to make comparison fruitful. I believe the assumption is warranted in that much can be learned. But studying countries in the international economy may be more like looking at the weather (an interactive system where different elements affect one another profoundly) than like studying salt compounds in freshman chemistry (where reactions are direct). Economic crises shape countries, but crises also express what is happening within those countries. Both crises and countries change over time, so that relationships change as well. And every country faces each crisis differently.

Because of these various contingencies, it is safer to say that in the previous three chapters I have not provided a "scientific" testing of alternative explanations. Rather, I have sought to outline a historical sociology of the trajectories of national responses to external changes.[1] The relationships among the explanatory variables are not constant but change overtime, and in this chapter I examine these changing relationships.

CRITICAL REALIGNMENTS: THE PATTERN AMONG SOCIETAL ACTORS

Each of the three crises has provoked deep changes in relation among societal actors; in sections of business, labor, and agriculture we have seen shifting patterns of cooperation and conflict. Students of elections and political parties have noted the development of "critical realignments" in voting behavior, where at moments of crisis deep partisan attachments are formed which persist over long periods of time.[2] Something similar seems to happen with groups.

The linchpin to these critical realignments among groups has been the linkage between international competition and intrabusiness relationships. Two interconnected matters deserve particular attention. First, the ability of labor and agriculture, and mass pressure generally, to influence an economic policy debate depends on the existence of acute disagreements within the business community. Capitalists have a common interest in limiting the claims of wage earners for wages, power, and social benefits, of course, but business elements always disagree and compete for predominance. In some periods their disagreements will be so profound that segments of capital will seek allies among nonbusiness groups in fights against their capitalist rivals. They thus give other groups greater influence over events. Conversely, however, when intracapitalist conflicts decline in intensity and business groups draw together around a particular policy, the influence of other groups declines. Similarly, business has an easier time prevailing when other groups are in conflict one with another.[3]

This leads to my second point. Business groups have different "marginal propensities" toward progressive or conservative alignment. Progressive alignments link business to labor and agriculture around programs of better wages and working conditions, institutionalized industrial relations, social insurance systems, and constitutional government involving some sharing of power. Conservative alignments link these groups around programs that favor investment-led growth, limited wages, weak unions, limited social insurance, and, in some instances, the use of state power to control labor.

For business conservatives, labor is a commodity, a factor of production for which they seek the lowest possible cost. Like a commodity, labor cannot be seen as having rights, nor any claims to power. It must take what the market offers. Unions, from this viewpoint, are obstacles to the market, illegitimate attempts to use state power to obtain leverage, and so for conservatives, the preferred source of market stabilization is not high wages and social programs to assure labor demand, but government purchases and cartels. Business-dominated corporatism, not tripartite bargaining, is what they prefer. Some conservatives have supported elements of social welfare, but this has been a controversial point. For business progressives, on the other hand, labor is not only an input to production but a major source of demand and a component of society with legitimate claims for resources and power. Progressives see benefits accruing to business from strong and stable labor demand, from an institutionalized system of labor relations, and from general conditions of good health, education, and living arrangements.

The emergence of progressive attitudes marked an important shift in the history of industrial societies. As long as workers made products that they could not afford to buy, labor-capital relations revolved around the price of the wage commodity. When mass purchasing power became fundamental to business prosperity, however, the possibilities of a collective game grew. Businesses began to think more broadly about the relationship between the situation of their particular firm and general conditions in the economy. Moreover, healthy workers, well-educated and respectfully treated and well-paid, contributed more to productivity than sick, harshly treated, poor ones. Unions could play an important role in the management of labor markets: stabilizing, organizing, disciplining, and recruiting. In politics some progressive property owners had come to see incorporation of the masses through democracy as a strategy superior to repression; some businessmen came to see that the same principle could be applied in economic life.

"Progressive" and "conservative" are ideological categories. Their social location has varied over time with their shifting relationships to the international economy. In the late nineteenth century the salient issue was trade, and conflicts over tariffs divided industrial elites. The internationalists became the progressives, looking for labor's help to achieve an open trading system. Progressive business seems to have been characterized by high technology, an export orientation, and the manufacture of finished consumption goods; and it also included shipping and international commercial banking. Electrical goods, chemicals, and household goods are particularly clear examples. Conversely, antilabor views seem to have prevailed among companies with labor-intensive manufacture, high geographical concentration of the labor force, less flexibility in shifting resources, and high debt burdens. Iron and steel producers and mining companies appear to have been conservative nearly everywhere.

When the international trading system collapsed in the 1930s, these relationships shifted. Faced with stiff competition and collapsing world markets, the progressives stepped back from collaboration with labor. Their need to cut costs meant cutting wages and taxes, and hence conflict with labor. At the same time inward-oriented companies sought allies of their own. Despite their traditional enmity, they and labor were both more desperate for help than the international groups, and in the worst days of the Depression each became willing to support similar policies and politics. Out of the tangle of conflicting goals emerged a consensus in favor of stabilization and the management of demand, but the political formula varied widely from country to country.

When the world economy revived in the mid-thirties, relationships among groups changed again. The internationalists re-formed their partnership with labor, though with one very important addition: they accepted the goal stabilization. Industries seeking this kind of market included those with high levels of investment debt, such as airlines and oil, and producers of consumer goods of many kinds. The postwar bargain would turn on this convergence of the old "anti-corn-law" tradition of progressive labor relations with a newer compromise on "stabilization." The two coincided after the war around a mixture of Keynes and free trade which endured for a quarter century.

International economic conditions in the 1970s and 1980s undermined those understandings. The internationalization of production and consumption has severed the link between domestic stability and economic advantage, and the logic of the international market now applies pressure to drive down the costs to business of wages and taxes. No longer is it possible through the deployment of high technology to pass on the costs of highly paid domestic labor, for international competition is too strong. No longer is it possible for business to be assured of stabilized demand for no country can provide that much security in its own markets or has the ability to impose arrangements on international markets. With greater uncertainty and stronger competition, all companies seek lower costs from labor, more freedom of maneuver in shifting labor and other resources around. High-technology producers and consumer goods producers all seek to produce at the world's lowest cost, whatever the price to domestic labor.

Labor has thus lost its business allies. In Europe and North America business elites see labor as living above its and their means. And the economies of all of these countries have evolved in ways that diminish the number of blue-collar workers and the chances that solidarity will develop around union conceptions of worker welfare. Such groups as "yuppies," and cadres of the emerging industrial economy, white-collar workers, and blue-collar workers in the new industries have little attachment to the concerns of the Rustbelt unions.

The relationship between labor and agriculture has also involved massive shifts. In the nineteenth century labor and agriculture were at loggerheads: the city wanted cheap food, the countryside cheap industrial goods. Other factors certainly hindered cooperation also, but my general point is that these two groups had a very difficult time collaborating against business forces. The crisis of the late nineteenth century split agriculture between growers of commodity crops for world markets and producers of high-quality foodstuffs for nearby urban-industrial markets. The latter, users of the grains and other commodities produced by the former, were available as a potential ally for industry oriented toward free trade. Commodity crop growers were available for a protectionist alliance. (In the United States, however, the positions were reversed; as efficient producers, commodity crop growers were free traders, while growers of high-quality food identified with the interests of protectionist manufacturing, their major market.) Both groupings directed their negotiations at business, not to labor and the populist alliances of the period failed.

The Great Crash of 1929 changed that pattern profoundly. Although farming continued to be internally complex, the universality of an agricultural distress that began in the twenties and became acute in the early thirties made all of its factions available for new politics and new policies. In several countries labor was willing to make a deal but business was not, and farmers were desperate enough to make the switch. Where farmer-labor alignments occurred, they were strong enough to attract some elements of business. The progressives, with their own policy goals, split off to accept pieces of the labor-agriculture programs and this formed the historical compromise that emerged in the 1930s and 1940s.

Labor's success in forming alliances with agriculture would not last. Agriculture stayed with labor when times were bad but moved away when things turned better. Extensive state programs stabilized agricultural markets, providing a floor for farmers' incomes. Improved industrial performance strengthened urban markets for farm goods and generated jobs for the marginal agricultural population. Business overcame its antipathy for intervention in markets and became quite willing to offer agriculture the same arrangements as labor had or better. With population falling in the countryside, in sum, agriculture was becoming an interest group, able to offer its support to the high-

225

est bidder. Its leverage as a swing group was already quite clear in the thirties, when it imposed limits on the reformism of the New Deal, the Swedish Social Democrats, and the French Popular Front.

In the 1970s and 1980s labor has lost agricultural support. The smaller rural population and the continuation of farming subsidies make agriculture less available as an ally. That loss is significant, not only in numbers of votes but in political ideology, particularly in arguments about the role of the state in capitalist democracies. Farmers, as owners of property, have bestowed on state intervention in the market a legitimacy that labor has always had difficulty sustaining by itself. Populist revolts based on the grievances of small capitalists against the market have extended the strength of the sellers of labor power when both groups are able to make common cause.

In the current period, however, the agricultural sources of such support have waned, and the current sources of populism (shopkeepers, small entrepreneurs, white-collar workers, professionals) appear to provide no such opportunities for alliance. On the contrary, their complaints seem directed particularly at labor. They link the economy's ills to unions and work rigidities, and to the expenses of the welfare state. Labor demands currently appear to have less legitimacy than those of other groups in the capitalist system.

Within the category of labor itself, two groups can be differentiated: unionized and nonunionized labor. The direction of and tendency for alliances seems quite different for the two. Union workers have been far more willing to follow their leaders within the labor-allied parties and the trade unions themselves than have nonunion workers. The latter instead have been available for mobilization around other principles of solidarity (such as nationalism, religion, race, and ethnicity) and other economic programs. As a result, the tracing of political and policy coalitions involves following the behavior both of leaders of the labor movement and of the nonunionized "masses."

In the late nineteenth century unions everywhere had a difficult time in finding allies. Most businesses hoped to prevent union growth; most of agriculture feared union radicalism. Labor did have an influence on policy and politics, but its role tended to be passive—though labor provided votes and other kinds of support, the movement's leaders did not share power. It took World War I and the Depression to end that exclusion. In all five countries labor entered the system during and after the Great War, lost ground in the twenties, and reentered more fully in the thirties. In Germany the unionized groups held firm against Nazi appeals, but the radical right could claim the legitimacy of mass strength by tapping, among other groups, the nonunionized work force. In Sweden, the United States, and France, labor union and labor party leaders became major participants in coalitional politics.

Part of the postwar compromise has been the institutionalization in the various countries of the rights and powers of labor unions. Industrial relations, plant management, social programs, and government administration all developed a great role for labor. In the seventies and eighties this position has come under attack, albeit to different degrees in different countries. Labor unions have become the central target of criticism by other groups of whatever is wrong with the economy. At the same time various factors have weakened labor solidarity. The growing complexity of the economy, new industries, new relationships in the workplace, geographical mobility, and prosperity have all made the tasks of collective mobilization more difficult. As long as other groups are able to contain their internal differences and direct criticism against "labor, welfare, and the state," unions and organized labor movements will continue to face problems. Labor parties may maintain themselves in office, but they will do so only by modifying their policies, not with the labor-defensive policies that they supported for many decades.

In the crisis of the late nineteenth century the free market was blamed, and protectionism plus some regulation was the response. In the depression of the 1930s the market was blamed again, only this time much more extensively. In both of those crises the state and public policy were seen as instruments of capitalism and plutocracy. The task of political mobilization was to capture the state for the people. With the policies of the thirties and the postwar compromise, the state came to serve social welfare and labor purposes as well as capitalist ones. When things deteriorated in the eighties, therefore, the political location of the state had changed. The state and its progressive allies could themselves become the objects of attack.[4]

THE STATE AND SOCIETAL ACTORS

The relationships among societal actors have changed over the three crises. So has the relationship between the state and specific societal actors (a matter of substance) and the role of the state in society (a matter of form). The two are linked. In all three crises the role of the state itself has been an issue in arguments over economic policy. The quarrel over role is mixed with the struggles over substance.

In the first crisis the state looked to encourage market conditions favorable for capitalist growth and deployed instruments of coercion against labor and other protest movements. Policy interventions promoted market conditions desired by capitalists, such as tariffs, transportation infrastructure, utilities, and the like. There was some social welfare regulation of working conditions, hours, safety, and the employment of women and children. There was also some social investment in education and health. Indeed, the state was far more active than primitive liberal or social Darwinist models suggest, but compared to what it would become in the twentieth century, it was very limited. And it was seen by the masses, in cities and on the farms, as dominated by business.

When the Depression, began, then, the state was generally perceived as limited in its market role and oriented toward business elites. Labor and agriculture had a variety of grounds for seeing the state as an instrument of their opponents. Market interventions and the restructuring of the state's links to other social groups could still be presented as new and workable policy. State structure grew and developed with increased state action in the 1930s, and as that happened, the political location of the state changed. The state became linked to a variety of social groups, including labor and agriculture, and it stopped being seen as relatively passive in the economy.

When the crisis of the seventies began, therefore, the political meaning of state action had changed. Activism was the incumbent philosophy, and the catchall welfare state had replaced the night watchman state. The state had never stopped helping capitalists, but now it was harder to portray it as serving capitalists alone. When economic troubles emerged, it became possible to argue that the problem was located deep in the incumbent model of state-society relations, in an active state that gave a strong voice to workers and the welfare poor.

So the political location of state action has changed from crisis to crisis. At the same time the articulation of state institutions has charged. States have varied widely in their organizational and constitutionalist forms, and they still do, but all states have developed large bureaucracies and massive capacities for intervention. The pattern of that development has not been linear; states have expanded their capacities and contracted them. Even the American state constructed extensive new capabilities during both world wars, only to dismantle them afterward. Institutional capabilities can thus be the products of creation or the products of destruction, according to the state of political conflict at a specific moment.

At any given decision point the presence or absence of institutional

228

machinery may play some role in the political struggle—if an apparatus exists, it does not have to be created. The French have techniques of financial intervention, for example, which the British or Americans would have to create, and the effort to do so would create a political battle separate from the content of the policy issue. Once machinery exists, moreover, it acquires its own lobby for use. French energy policy, for example, may be interpreted as expressing the inclinations of the energy-sector civil service to use its capacities. Nationalization may seem a more plausible option in a country whose state bureaucracy has a high reputation for competence.

Rules operate in a manner similar to bureaucratic machinery. A constitution may express the politics of the moment, but once in place it shapes the strengthening or weakening of social groupings. Rules can be changed, but the fight will take resources and may drain energy from a policy quarrel.

State institutions, both the rules and the machinery, affect policy battles in ways that we can trace by examining the relationship between the state and the societal actors with which it interacts. With political support, rules and institutions can be changed: Hitler is the most spectacular example of a leader who brought about change, but de Gaulle and Bismarck are others. Even in the absence of major change, the same institutions can be used for different purposes according to the political mobilization of the officeholders, as the policy shifts from de Gaulle to Giscard and from Giscard to Mitterrand, or from LBJ to Reagan, illustrate. The behavior of state institutions is colored by the outlook of those who staff them, which is in turn linked to social background, education, and social cohesion: the "Prussian" nature of army, bureaucracy, and judiciary at the time of Weimar stands out in one obvious example.

In shaping policy, societal actors and the state interact; the one requires the other. The interaction of societal actors is affected by the rules and institutions through which they act. But the impact of rules and institutions depends on who tries to use them and for what purposes. Many proponents of each argument tend to underplay the importance of the other and often do so by blurring their position to include an important factor that is actually distinct unto itself: the intermediate associations of parties and interest groups.

Associations

As the relationship between state and society has changed, so has the way that associations mediate that relationship. With the growth of mass politics, organization matters more; with the expansion of the state, the structures that link society to the state matter more. From the first crisis to the third, therefore, the role of associations has increased, and with it their role in explaining outcomes.

As the political location of state action has changed from crisis to crisis, so the articulation of state institutions and their importance has changed. As the state's activism in the economy has grown, so has the role of social groupings in that activism. The state, that is to say, may be more active, more able to intervene, but it is not necessarily stronger or more autonomous from society. Indeed, its interventions frequently require the complicity of forces it seeks to regulate or direct. State action is frequently corporatistic, in that state and groups borrow from each other the authority to do what they cannot do alone.

As this has happened the machinery that links state and societal actors has grown in importance, and the variance among countries on that point has also grown. At the onset of the first crisis, in the last third of the nineteenth century, organizations were relatively weak. Functional interests worked directly on politics and policy debate in a relatively unmediated way, and outcomes could be inferred fairly directly from the struggles of societal actors. Moreover, organizations shifted positions rapidly as their members' preferences shifted with new economic situations; the changes in Germany during the 1870s form the most spectactular example.

The struggle over policy itself rewarded organization. The late nineteenth century was a period of considerable developments in mass politics. Universal suffrage, the growth of cities, and ever-larger factories combined with severe battles over policy, both economic and other, to induce a race to organize. The payoff was large and the process correspondingly rapid. The organizational space was relatively open, amenable to varying outcomes, but by the end of the century the organizational "vacuum" was filled in and the space preempted.[5] Parties and interest groups had shaped the political landscape in Europe and North America, and subsequent issues and groups would henceforth have to deal with them. These existing structures mediated relations between society and the state quite strongly.

In the story of the second crisis, the Depression of the 1930s, parties and interest groups loom much larger than in the first. In the United Kingdom one has to note the fight within the Labour party of Ramsay MacDonald, the tactics of Lloyd George and John Maynard Keynes. In Germany one cannot ignore the raiding by Hitler of parties and interest groups, the relations between unions and Social Democrats, and the effectiveness of strikes in stopping the Kapp

Putsch of 1920 contrasted with the absence of strikes in 1932. Sweden saw negotiations between Agrarians and the SAP, and the trilateral discussions at Saltsjöbaden. The Communist party switched tactics in the France of 1936; union organizations and farm and industrial producer associations were crucial in the United States. The list could continue, but the message is clear: party and interest group organizations interacted in complex ways with societal actors to produce policy and political results.

Societal actors had to act through parties and associations that had their own agendas, goals, and categories. Sometimes, when these organizations were unresponsive to members' pressures, their troops would desert for another group, as Hitler's successes demonstrate most spectacularly. Many forms of action operated independently of organizational behavior, of course, capital flight or passivity, wildcat strikes, and voting among them, but as union-party relations in the United Kingdom and Germany suggest, societal groups were often restrained in action by their organization commitments. Organizations shaped how their members interpreted the choices that they faced, just as church and union "shielded" Catholics and organized workers from Nazi appeal.[6]

The role of parties and interest groups in this second crisis lay in mediating the bargaining among societal actors. With that crisis, new policies were devised which increased the role of these associations in forming and implementing policy, with consequences for the third crisis. The policy responses of all countries to the Depression greatly extended state activism in the economy, particularly in "corporatist" directions. From agriculture to oil, from health to transportation, whole areas of the economy were structured by a variety of regulatory devices. State activism extends state power, of course, but it also extends the leverage that social groups can exert on the exercise of that power. Groups become involved in their own regulation as the need for advice and consent gives them considerable power. States and groups borrow authority from each other, and each thereby acquires an ability to influence the other.

The structures set up to manage policy are themselves important allocators of power. Decisions about who is represented, how, and with what perquisites affect how policy is formed and implemented. Regulatory mechanisms differ considerably across countries in extent, type, and content. It is outside our sample of five countries that the most extensive corporatist arrangements are to be found in postwar Europe—in Austria, where every major interest group and political party has its institutional place, not only in consultation but in decision making and the allocation of resources.[7] Major and minor decisions on the economy are made not by the free market, whether political or economic, but by a constant bargaining. Among our five, Sweden comes closest to this corporatist extreme. At the opposite pole is the United States, where no general mechanism exists for collective decision making among societal actors. But even there, such mechanisms have been brought to bear, de jure or de facto, on large areas of economic life.

With the growing importance of associations in shaping the behaviors of societal actors and participating in the actual making and implementation of policy, differences among associations have come to play a greater role in accounting for choice of policy. The differences among corporatist mechanisms derive from the different politics of the various countries, but the result makes for other differences in subsequent policy debates. Three features of associations seem particularly important: the institutionalization of corporatist policy bargaining, the formal systems of party and interest group organization, and the substantive programs and strategies to which these groups are attached.

Mercantilist policy approaches have a far harder time in the United States than in Sweden or Austria, because the mechanisms that they require have to be created. When Felix Rohatyn worked out a solution to the fiscal crisis of New York City through tripartite negotiations, he was actually inventing the machinery. In calling for the same thing at the national level, he and like-minded people face the same problem: creating the necessary mechanisms would generate its own political quarrel over the distribution of power, a quarrel separate from debate over the purpose for which the mechanism would be used.

Not only is the tissue of corporatist mechanisms different among countries; so also, more directly, are the systems of party and interest group. In Sweden the labor unions are centralized and comprehensive in scope; in the United Kingdom, fragmented and parcelized; and in France, split among political parties. Similar differences can be explored for other interest groups, in business and in agriculture. Some policies require collective agreements among societal actors, and fragmented systems are less likely to produce them. High levels of competition among interest groups may prevent the identification and attainment of positive-sum games. Egotism, as several theorists have shown, may lead to cooperation, but institutional mechanisms are likely to make some difference to the chances of doing so. The probability that the United States will adopt mercantilist policies is thus diminished, not only by the absence of formal state institutions suited to such policies but also by the absence of mechanisms to link interest groups to the state and by the low levels of concentration among interest groups themselves.[8]

This feature of associations is formalistic, in that it focuses on the structure of parties and groups rather than the "content" of their political and economic outlook. It is this content, the understandings to which parties and groups are attached, which integrates associations internally and shapes their responses to policy debates. The difference among labor-allied parties is not simply a formal one of organizational characteristics but also a matter of strategy and ideology. The United States has no communist party of any significance, nor even much of a socialist party; France has both. As a consequence, nationalization and other types of intervention have a far greater chance of becoming policy in France than in the United States.

Intermediate associations have become more important in shaping policy, and so their internal properties are of consequence. Like the other variables, they have their own rigidities and continuities, but they are also mechanisms created by politics, not immutable features of the landscape. Like the institutions of the state, they can be created and dismantled, mutate and be transformed, torn down and built up. The effects of institutions, in sum, are not automatic: there is a politics to their creation, maintenance, and use.

Economic Ideology

As the importance of organizations has grown with growth of the state, so the importance of ideology has grown in accounting for the purposes to which organizational power is put. Economic reality is rarely so clear that objective circumstances impose themselves on behavior with no mediation from ideas. The tools for analyzing economic situations have grown from one crisis to another, and many current ways of thinking about problems did not exist a century ago. Yet there is little reason to think that the dismal science is better able to control the myriad considerations of politics which affect policy than it was a hundred years ago.

Economic theory did not stop the Junkers from abandoning three centuries of free trade in the 1870s, did not stop Congress from passing Hawley-Smoot in 1930 over the objections of one thousand economists, and has not stopped the growth of nontariff barriers in the 1980s. That is one set of examples to set against the purported explanatory power of economic theory. But the issue here is not economic theory as practized by specialists; it is the role of economic ideas in the forum of political debate. And it is certainly possible to find instances where ideas matter, even if no secular change occurs. The choice of policy by the Socialist government in 1981 was surely connected to the development of ideas in the French left and more important, in the ideas held by organizations that represent the French left. The policy shifts of Ronald Reagan and Margaret Thatcher are connected to the evolution of argument in the conservative movements of their countries. The sociology of those movements is important, but the idea systems that they hold and express help in themselves to shape public understandings of options. Nationalization may be self-destructive for France, and supply-side egotism may prove costly for America. But these arguments have effects in shaping the universe of alternatives from which other groups— societal actors and electors—have to choose.

Ideas also play an important role in forming and integrating social coalitions. Policies require bargains, explicit or de facto. Usually these bargains require the burying of one set of contradictions or points of conflict in order to draw out points held in common along another dimension. Ideologies help construct these coalitions by providing a framework of collective purpose, obscuring egotistical goals for a larger common good, minimizing elements of conflict, drawing out realms of agreement.

Each of the major economic policy alternatives examined here models society differently. Each has a different conception of groups and their interests. Each thereby provides different signals to politicians in need of strategies for the mobilization of support. Politicians may pick political strategies as a function of economic ideology, as in the cases of Hilferding and Snowden; or they may be more adaptive and look for economic ideologies that enable them to adopt different political strategies, as did figures as diverse as Wigfors, Roosevelt, and Hitler. In either case, economic ideology provides important cues for analyzing both political and policy options.

International System

The central concern of this book is to account for the ways in which countries respond to changes in the international system. What degrees of freedom do units have in shaping their behavior within the system of which they and their behavior are a part? And to the extent that degrees of freedom exist, what explains choice within that system?

Interdependence, the involvement of countries in an international economy, is certainly an old phenomenon; so are its effects. From the first crisis examined here to the present one, the international division of labor has intensified. More and more countries have come to rely on specialization to increase living standards, and more and more are thereby "dependent" on the international economy, and hence subject to its pressures. More specialization means more dependence, and this means that the international economy presses ever more heavily on its units. Countries are, in a sense, smaller, less able to control the environment that bears on their future. Currency devaluations demonstrate this claim forcefully: no country has escaped that pressure, not even the world's largest economy, that of the United States.

As the largest economy, the United States has the greatest degree of control over its fate. More than any other country it shapes the system of which it is a part. More than any other country, it can afford its mistakes or can even exert the power to convert them to soundness. What the United States does depends therefore very greatly on its internal decisions.

But even the small countries, such as Sweden, have some leeway. The international system rewards some behaviors, punishes others, yet countries do not automatically choose the actions that lead to rewards. Sometimes they tilt the other way and suffer. Meeting the demands of the system thus requires explanation. All the small countries may have developed corporatist mechanisms for managing their relations with the international economy, and smallness may increase the chances that domestic actors will see the advantages of such a strategy. But smallness does not guarantee that they will. Contemporary Lebanon is perhaps the most obvious recent example.

Domestic politics thus matters in the shaping of responses to the international economy, even where these responses are intense. The convergence of policy behaviors toward neoclassical approaches does not disconfirm this argument: convergence despite partisan variance demonstrates the constraints that the international economy imposes, but it does so by pressing governments to worry about the same political effects. All governments seek some kind of prosperity; all governments have to worry about market confidence. As a consequence all governments accept market-induced austerity—the impact of the system on governments passes through politics.

The international economy presses on individual countries, and it does so through working on domestic actors. It is these domestic actors who are affected by changes in international market conditions

235

and who, as result, seek changes in national policy. To understand how nations respond to changes in the international economy, therefore, we cannot seek simply to correlate attributes of the country as a whole with policy behavior. Rather, we must disaggregate, to ascertain who advances one or another understanding of how the country should respond. And that leads back to the explanations of domestic politics explored above.

This reasoning about international-domestic linkages applies to the other main dimension of the international system, political-military pressures. Military rivalries have effects similar to those of the market: countries are involved in a competitive struggle for the rewards of military capability. More crudely than the market, with fewer "events" testing military competence, political-military relations press countries into considering the security implications of all issues, including economic policy.

From the first crisis to the third, military considerations have always been involved in economic policy debates. In each case, military situations have reinforced or weakened one policy option or another. Size also matters here, too. Sweden could not try an imperialist solution to its problems; the other countries could and did. Tariffs, government contracts, mercantilism, demand management—all sorts of policies have been justified by security considerations.

But the leeway for individual countries has nonetheless been large, for security problems have always been susceptible to very different interpretations. Within each country, actors have quarreled over what the security problems are and what should be done about them. Like questions of economics, international security issues thus affect countries through the "agency" of actors within each nation. Arguments win because their proponents have the power to prevail.

Arguments over security are partly a matter of competing conceptions of the world. They are also arguments for political advantage and material gain. The reality of international tensions mingles with the quarrels of place and position. Spending on guns has effects on the economy. It increases both general demand and the demand for specific goods produced by specific sectors and firms. It can comprise de facto versions of countercyclical, protectionist, and mercantilist policies, and even nationalization policies, especially by governments whose rhetoric rejects each of these courses of action.

The political location of extensive military spending in periods of economic difficulty is not random. In all three crises, it is far more likely to emerge from the right than from the left. There have been

236

cases of left-wing nationalism and left-wing support for national defense, but by and large left and center-left solutions to economic difficulties focus on the redistribution of income and power, on social welfare programs, on protectionism and market regulation. From Bismarck to Reagan, military spending has been a way of intervening in the economy used by actors who on other grounds deny the ligitimacy of state action in the economy. In each case, military issues linked to nationalism have undercut leftist programs for social spending or redistributive approaches to economic ills. Long before Keynes, military Keynesianism was a reality, a way of helping industries in trouble which was quite different from the civilian way. Military approaches gain ground, moreover, in periods of economic difficulty: orders for battleships increased when the railroad boom ran out, regional imperialisms increased in importance when the reconstruction after World War I ran out, military buildup continued when the strong years of the postwar boom went into decline. There are always many factors involved in the expansion of military spending, but the utility of such expenditures in aiding certain industries and in blocking certain types of reform is undeniable.

Here we see how size and geographical location contribute to economic policy debate. In Sweden arguments for a military Keynesian solution to national ills could not be plausibly made in the thirties because of the country's size. In the United States, geographical isolation had the same effect. World War II did more than domestic policy initiatives to end the Depression in the United States, but war did not arise from internal American politics. That war rendered geographical isolation impossible, and with American activism in international politics, the balance has shifted quite dramatically. Reagan has been able to increase the role of the state in the economy, increase fiscal stimulus, extend protection through military purchasing, sustain an industrial policy through military procurement, and even effectively nationalize certain companies wholly involved in military production, all the while attacking the notion of active state involvement in the economy.

Oddly, many analysts of political economy treat military spending as deriving wholly from strategic calculations, not as an instrument in itself of economic policy or political advantage. Although strategic issues are certainly involved, the historical record indicates that such an approach is seriously distorted. Strategic conceptions, like economic ideas, have a claim to independence from other goals and processes no greater than that of any other motives. International military pressures, like international economic pressures, turn on analyses of the world which are themselves part of a broader struggle of political economy.

POLITICS AND THE SOCIAL BASES OF THE AUTONOMOUS STATE

In exploring the politics of choosing an economic policy to respond to international economic crisis, I have put particular emphasis on the political problem of mobilizing support. Politicians sitting at the center of state decision making must find support for policies from a number of actors who have varying modes of resistance or assistance at their disposal. No policy act is without the need for support, and all ways of getting support come with a price tag attached—they all have opportunity costs. Where the state has massive coercive powers, it is often unable to elicit initiative. Where the state permits considerable freedom, it often has difficulties that stem from the need for coordination.

The state's autonomy or the lack thereof, the power of society or its lack of power, both turn on the interaction between goals and systems of decision making. In this sense, the autonomy of the state has a social base: for state autonomy to exist for specific purposes, the state must be able to obtain support, of differing kinds, from societal actors. The strong state is one with the political support to be strong, a state with the compliance or enthusiasm of at least some societal actors that support the actions of strength. When that support disappears, so does state strength.

By starting with state actors, with politicians, it is possible to trace the impact of societal actors on decision making without tumbling into the traps to which such approaches are often vulnerable. Politicians make decisions. To do so, they need support, but whose and how is that support manifested? By linking alternative policies to alternative support coalitions in different countries, it is possible to probe the effects that societal actors do or do not have in constraining or influencing politicians and policy choices.

Often the societal actors tradition of explanation tries to "derive" policy from a group or groups: one defines a set of groups, looks at a policy, and draws links from one to the other. The critique of that approach properly focuses on the many ambiguities and uncertainties of who wants what and how. And the societal actors approach frequently derives cause from an analysis of benefits, leading to deserved criticism concerning unintended consequences. But that exchange of assertions and critiques misses a crucial relationship, the one between the policies chosen and the groups whose support or compliance is needed to carry it out—more broadly, between the goals of the decision makers and the goals of societal actors.

Policies require politics. Politicians have goals and look for policies that suit them; societal actors have goals and look for the politics that suits them.[9] Stitching these elements together is the task of politics, the creative construction of choices of value and the authority to realize those choices, or "the authoritative allocation of value" in David Easton's apt formulation. To understand those linkages requires the analyst to work from both ends of the chain, to examine both politicians seeking to construct coalitions, and actors seeking benefits.

I have argued in this book that freedom of politicians is circumbscribed by their need to construct support coalitions. Just what are the limits they face? Metaphors are more telling than indicators. On one side is an image borrowed from plate tectonics: huge blocks pushed by magma, sluggish and slow-moving, hard to maneuver, hard to shift, changing course massively but rarely, possessed of considerable inertia. By such an analogy, politicians are greatly constrained. There may be moments of open choice, like earthquakes or volcanic eruptions, when concrete action can affect the direction in which the elements move, but even these allow choice only within sharply conscribed limits. Or there is an image borrowed from the play of children, of toy sailboats on a shallow park pond: small pieces, light, with shallow drafts, very maneuverable, easily moved, responding to the lightest touch or breeze. By such an analogy, politicians have great freedom. Not only are there moments of choice, but there is considerable play in where social groups can be pushed or guided.[10]

The aptness of each metaphor turns on an attitude toward history. Analytically, it may indeed be possible to identify the choices made by countless human actors (the breezes that move the sailboat). But those choices are likely to be heuristic constructs, imposed by the observer. Sociologically, actors are not so free. Commitments once made tend to persist; they are hard to change in practice, even if in analytical terms the observer may see the possibility of choice.

Students of the U.S. Congress have observed that two senators of quite different ideological coloration and policy bent have often managed to represent the same constituency at one time: senators Douglas and Dirksen from Illinois, for instance, or senators Cranston and Wilson from California. Politicians appear to have considerable leeway in defining how they are to be judged and hence in defining the pressures to which they are subject. Once they have made their choices, however, they will find it very difficult to switch. The choices are shaped by the system in which politicians operate, and those systems are very sluggish and hard to change (the sluggish movement of geological plates).

The moments of greatest freedom are crisis points, and that is why I have focused this book on crises. Choices are more constrained in stable times, but stability makes analysis easier by producing stable systems. In moments of flux, on the other hand, choices widen, but analysis becomes more complicated because relationships change.

Crisis are times of danger, as the career of Adolf Hitler constantly reminds us. But they are also moments for hope, as Swedish social democracy suggests. The future always requires imagination: politicians require imagination to find new ways of linking policy goals to coalitions; social scientists require imagination to conceptualize policy options, social categories, ideologies and structures, and the various ways that these elements may combine. I tend to favor the metaphor of plate tectonics, but that proclivity is the pessimistic side of a hope in the possible. My optimistic side favors the metaphor of sailboats on a pond: it sees choice and has heroes. In this tale my heroes are those activists who thought up combinations that linked progressive political ideals with the realities of markets and power: Wigfors in Sweden, Woytinski in Germany, Bevin and Keynes in the United Kingdom, and, in the United States, FDR. Alas, creativity can be demonic in a Hitler or a Stalin. But even the demons have lessons to teach; and from them we can learn whether there are ways to avoid them.

Notes

Chapter 1. *The Politics of Economic Policy*

1. Andrew Shonfield, *Modern Capitalism* (London: Oxford University Press, 1965), is one of the best-known accounts of the emergence and extension of the postwar approach to macroeconomic policy. Sequels to this important book are Shonfield's *The Uses of Public Power* (Oxford: Oxford University Press, 1982), and *In Defence of the Mixed Economy*, ed. Zuzanna Shonfield (Oxford University Press, 1984). For comprehensive analyses of different responses to the 1970s and 1980s, see the work in progress of Jeffrey Sachs, Dept. of Economics, Harvard University, and Fritz Scharpf of the Free University of Berlin. For example, Michael Bruno with Jeffrey Sachs, *Economics and Worldwide Stagflation* (Cambridge: Harvard University Press, 1985); Fritz Scharpf, "Economic and Institutional Constraints of Full Employment Strategies: Sweden, Austria, and West Germany, 1973–1982," in John Goldthorpe, ed., *Order and Conflict in Contemporary Capitalism* (Oxford: Oxford University Press, 1984).

2. In discussing coalitions I draw on a diverse tradition: Barrington Moore, Jr., *Social Origins of Dictatorship and Democracy* (Boston: Beacon, 1966); Alexander Gerschenkron, *Bread and Democracy in Germany* (1943; New York: Fertig, 1966); Walter Dean Burnham, *Critical Elections and the Mainsprings of the American Party System* (New York: Norton, 1970); and other applications of this approach to specific situations.

3. References on these approaches appear in Chapter 2, notes 14–18.

4. On each crisis period and country see the references in Chapters 3–5.

Chapter 2. *Explaining Policy Choices*

1. The different meanings of the term "liberal" pose problems. The European usage refers to a tradition of individualism and sympathy for the market, whereas the American usage refers to progressive social policies and market intervention. I have tried to avoid the confusion by using "classical"; it

evokes time rather than substance but will be less confusing than "liberal." My typology of policy options and my general thoughts on economic doctrines have been influenced by a wide variety of sources. I continue to admire the first book I read on economic doctrines, Robert Heilbronner's *The Worldly Philosophers* (New York: Simon & Schuster, 1953). See also David Landes, *The Unbound Prometheus* (Cambridge: Cambridge University Press, 1969); H. W. Arndt, *The Economic Lessons of the 1930s* (Oxford: Oxford University Press, 1944); Andrew Shonfield, *Modern Capitalism* (London: Oxford University Press, 1965); and the literature debating Swedish economic policy in the 1930s (see Chapter 4, notes 4–7).

2. On the product cycle see Raymond Vernon, *Sovereignty at Bay* (New York: Basic, 1971), and James Kurth, "The Political Consequences of the Product Cycle: Industrial History and Political Outcomes," *International Organization* 33 (Winter 1979), 1–34.

3. Many nonsocialists, from Veblen to Galbraith, have made such criticisms of capitalism, showing that indeed advanced capitalism does not wish to live fully by the logic of the market but, rather, tries to plan, allocate, control, and stabilize. See also Robert H. Weibe, *The Search for Order; 1877–1920* (New York: Hill & Wang, 1966), and the German discussion of "organized capitalism," especially Heinrich Winkler, *Organizierte Capitalismus* (Gottingen: Vandenhoeck & Ruprecht, 1974).

4. On German and British steel tariffs see Stephen B. Webb, "Tariff Protection for the Iron Industry, Cotton Textiles and Agriculture in Germany, 1879–1914," *Jahrbucher für Nationalökonomie und Statistik* 192, nos. 3–4 (1977), 336–57.

5. Thus devaluation has an effect similar to that of raising tariffs: the price of imports rises while that of exports declines. If export production depends very heavily on imported materials, the higher cost of inputs may wipe out the advantage of cheaper finished export goods.

6. Classic on the difference timing makes for the environment for industrialization is Alexander Gerschenkron, "Economic Backwardness in Historical Perspective," in his *Economic Backwardness in Historical Perspective* (Cambridge: Harvard University Press, 1962). The dependencia literature is vast; see the references in my review essay on the international influences upon domestic politics: "The Second Image Reversed," *International Organization* 32 (Autumn 1978), 881–912.

7. On the relation between the market and military manufacturing see William H. McNeill, *The Pursuit of Power* (Chicago: University of Chicago Press, 1982).

8. I do not label this policy option Keynesianism, because I wish to separate it from its most famous theoretician. Giving the option his name implies a statement of cause (from theory to policy) which is debatable.

9. John A. Hobson, *Imperialism: A Study* (1902; Ann Arbor: University of Michigan Press, 1965).

10. "Mercantilism" has a classical reference to the flow of bullion—countries increased wealth by getting more of a fixed quantity of bullion from other countries, which they could do through government aid to manufacturing. In modern usage this historical referent has all but disappeared. Other terms often used in connection with this type of policy include corporatism, industrial policy, and sectoral policy.

11. See Charles Kindleberger, "The Postwar Resurgence of the French Economy," in Stanley Hoffmann et al., eds., *In Search of France* (Cambridge: Harvard University Press, 1963), and Richard Kuisel, *Capitalism and the State in Modern France* (Cambridge: Cambridge University Press, 1981).

12. Chalmers Johnson, *MITI and the Japanese Miracle: The Growth of Industrial Policy, 1925–75* (Stanford: Stanford University Press, 1982). See also the effort by Daniel Okimoto to sort out how the role of the Japanese state varies according to type of industry and its linkage to politics, in *Between MITI and the Market* (Stanford: Stanford University Press, forthcoming).

13. E. E. Schattschneider, *Politics, Pressure Groups and the Tariff* (1935; Hamden, Conn.: Archon, 1963).

14. The classic sources of this approach include Bentley and Marx. The argument over "reductionism"—whether this approach "reduces" politics to interests, and the costs of so doing—is as old as the approach itself. Treatments of U.S. politics dealing with these issues include Theodore Lowi, *The End of Liberalism: Ideology, Policy and the Crisis of Public Authority* (New York: Norton, 1969), and Grant McConnell, *Private Power and American Democracy* (New York: Knopf, 1966).

15. In American discourse the locus classicus for the importance of "intermediate associations" is Alexis de Tocqueville and his explorations of the difference between the American and French systems in *Democracy in America* and *The Old Regime*. Stanley Hoffmann, in lectures on French politics at Harvard University, has called such associations "transmission belts"; see also Hoffmann's "Paradoxes of the French Political Community," in Hoffmann et al., *In Search of France*.

With the phrase "policy networks," Peter Katzenstein combines state institutions with intermediate associations such as parties and interest groups. He thereby helps simplify matters, using one dimension to differentiate polities, but like all useful simplifications, this one has some cost: institutions such as bureaucracies and rules do not necessarily fit together with transmission belts. They do so most clearly in the highly corporatist states but not in the more "pluralized" ones. See Katzenstein's essays in *Between Power and Plenty: Foreign Economic Policies of Advanced Industrial States* (Madison: University of Wisconsin Press, 1978), as well as his recent books on the smaller European democracies: *Corporatism and Change: Austria, Switzerland, and the Politics of Industry* (Ithaca: Cornell University Press, 1984), and *Small States in World Markets: Industrial Policy in Europe* (Ithaca: Cornell University Press, 1985).

The literature on corporatism has increased the attention given to intermediate associations and thus stimulated valuable research on the structure of these associations. Less clear at times is ability to demonstrate clear linkages between these structures and policy outcomes. Philippe Schmitter has done a great deal of work on corporatism; see, among other sources, his "Interest Intermediation and Regime Governability in Contemporary Western Europe and North America," in *Organizing Interests in Western Europe*, ed. Suzanne Berger (New York: Cambridge University Press, 1981). For a strong statement of the policy effects of these structures, see Mancur Olson, *The Rise and Decline of Nations* (New Haven: Yale University Press, 1982). For criticism of Olson's findings, see among others Ronald Rogowski, "Structure, Growth, and Power," *International Organization* 37 (Autumn 1983), 713–38.

16. Theda Skocpol has emphasized this variable, particularly in recent

work comparing the development of welfare systems in different countries. See Margaret Weir and Skocpol, "State Structures and the Possibilities for 'Keynesian' Responses to the Great Depression in Sweden, Britain and the United States," in *Bringing the State Back In,* ed. Peter Evans, Dietrich Rueschmeyer, and Skocpol (Cambridge: Cambridge University Press, 1985), 107–68.

17. For example, Charles Kindleberger, "The Rise of Free Trade in Western Europe, 1820–1875," *Journal of Economic History* 35 (1975), 20–55.

18. One classic statement is Otto Hintze, "Military Organization and the Organization of the State," in *The Historical Essays of Otto Hintze,* ed. Felix Gilbert (New York: Oxford University Press, 1975). See also my "Second Image Reversed."

19. See Richard Neustadt, *Presidential Power: The Politics of Leadership* (New York: Wiley, 1960).

20. How to conceptualize society remains a root controversy of political sociology. Most analysts of elections in the United States see society as a mass of individuals: see Angus Campbell et al., *The American Voter* (New York: Wiley, 1960); Anthony Downs, *An Economic Theory of Democracy* (New York: Harper & Row, 1957); and Sam Popkin et al., "What Have You Done for Me Lately? Toward an Investment Theory of Voting," *American Political Science Review* 70 (September 1976), 779–805.

Conceptualizations of class derive from Marx, strongly influenced by political economists of his day, and from Max Weber, particularly the well-known essay "Class, Status and Party." Some contemporary authors stress the class context of individual action. In the voting tradition see Douglas Hibbs, "Political Parties and Macroeconomic Policy," *American Political Science Review* 71 (1977), 1467–87, and Robert Alford, "Class Voting in the Anglo-American Political Systems," in S. M. Lipset and Stein Rokkan, eds., *Party Systems and Voter Alignments* (New York: Free, 1967).

Society seen as groups derives, among other sources, from the old "functionalists," as Samuel Beer calls them in *British Politics in the Collectivist Age* (New York: Random House, 1965)—the old Tory and Whig theorists who spoke of major functions in society and those who carried them out. A contemporary version of this approach stresses "sectors" in the economy or major product families in industry and agriculture. Alexander Gerschenkron uses this approach in *Bread and Democracy in Germany* (1943; New York: Fertig, 1966), as have other economic historians, such as Landes, *Unbound Prometheus,* and Erik Dahmen, *Entrepreneurial Activity and the Development of Swedish Industry, 1919–1939,* trans. Axel Leijonhufvud (Homewood, Ill.: Irwin, 1970). See the very imaginative essay using the sectoral approach by James R. Kurth, "The Political Consequences of the Product Cycle: Industrial History and Political Outcomes," *International Organization* 33 (Winter 1979), 1–34.

21. See Gerschenkron, *Bread and Democracy,* and William Appelman Williams, *Roots of the Modern American Empire* (New York: Random House, 1969).

22. Stephen Webb makes this point in his discussion of competition between German and British steel at the turn of the century. (See references in Chapter 3, note 16). See the discussion of stable demand and Fordism vs. fluctuating demand and flexible adaptation in Michael Piore and Charles Sabel, *The Second Industrial Divide* (New York: Basic, 1985).

23. So argue Tom Ferguson, "From Normalcy to New Deal: Industrial Structure, Party Competition, and American Public Policy in the Great Depression," *International Organization* 38 (Winter 1984), 41–94, and David Abraham, *The Collapse of the Weimer Republic* (Princeton: Princeton University Press, 1981).

24. See Piore and Sabel, *Second Industrial Divide*, and McNeill, *Pursuit of Power*.

25. On the role of banking structures in shaping policy see Gerschenkron, "Economic Backwardness"; Kurth, "Political Consequences of the Product Cycle"; and John Zysman, *Government, Markets and Growth: Financial Systems and the Politics of Industrial Change* (Ithaca: Cornell University Press, 1984).

26. See Gerschenkron, *Bread and Democracy;* Williams, *Roots of the Modern American Empire;* Lowi, *End of Liberalism;* and McConnell, *Private Power.*

27. John Goldthorpe and David Lockwood, *The Affluent Worker in the Class Structure* (Cambridge: Cambridge University Press, 1969).

28. See Robert Dahl, *Preface to Modern Democratic Theory* (Chicago: University of Chicago Press, 1956). His discussion remains the clearest treatment of such problems as circularity and tautology.

29. Various words are used in the discussion of intermediate groupings: "interest groups" and "social forces" have been frequently used in the past. Each makes a conceptual point, and each has become associated with political tendencies as well. The phrase "interest groups" means both the category of people with a particular interest or point of view and the organization that represents them; it downplays the existence of a "function" or a form of power which shapes outcomes independently of any conscious group action. The phrase "social forces" does exactly that, but at the expense of bypassing the organizations that give voice to the form of power or point of view. The latter phrase has been used by Marxists, the former by American pluralist theorists critical of Marxism. To avoid the highly charged associations of each, I use "societal actors."

30. See note 15 above for the writings of Stanley Hoffmann.

31. See Weir and Skocpol, "State Structures."

32. On the last distinction see Stephen Krasner, *Defending the National Interest* (Princeton: Princeton University Press, 1978).

33. Kenneth Waltz, *Man, the State and War* (New York: Columbia University Press, 1959).

34. See Gourevitch, "Second Image Reversed."

35. Fernando Henrique Cardoso and Enzo Faletto, *Dependency and Development in Latin America* (Berkeley: University of California Press, 1979); Theotonio dos Santos, "The Structure of Dependence," *American Economic Review* 60 (May 1970), 231–36.

36. Hintze, "Military Organization."

37. See especially McNeill, *Pursuit of Power.*

38. See André Gunder Frank, *Capitalism and Underdevelopment in Latin America* (New York: Monthly Review, 1967), and Immanuel Wallerstein, *The Modern World System: Capitalist Agriculture and the Origins of the European World-Economy in the Sixteenth Century* (New York: Academic, 1974).

39. Cf. Arend Lijphart, "Comparative Politics and the Comparative Method," *American Political Science Review* 65 (1971), 682–93.

40. The first may be called Marshallian after the theorist of business cycles;

the second, Schumpeterian after one of the pioneers of structural interpretations of the economy.

Chapter 3. *Protectionism and Free Trade: The Crisis of 1873–96*

1. In his analysis of the product cycle and economic cycles, James Kurth correctly begins the sequence earlier than I do, with the difficult years of the 1840s. To economize on space, time, and energy, I begin with the 1870s. See Kurth, "The Political Consequences of the Product Cycle: Industrial History and Political Outcomes," *International Organization* 33 (Winter 1979), 1–34.

2. Charles Kindleberger, "The Rise of Free Trade in Western Europe, 1820–1875," *Journal of Economic History* 35 (1975), 20–55.

3. See Hans Rosenberg, "The Depression of 1873–1896 in Central Europe," *Journal of Economic History* 13 (1943), 58–73; Joseph Schumpeter, *Business Cycles* (New York: McGraw Hill, 1939); Charles P. Kindleberger, "Group Behavior and International Trade," *Journal of Political Economy* 59 (1951), 30–46; David Landes, *The Unbound Prometheus* (Cambridge: Cambridge University Press, 1969); S. B. Saul, *The Myth of the Great Depression* (New York: Humanities, 1969); W. W. Rostow, *The British Economy of the 19th Century* (Oxford: Oxford University Press, 1948); and Peter Flora, *State, Economy and Society in Western Europe*, vol. 1 (London: Macmillan, 1983).

4. Immanuel Wallerstein, *The Modern World System: Capitalist Agriculture and the Origins of the European World-Economy in the Sixteenth Century* (New York: Academic, 1974). It would be interesting to compare the responses of the "plains countries," exploring the consequences of different types of industrial "presences" (strong domestic capital, foreign capital, shippers, and bankers) in the United States, Russia, Argentina, Canada, Australia, and elsewhere. See Theodore H. Moran, "The Development of Argentina and Australia: The Radical Party of Argentina and the Labor Party of Australia in the Process of Economic and Political Development," *Comparative Politics* 3 (1970), 71–92. It would also be stimulating to apply the categories of specialized function in the world economy, such as core, semiperiphery, and periphery, worked out by Wallerstein and others. Britain could pursue free trade because it was the core country; the others had to protect. This idea works in a broad way, but it is less useful in matters of timing, especially in explaining why it took Britain so long to react after losing its hegemony. In addition to the works just cited see also Tom Naylor, "The Rise and Fall of the Third Commercial Empire of the St. Lawrence," in *Capitalism and the National Question in Canada*, ed. Gary Teeple (Toronto: University of Toronto Press, 1972); Naylor, *The History of Canadian Business, 1867–1914*, 2 vols. (Toronto: Lorimer, 1975); and Naylor's work in progress, situating Canadian economic development in an international context.

5. See especially Michael Tracy, *Agriculture in Western Europe* (London: Cape, 1964); J. D. Chambers and G. E. Mingay, *The Agricultural Revolution, 1750–1880* (London: Batsford, 1966); and Alexander Gerschenkron, *Bread and Democracy in Germany* (1943; New York: Fertig, 1966).

6. See Landes, *Unbound Prometheus*, 191–94, and E. J. Hobsbawm, *Industry and Empire* (London: Weidenfeld & Nicolson, 1968).

7. Alexander Gerschenkron, "Economic Backwardness in Historical Per-

spective," in his *Economic Backwardness in Historical Perspective* (Cambridge: Harvard University Press, 1962).

8. See cited works by Landes, Aldcroft, Rostow, Saul, Hobsbawm; also Benjamin Brown, *The Tariff Reform Movement in Great Britain, 1881–1895* (New York: Columbia University Press, 1943); J. H. Clapham, *An Economic History of Modern Britain* (Cambridge: Cambridge University Press, 1958); P. J. Perry, ed., *British Agriculture, 1875–1914* (London: Methuen, 1973); Leland Hamilton Jenks, *The Migration of British Capital* (New York: Knopf, 1927); and S. B. Saul, *Studies in British Overseas Trade, 1870–1914* (Liverpool: Liverpool University Press, 1960).

9. Gerschenkron, *Bread and Democracy.*

10. See Chambers and Mingay, *Agricultural Revolution;* C. S. Orwin and E. H. Whetham, *A History of British Agriculture, 1864–1914* (Hamden, Conn.: Archon, 1964). Interestingly, the literature on Britain concentrates not on why there was no restoration of protection in the 1870s but on whether and why agriculture did a poor job of modernizing. One of the reasons offered is the same as that given in the German case—the concentration of ownership meant too few of the middling farmers needed to do the job.

11. Cf. F. M. L. Thompson, *English Landed Society in the 19th Century* (London: Routledge & Kegan Paul, 1963), and Barrington Moore, Jr., *Social Origins of Dictatorship and Democracy* (Boston: Beacon, 1966).

12. See Paul Smith, *Disraelian Conservatism and Social Reform* (London: Routledge & Kegan Paul, 1967), and Robert Blake, *Disraeli* (New York: St. Martin's, 1966). As Benjamin Brown says, "as an imperialist movement, Fair Trade was suspect. The league was never quite able to overcome the impression that many of its members were merely stowaways on the good ship Empire because their own protectionist ship had little prospect of making port" (*Tariff Reform Movement*, p. 89). Later he amplifies the point: "Men became protectionist usually because they wanted to secure their bread and butter; but often because they were Conservatives and wanted ammunition to snipe at Liberals; often because they believed in the empire; and sometimes, indeed because they revered their grandfathers or were members of the Church of England" (p. 102).

13. See P. F. Clarke, *Lancashire and the New Liberalism* (Cambridge: Cambridge University Press, 1971); Smith, *Disraelian Conservatism;* and Blake, *Disraeli.*

14. Important is Christopher Hill, *Puritanism and Revolution* (London: Secker & Warburg, 1958).

15. Kindleberger, "Rise of Free Trade."

16. Robert Gilpin, *U.S. Power and the Multinational Corporation* (New York: Basic, 1975). On the British steel industry see by Steven Webb, "Tariff Protection for the Iron Industry, Cotton Textiles and Agriculture in Germany, 1879–1914," *Jahrbucher für Nationalökonomie und Statistik* 192, nos. 3–4 (1977), 336–57; "Tariffs, Cartels, Technology and Growth in the German Steel Industry, 1879 to 1914," *Journal of Economic History* 40 (March 1980), 309–29; and "Cartels and Business Cycles in Germany, 1800 to 1914," *Zeitschrift für die gesamte Staatswissenchaft* 138 (June 1982), 205–24. See also Robert McCloskey, *Economic Maturity and Entrepreneurial Decline: British Iron and Steel, 1870–1913*, Harvard Economic Series 142 (Cambridge: Harvard University Press, 1973).

17. Cf. Paul Kennedy, *The Rise of the Anglo-German Antagonism, 1860–1914* (London: Allen & Unwin, 1980).

18. Gerschenkron, *Bread and Democracy.*

19. See Einar Jensen, *Danish Agriculture: Its Economic Development* (Copenhagen: Schultz, 1937).

20. On German agriculture see especially Gordon Craig, *Germany, 1866–1945* (Oxford: Clarendon, 1978); Gerschenkron, *Bread and Democracy*, passim; Ivo Lambi, *Free Trade and Protection in Germany, 1868–1896* (Weisbaden: Steiner, 1963); Hans-Jürgen Puhle, *Politische Agrarbewegungen in kapitalistischen Industriegesellschaften: Deutschland, USA und Frankreich im 20. Jarhrhundert* (Gottingen: Vandenhoeck & Ruprecht, 1975); J. Aldon Nichols, *Germany after Bismarck: The Caprivi Era* (Cambridge: Harvard University Press, 1958); and Sarah Tirrell, *German Agrarian Politics after Bismarck's Fall,* Studies in the Social Sciences 566 (New York: Columbia University Press, 1951). On corporatist arguments and peasant organizations see Suzanne Berger, *Peasants against Politics* (Cambridge: Harvard University Press, 1972).

21. Robert G. Moeller, "Peasants and Tariffs in the Kaiserreich: How Backward were the 'Bauern'?" *Agricultural History* 55 (1981), 370–84.

22. See particularly Gerschenkron, *Bread and Democracy.*

23. See Lambi, *Free Trade and Protectionism;* Hans-Ulrich Wehler, "Bismarck's Imperialism, (1862–1890)," *Past and Present* 48 (1970), 119–55, which is a summary of *Bismarck und der Imperialismus* (Cologne: Kiepenheuer & Witsch, 1969); Hartmut Kaelble, *Industrielle Interessenpolitik in der Wilhelminischen Gesellschaft* (Berlin: de Gruyter, 1967); Helmut Böhme, "Big Business Pressure Groups and Bismarck's Turn to Protectionism, 1873–79," *The Historical Journal* 10, 2 (1968), 218–36, which is an abridgement of *Deutschlands Weg zur Grossmacht* (Cologne: Kiepenheuer & Witsch, 1966); David Calleo, *The German Problem Reconsidered: Germany and the World Order, 1870 to the Present* (New York: Cambridge University Press, 1978); and Kenneth D. Barkin, *The Controversy over German Industrialization 1890–1902* (Chicago: University of Chicago Press, 1970).

24. Cf. the discussion of "creating comparative advantage" in John Zysman and Laura Tyson, eds., *American Industry in International Competition: Government Policies and Corporate Strategies* (Ithaca: Cornell University Press, 1983).

25. See works by Webb and McCloskey cited in note 16; Derek Aldcroft, "Introduction: British Industry and Foreign Competition," in *British Industry and Foreign Competition,* ed. Aldcroft (London: Allen & Unwin, 1968), 11–36. See also the discussion about the advantage of supposedly obsolete, smaller, and less capital-intensive economic forms in Michael Piore and Charles Sabel, *The Second Industrial Divide* (New York: Basic, 1985).

26. Cf. Gerschenkron, "Economic Backwardness," and Kurth, "Political Consequences of the Product Cycle."

27. See Nichols, *Germany after Bismarck,* and Tirrell, *German Agrarian Politics.*

28. Böhme, "Big Business Pressure Groups," p. 218.

29. Cf. Samuel P. Huntington, *Political Order in Changing Societies* (New Haven: Yale University Press, 1969); Theda Skocpol, "Bringing Back the State," in *Bringing the State Back In,* ed. Peter B. Evans, Dietrich Rueschmeyer, and Skopol (New York: Cambridge University Press, 1985).

30. See especially Gordon Craig, *The Politics of the Prussian Army, 1640–1945* (New York: Oxford University Press, 1956).

31. Arthur Rosenberg, *Imperial Germany,* trans. Ian Morrow (Boston:

Beacon, 1964); A. J. P. Taylor, *The Course of German History* (New York: Coward-McCann, 1964); Craig, *Germany;* and Henry Kissinger, "The White Revolutionary," *Daedalus,* Summer 1968.

32. Wehler, "Bismarck's Imperialism," p. 143.

33. On the importance of economic ideology see Charles P. Kindleberger, "The Rise of Free Trade in Western Europe, 1820–1875," *Journal of Economic History* 35, 1 (1975), 20–55.

34. On international system explanations and the domestic internal issues, a good summary of the arguments can be found in Calleo, *German Problem Reconsidered.* Classic statements of the internal sources of foreign policy can be found in Eckart Kehr, *Schlachtflottenbau und Parteipolitik* (Berlin, 1930), trans. into English by Pauline R. and Eugene N. Anderson as *Battleship Building and Party Politics in Germany, 1894–1901* (Chicago: University of Chicago Press, 1973); and Kehr, *Der Primat der Innenpolitik* (Berlin: de Gruyter, 1965).

See also Theodore Hamerow, *Restoration, Revolution and Reaction: Politics in Germany, 1815–1871* (Princeton: Princeton University Press, 1958). In the German literature the primacy of foreign policy was the statement of the conservative, nationalist school; liberals, radicals, and internationalists challenged it by stressing the primacy of internal politics. The debate continues to the present day.

35. See the debate on the formation and erosion of "regimes," particularly the recent dispute about the importance of a hegemon, and in particular Robert O. Keohane, *After Hegemony: Cooperation and Discord in the World Political Economy* (Princeton: Princeton University Press, 1984); Stephen Krasner, "State Power and the Structure of International Trade," *World Politics* 28 (April), 317–43; Gilpin, *U.S. Power;* Charles Lipson, "The Transformation of Trade: The Source and Effects of Regime Change," in *International Regimes,* ed. Krasner (Ithaca: Cornell University Press, 1983); and Charles Kindleberger, *The World in Depression, 1929–1939* (Berkeley: University of California Press, 1973).

36. Thomas Kemp, *Economic Forces in French History* (London: Dobson, 1971); C. P. Kindleberger, *Economic Growth in Britain and France* (Cambridge: Harvard University Press, 1967); and Kindleberger, *Economic Response: Comparative Studies in Trade, Finance and Growth* (Cambridge: Harvard University Press, 1978).

37. Eugene Golob, *The Meline Tariff* (New York: Columbia University Press, 1944); J. H. Clapham, *Economic Development of France and Germany,* 4th ed. (Cambridge: Harvard University Press, 1968); Michel Augé-Laribé, *La politique agricole de la France de 1880 à 1940* (Paris: Presses Universitaires de la France, 1950); and Michael Tracy, *Agriculture in Western Europe* (London: Cape, 1964).

38. Sanford Elwitt, *The Making of the Third Republic: Class and Politics in France, 1868–1884* (Baton Rouge: Louisiana State University Press, 1975), 270–72.

39. John McManners, *Church and State in France* (London: S.P.C.K. for the Church Historical Society, 1972); Stanley Hoffmann, "Paradoxes in the French Political Community," *In Search of France,* ed. Hoffmann (Cambridge: Harvard University Press, 1963).

40. Robert Wiebe, *The Search for Order, 1877–1920* (New York: Hill & Wang, 1967).

41. The Compromise of 1876, which put Hayes in the White House, had less to do with the end of Reconstruction, which was ending anyway, than with the desire of Southerners to obtain patronage and a railroad through the southwest. See C. Van Woodward, *The Origins of the New South* (Baton Rouge: Louisiana State University Press, 1951); *Reunion and Reaction* (Boston: Little, Brown, 1951); and *Tom Watson: Agrarian Rebel* (New York: Macmillan, 1938). See also Gabriel Kolko, *The Triumph of Conservatism* (New York: Free, 1963); Kolko, *Railroads and Regulation* (Princeton: Princeton University Press, 1965); William Appelman Williams, *Roots of the Modern American Empire* (New York: Random House, 1969); Frank Taussig, *A Tariff History of the United States*, 8th rev. ed. (New York: Capricorn, 1964); Paul Glad, *McKinley, Bryan and the People* (Philadelphia: Lippincott, 1964); and John Hope Franklin, *Reconstruction: After the Civil War* (Chicago: University of Chicago Press, 1961).

42. Moore, *Social Origins*, 111–55.

43. Letter of 8 November 1892 quoted in Joseph Wall, *Andrew Carnegie* (New York: Oxford University Press, 1970), p. 569.

44. Eric Foner, *Free Soil, Free Labor, Free Men* (New York: Oxford University Press, 1970).

45. Walter Dean Burnham, *Critical Elections and the Mainsprings of American Politics* (New York: Norton, 1970); James L. Sundquist, *Dynamics of the Party System* (Washington, D.C.: Brookings, 1973); and S. M. Lipset and Stein Rokkan, *Party Systems and Voter Alignments* (New York: Free, 1967).

46. For material on Sweden, I have relied on many sources and benefited from useful criticism from several Swedish scholars. Steven Koblik, ed., *Sweden's Development from Poverty to Affluence, 1750–1970* (Minneapolis: University of Minnesota Press, 1975), has a good bibliography; Eli Hecksher, *An Economic History of Sweden* (Cambridge: Harvard University Press, 1954); Donald Hancock, *Sweden: The Politics of Post-Industrial Change* (Hinsdale, Ill.: Dryden, 1972); Kurt Samuelsson, *From Great Power to Welfare State* (London: Allen & Unwin, 1968); Robert Dahl, *Political Oppositions in Western Democracies* (New Haven: Yale University Press, 1966); Lennart Jorberg, *The Industrial Revolution in Scandinavia, 1850–1914*, Fontana Economic History of Europe 4 (London: Collins, 1970); Jorberg, *Growth and Fluctuations of Swedish Industry, 1869–1912* (Stockholm: Almquist & Wiksell, 1961); Leif Lewin et al., *The Swedish Electorate, 1887–1968* (Stockholm: Almquist & Wiksell, 1972); Herbert Tingsten, *The Swedish Social Democrats: Their Ideological Development*, trans. Greta Frankel and Patricia Howard-Rosen (Totowa, N.J.: Debminster, 1973); Tingsten, *The Debate on the Foreign Policy of Sweden, 1918–1939*, trans. Joan Bulman (London: Oxford University Press, 1949); Douglas Verney, *Parliamentary Reform in Sweden, 1866–1921* (Oxford: Clarendon, 1957). For more references, see Peter A. Gourevitch, "Breaking with Orthodoxy: The Politics of Economic Policy Responses to the Depression of the 1930s," *International Organization* 38 (Winter 1984), 95–130.

47. See Robert Dahl, *Preface to Modern Democratic Theory* (Chicago: University of Chicago Press, 1956); John Gaventa, *Power and Powerlessness: Quiescence and Rebellion in an Appalachian Valley* (Urbana: University of Illinois Press, 1980).

48. Max Weber, "Class, Status and Party," in Hans Gerth and C. Wright Mills, eds., *Readings from Max Weber* (New York: Oxford University Press, 1946). Clifford Geertz, "Ideology as a Cultural System," in *Ideology and Discon-*

tent, ed. David Apter (New York: Free, 1964); and David Laitin, "Religion, Political Culture and the Weberian Tradition," *World Politics* 30 (July 1978), 563–92.

49. On arguments over the role of state structures, see the discussion in Evans, Rueschmeyer, and Skocpol, *Bringing the State Back In.*

50. See Kehr, *Primat der Innenpolitik.*

51. Peter Gourevitch, "The Second Image Reversed: The International Sources of Domestic Politics," *International Organization* 32 (Autumn 1978), 881–912.

52. P. F. Clarke, *Lancashire and the New Liberalism* (Cambridge: Cambridge University Press, 1971).

53. Woodward, *Origins of the New South.*

54. The relation between policy content and regime types ought to be elucidated by comparative policy studies. See Arnold J. Heidenheimer, "The Politics of Public Education, Health, and Welfare in the USA and Western Europe: How Growth and Reform Potentials Have Differed," *British Journal of Political Science* 3 (1973), 315–40.

CHAPTER 4. *Breaking with Orthodoxy: The Formation of the Mixed Economy, 1929–49*

1. For an overview of the policy debate in the 1930s, see H. W. Arndt, *The Economic Lessons of the Nineteen-Thirties* (Oxford: Oxford University Press, 1944); David S. Landes, *The Unbound Prometheus: Technological Change and Industrial Development in Western Europe from 1750 to the Present* (Cambridge: Cambridge University Press, 1969); W. Arthur Lewis, *Economic Survey, 1919–1939* (London: Allen & Unwin, 1960); John A. Garaty, "The New Deal, National Socialism, and the Great Depression," *American Historical Review* 78 (1973), 907–44; and chaps. 7–9 of William H. McNeill, *The Pursuit of Power* (Chicago: University of Chicago Press, 1982). See also Ekkart Zimmermann, "Economic and Political Reaction to the World Economic Crisis of the 1930s in Six European Countries" (paper delivered at the annual meeting of the Midwest Political Science Association, Chicago, April 1986).

2. On the postwar compromise the literature is large. See Andrew Shonfield, *Modern Capitalism* (London: Oxford University Press, 1969). For a view from the standpoint of the role of the labor movements, see Peter Lange et al., *Unions, Change and Crisis: French and Italian Union Strategy and the Political Economy, 1945–80* (London: Allen & Unwin, 1982), and Peter Gourevitch et al., *Unions and Economic Crisis: Britain, West Germany and Sweden* (London: Allen & Unwin, 1984). For a view exploring the political economic origins of postwar consociationalism and democratic corporatism, see Peter Katzenstein, *Corporatism and Change* (Ithaca: Cornell University Press, 1984).

3. On the relation between Keynesianism and political struggles, see Robert Skidelsky, "The Decline of Keynesian Politics," and Colin Crouch, "The State, Capital, and Liberal Democracy," both in *State and Economy in Contemporary Capitalism,* ed. Colin Crouch (London: Croom Helm, 1979).

4. Steven Koblik, ed., *Sweden's Development from Poverty to Affluence,* trans. Joanne Johnson (Minneapolis: University of Minnesota Press, 1975).

5. From the large literature on Sweden in this period, note Andrew Martin,

"The Dynamics of Change in a Keynesian Political Economy: The Swedish Case and Its Implications," in Crouch, *State and Economy; Erik Dahmen, Entrepreneurial Activity and the Development of Swedish Industry, 1919–1939*, trans. Axel Leijonhufvud (Homewood, Ill.: Irwin, 1970); Eli F. Heckscher, *An Economic History of Sweden*, trans. Goran Ohlin, Harvard Economic Studies 95 (Cambridge: Harvard University Press, 1954); Walter Korpi, *The Working Class in Welfare Capitalism: Work, Unions, and Politics in Sweden* (London: Routledge & Kegan Paul, 1978); Leif Lewin, Bo Jansson, and Dag Sorbom, *The Swedish Electorate, 1887–1968*, Publications of the Political Science Association in Uppsala 60 (Stockhom: Almquist & Wiksell, 1972); Assar Lindbeck, *Swedish Economic Policy* (London: Macmillan, 1975); Arthur Montgomery, *How Sweden Overcame the Depression, 1930–1933* (Stockholm, 1938; New York: Johnson, 1972); Sven Anders Soderpalm, *Direktorsklubben-storindustrin i svensk politik under 1930- och 40-talen*, TemaTeori 12 (Zenit: Raben & Sjogen, 1976); Herbert Tingsten, *The Swedish Social Democratics: Their Ideological Development*, trans. Greta Frankel and Patricia Howard-Rosen (Totowa, N.J.: Bedminster, 1973); and Olle Nyman, *Svensk parlamentarism, 1932–1936: Fon minoritiets parlamentarism till majoritetskoalition* (Uppsala: Almquist & Wiksell, 1947).

6. Dahmen, *Entrepreneurial Activity*, is a particularly interesting economic history for the approach taken here, because it is one of the few to disaggregate by industrial sector.

7. For critical evaluations of the course of Swedish policy in the 1930s see Bo Gustafsson, "A Perennial of Doctrinal History: Keynes and the 'Stockholm' School," *Economy and History* 16 (1973), 114–28; Lars Johnung, "Knut Wicksell's Norm of Price Stabilization and Swedish Monetary Policy in the 1930s," *Journal of Monetary Economics* 5 (1979), and "The Depression in Sweden and the United States: A Comparison of Causes and Policies," in Karl Brunner, ed., *The Great Depression Revisited* (Boston: Nijhoff, 1981); T. A. Tilton, "A Swedish Road to Socialism: Ernst Wigfors and the Ideological Foundations of Swedish Social Democracy," *American Political Science Review* 73 (June 1979), 505–20; Donald Winch, "The Keynesian Revolution in Sweden," *Journal of Political Economy* 74 (April 1966), 168–76; and Carl G. Uh, "The Emergence of the 'New Economics' in Sweden: A Review of a Study by Otto Steiger," *History of Political Economy* 5 (Spring 1973), 243–60.

8. Arndt, *Economic Lessons;* Derek H. Aldcroft and Harry W. Richardson, *Building in the British Economy between the Wars* (London: Allen & Unwin, 1968); Richardson, *Economic Recovery in Britain, 1932–39* (London: Weidenfeld & Nicolson, 1967); Alexander Youngson, *The British Economy, 1920–57* (Cambridge: Harvard University Press, 1960); Donald Winch, *Economics and Policy: A Historical Study* (New York: Walker, 1969); Keith J. Hancock, "Reduction of Unemployment as a Problem of Public Policy, 1920–29," *Economic History Review*, 2d ser., 15 (December 1962), 328–43, and "Unemployment and the Economists in the 1920's," *Economica*, n.s., 27 (1960), 305–21; Alfred Kahn, *Great Britain in the World Economy* (New York: Columbia University Press, 1946); and Susan Strange, *Sterling and British Policy* (London: Oxford University Press, 1971). On British tariff controversies see Benjamin Brown, *The Tariff Reform Movement in Britain, 1881–1895* (New York: Columbia University Press, 1943), and Aldcroft and Richardson, *The British Economy, 1870–1939* (London: Macmillan, 1969).

9. Alan Bullock, *The Life and Times of Ernest Bevin*, vol. 1 (London:

Heinemann, 1960), and Robert Skidelsky, *Politicians and the Slump* (London: Macmillan, 1967).

10. Dennis A. Kavanagh, "Crisis Management and Incremental Adaptation in British Politics: The 1931 Crisis of the British Party System," in *Crisis, Choice, and Change: Historical Studies of Political Development*, ed. Gabriel Almond et al. (Boston: Little, Brown, 1973).

11. Frank Longstreth, "The City, Industry and the State," in his *State and Economy in Contemporary Capitalism* (London: Croom Helm, 1979); Robert Gilpin, *U.S. Power and the Multinational Corporation* (New York: Basic, 1975); Stephen Blank, "Britain: The Politics of Foreign Economic Policy," in *Between Power and Plenty*, ed. Peter Katzenstein (Madison: University of Wisconsin Press, 1977); and Samuel H. Beer, *British Politics in the Collectivist Age* (New York: Knopf, 1965).

12. From the vast literature on Germany before WWI, see the references provided in the previous chapter.

13. David Abraham, *The Collapse of the Weimar Republic* (Princeton: Princeton University Press, 1981), contains an extremely useful and interesting account of the substantive policy goals of different interest groups and the possible combinations. On the turbulent debate surrounding this book and Henry Ashley Turner, Jr., *German Big Business and the Rise of Hitler* (New York: Oxford University Press, 1985), see the comments of James Joll, "Storm over German History: Business as Usual," *New York Review of Books* 32, no. 14 (26 September 1985), 5–10: "Abraham's account of the polarization of the advocates and opponents of the Weimar Republic's social welfare schemes shows clearly the extent to which in this as in other cases economic differences led to political divisions. The curious thing that emerges from both Turner's and Abraham's books is in fact how little the leaders of the various economic pressure groups understood where their interests lay; and the Nazis were able to profit from this." Joll goes on to note that "not all the errors vitiate all the arguments . . . [and] In any case the questions raised by Abraham's theoretical analysis won't go away."

The core of Abraham's argument is the point stressed by Joll—that the conflict over policy contributed to political deadlock, which the Nazis exploited. The core of Turner's argument is that the Nazis were not the first choice of big businesss among politicians—a point with which Abraham fully agrees. This is an important statement because of decades of belief in the more primitive, reductionist explanations of the Nazi seizure of power. But if business, or other groups, contributed to the paralysis of Weimar, then surely they play some causal role, which "smoking gun" epistemology ignores.

In his effort to map social preferences by different societal actors on a range of issues, then to model the possible terms of trade along which various alignments could occur, Abraham's work resonates strongly with that of Tom Ferguson on the United States and Denis Kavanagh on the United Kingdom. See note 24 on Ferguson and note 10 on Kavanagh.

14. The classic treatments of the mass electorate—S. M. Lipset, *Political Man* (Garden City, N.Y.: Doubleday, 1963), and Rudolf Haberle, *From Democracy to Nazism* (Baton Rouge: Louisiana State University Press, 1970)—have been surpassed by Richard Hamilton, *Who Voted for Hitler?* (Princeton: Princeton University Press, 1982), who stresses the social diversity of the Nazi electorate and the importance of Nazi organizational skills.

15. Vladimir Woytinski, *Stormy Passage* (New York: Vanguard, 1961). Michael Schneider, *Das Arbeitsbeschaffungsprogramm des ADGB*, Friedrich-Ebert-Stiftung 120 (Bonn: Neu Gesellschaft, 1975) English introduction by George Garvy.

16. Gerschenkron, "Economic Backwardness in Historical Perspective."

17. Kurth, "Political Consequences of the Product Cycle"; Joseph Borkin, *The Crime and Punishment of I. G. Farben* (New York: Free, 1978).

18. In addition to Abraham's *Collapse of the Weimar Republic* and Turner's *German Big Business*, see Gerald Feldman, "The Social and Economic Policies of German Big Business, 1918–29," *American Historical Review* 75 (October 1969), 47–55, and several earlier works by Henry Ashby Turner, Jr.: "Big Business and the Rise of Hitler," *American Historical Review* 75 (October 1969), 56–70; "Emil Kirdorf and the Nazi Party," *Central European History* 1 (December 1968), 324–44; "Hitler's Secret Pamphlet for Industrialists, 1927," *Journal of Modern History* 11 (September 1968), 348–74; "The Ruhrlade, Secret Cabinet of Heavy Industry in the Weimar Republic," *Central European History* 3 (September 1970), 195–228; and *Stresemann and the Politics of the Weimar Republic* (Princeton: Princeton University Press, 1963).

19. John D. Heyl, "Hitler's Economic Thought: A Reappraisal," *Central European History* 6 (March 1973), 83–96; Arndt, *Economic Lessons;* and Alan S. Milward, "Fascism and the Economy," in *Fascism, A Reader's Guide: Analyses, Interpretations, Bibliography*, ed. Walter Laqueur (Berkeley: University of California Press, 1976). On foreign economic policy see David Kaiser, *Economic Diplomacy and the Origins of the Second World War* (Princeton: Princeton University Press, 1980); Albert Hirschman, *National Power and the Structure of Foreign Trade* (1945; Berkeley: University of California Press, 1980).

20. See Charles Kindleberger, *The World in Depression, 1929–1939* (Berkeley: University of California Press, 1973); Chalmers Johnson, *MITI and the Japanese Miracle: The Growth of Industrial Policy, 1925–75* (Stanford: Stanford University Press, 1982); and Daniel Okimoto, *Between MITI and the Market* (Stanford: Stanford University Press, forthcoming).

21. U.S. tariff policy has received numerous treatments from different sorts of specialists. For emphasis on politics, see E. E. Schattschneider, *Politics, Pressure and the Tariff* (1935; Hamden, Conn.: Archon, 1963), and William Appleman Williams, *Roots of the Modern American Empire* (New York: Random House, 1969), as well as his other books. For emphasis on economics, see Frank Taussig, *A Tariff History of the United States*, 8th rev. ed. (New York: Capricorn, 1964). For a work that argues against the importance of producer group interests, see Raymond Bauer et al., *American Business and Public Policy* (New York: Atherton, 1967).

22. Walter Dean Burnham, *Critical Elections and the Mainsprings of the American Party System* (New York: Norton, 1970).

23. Herbert Stein, *The Fiscal Revolution in America* (Chicago: University of Chicago Press, 1969); Albert U. Romasco, *The Politics of Recovery: Roosevelt's New Deal* (New York: Oxford University Press, 1983); and Daniel Fusfeld, *The Economic Thought of Franklin D. Roosevelt and the Origins of the New Deal* (New York: Columbia University Press, 1954).

24. The literature on the New Deal is, of course, immense. In addition to the well-known materials, I have found particularly useful some newer work. See Tom Ferguson's "From Normalcy to New Deal: Industrial Structure,

Party Competition, and American Public Policy in the Great Depression," *International Organization* 38 (Winter 1984), 41–94, and his *Critical Realignment: The Fall of the House of Morgan and the Origins of the New Deal* (New York: Oxford University Press, forthcoming). Theda Skocpol has published several articles with a stress on institutions; see "Political Responses to Capitalist Crisis: Neo-Marxist Theories of the State and the Case of the New Deal," *Politics and Society* 10, 2 (1980), 155–201; Skocpol and Kenneth Finegold, "State Capacity and Economic Intervention in the Early New Deal," *Political Science Quarterly* 97 (Summer 1982), 255–78; and Margaret Weir and Skocpol, "State Structures and the Possibilities for 'Keynesian' Responses to the Great Depression in Sweden, Britain and the United States," in *Bringing the State Back In,* ed. Peter Evans, Diekrich Rueschmeyer, and Skocpol (New York: Cambridge University Press, 1985), 107–68. On the role of the state see Steven Skowronek, *Building a New American State: The Expansion of National Administrative Capacities, 1877–1920* (New York: Cambridge University Press, 1982).

25. Stein, *Fiscal Revolution in America.*

26. See ibid.

27. François Goguel, *La politique des partis sous la IIIe République* (Paris: Seuil, 1946).

28. Charles Maier, *Recasting Bourgeois Europe* (Princeton: Princeton University Press, 1975); Stephen Schuker, *The End of French Predominance in Europe* (Chapel Hill: University of North Carolina Press, 1976).

29. Michel Auge-Laribe, *La politique agricole de la France* (Paris: Presses Universitaires de la France, 1950); Charles K. Warner, *Winegrowers of France and the Government since 1875* (New York: Columbia University Press, 1960).

30. Georges Dupeux, *Le Front Populaire et les élections de 1939* (Paris: Colin, 1959).

31. Henry Ehrmann, *Organized Business in France* (Princeton: Princeton University Press, 1957); Richard Kuisel, *Ernst Mercier: French Technocrat* (Berkeley: University of California Press, 1967).

32. Jean Bouvier, "Un débat toujours ouvert: La politique économique du Front Populaire," *Le mouvement social* no. 54 (January–March 1966), 175–81; Daniel Guérin, *Front populaire, révolution manquée,* rev. ed. (Paris: Maspero, 1970); M. Kalecki, "Lessons of the Blum Experiment," *Economic Journal* 48 (March 1938), 26–41; Georges Lefranc, *Histoire du front populaire,* 2d ed. (Paris: Payot, 1974); Robert Marjolin, "Reflections on the Blum Experiment," *Economica,* n.s., 5 (May 1938), 177–91; and Alfred Sauvy, *Histoire économique de la France entre les deux guerres,* vol. 2: *1931–39* (Paris: Fayard, 1967), and also some interesting articles in vol. 4.

33. Daniel Brower, *The New Jacobins: The French Communist Party and the Popular Front* (Ithaca: Cornell University Press, 1968); Louis Bodin and Jean Touchard, *Le front populaire de 1936* (Paris: Colin, 1961); Nathaniel Greene, *Crisis and Decline: The French Socialist Party in the Popular Front Era* (Ithaca: Cornell University Press, 1969); Pierre Broué and Nicole Dorey, "Critiques de gauche et opposition révolutionnaire au front populaire (1936–38)," *Le mouvement social* no. 54 (January–March 1966), 91–133; Joel Colton, *Leon Blum* (Cambridge: MIT Press, 1974); Henry Ehrmann, *French Labor from Popular Front to Liberation* (New York: Oxford University Press, 1947); and Jean Lacouture, *Léon Blum* (Paris: Seuil, 1977). On economic policy and

nationalism in the 1930s see Albert Hirschman, *National Power and the Structure of Foreign Trade* (Berkeley: University of California Press, 1945), and David Kaiser, *Economic Diplomacy and the Causes of the Second World War* (Princeton: Princeton University Press, 1980).

34. On the emergence of this "stabilization" compromise, see Michael Piore and Charles Sabel, *The Second Industrial Divide* (New York: Basic, 1984). Piore and Sabel cite the French literature on "regulation" (by which is meant internal stabilization), in particular Robert Boyer, "La crise actuelle: Une mise en perspective historique," *Critique de l'économie politique* nos. 7–8 (May 1979), 5–113; Boyer and Jacques Mistral, *Accumulation, inflation, crises* (Paris: Presses Universitaires de France, 1978); and Michel Aglietta, *Regulation et crises du capitalisme: L'example des Etats-Unis* (Paris: Calmann-Levy, 1976).

35. See Mancur Olson's discussion of all-encompassing vs. particularistic organizations in *The Rise and Decline of Nations* (New Haven: Yale University Press, 1982).

36. Louis Hartz, *The Liberal Tradition in America* (New York: Harcourt, Brace, 1955).

37. Edwin Hartrich, *The Fourth and Richest Reich* (New York: Macmillan, 1980); Henry C. Wallich, *Mainsprings of the German Revival* (New Haven: Yale University Press, 1955); Karl Hardach, *The Political Economy of Germany in the Twentieth Century* (Berkeley: University of California Press, 1980); Geoffrey Denton, Murray Forsyth, and Malcolm Maclennan, *Economic Planning and Policies in Britain, France and Germany* (London: Allen & Unwin, 1968); and Andrew Martin and Christopher Allen, "Trade Unions and Economic Crisis: The West German Case," in Peter Gourevitch et al., *Unions and Economic Crisis: Britain, West Germany and Sweden* (London: Allen & Unwin, 1984).

38. Charles Kindleberger, "The Postwar Resurgence of the French Economy," in Stanley Hoffmann et al., *In Search of France* (Cambridge: Harvard University Press, 1963), and Hoffmann's "Paradoxes of French Political Community" in the same book.

39. Richard F. Kuisel, *Capitalism and the State in Modern France* (New York: Cambridge University Press, 1981); Gordon Wright, *Reshaping French Democracy* (New York: Reynal & Hitchcock, 1948).

40. See Philip Williams's classic work on the Fourth Republic, *Crisis and Compromise* (London: Longmans, Green, 1964).

41. Samuel Beer, *British Politics in the Collectivist Age* (New York: Random House, 1965); Leo Panitch, *Social Democracy and Industrial Militancy: The Labour Party, the Trade Unions and Income Policy, 1945–74* (Cambridge: Cambridge University Press, 1976).

42. Piore and Sabel, *Second Industrial Divide*.

43. Andrew Martin, "Trade Unions in Sweden: Strategic Responses to Change and Crisis," in Gourevitch et al., *Unions and Economic Crisis;* Dankwart Rustow, *The Politics of Compromise* (Princeton: Princeton University Press, 1955); and Walter Korpi, *The Working Class in Welfare Capitalism* (London: Routledge & Kegan Paul, 1978).

CHAPTER 5. *Reopening the Debate: The Crisis of the 1970s and 1980s*

1. In a huge literature see Andrea Boltho, *The European Economy: Growth and Crisis* (Oxford: Oxford University Press, 1982); Michael Bruno with Jeffrey Sachs, *Economics and Worldwide Stagflation* (Cambridge: Harvard Uni-

versity Press, 1985); L. Lindberg, R. Alford, C. Crouch, and C. Offe, eds., *Stress and Contradiction in Contemporary Capitalism* (Lexington: Health, 1977); Crouch and A. Pizzorno, *The Resurgence of Class Conflict in Europe* (New York: Holmes & Meier, 1978); Lindberg and Charles Maier, eds., *The Politics of Inflation and Recession* (Washington: Brookings, 1985); John Goldthorpe, *Order and Conflict in Contemporary Capitalism* (Oxford: Clarendon, 1984); Peter Katzenstein, ed., *Between Power and Plenty: Foreign Economic Policies of Advanced Industrial States* (Madison: University of Wisconsin Press, 1978); Crouch, *State and Economy in Contemporary Capitalism* (London: Croom Helm, 1979); Katzenstein, *Corporatism and Change* (Ithaca: Cornell University Press, 1984), and *Small States in World Markets: Industrial Policy in Europe* (Ithaca: Cornell University Press, 1985); Suzanne Berger, ed., *Organizing Interests in Western Europe* (New York: Cambridge University Press, 1981); Mancur Olson, *The Rise and Decline of Nations: Economic Growth, Stagflation and Social Rigidities* (New Haven: Yale University Press, 1981); Andrew Shonfield, *Modern Capitalism* (London: Oxford University Press, 1965); Walter Korpi, *The Democratic Class Struggle* (London: Macmillan, 1983); and S. M. Lipset and S. Rokkan, *Party Systems and Voter Alignments* (New York: Free, 1967).

2. See Philip G. Cerny and Martin A. Schain, *Socialism, The State and Public Policy in France* (New York: Methuen, 1985), and Stephen Cohen and Peter Gourevitch, eds., *France in the Troubled World Economy* (London: Butterworth, 1982).

3. Richard W. Johnson, *The Long March of the French Left* (New York: St. Martin's, 1981).

4. Cf. Pierre Rosanvallon and Patrick Viveret, *Pour une nouvelle culture politique* (Paris: Seuill, 1977).

5. See the discussion in Katzenstein, *Between Power and Plenty*. John Zysman emphasizes the role of specific institutions in inhibiting or encouraging a type of policy in providing (or not providing) particular policy instruments; see his *Government, Markets, and Growth: Financial Systems and the Politics of Industrial Change* (Ithaca: Cornell University Press, 1983). See also Peter Hall, "Socialism in One Country: Mitterrand and the Struggle to Define a New Economic Policy for France," in Cerny and Schain, *Socialism . . . in France,* pp. 81–107, and Hall, "Economic Planning and the State: The Evolution of Economic Challenge and Political Response in France," in Maurice Zeitlin et al., eds., *Political Power and Social Theory,* vol. 3 (Greenwich, Conn.: Jai, 1982). On planning see Stephen Cohen, *Modern Capitalist Planning: The French Model* (Cambridge: Harvard University Press, 1969), and James Sheahan, *Promotion and Control of Industry in Postwar France* (Cambridge: Harvard University Press, 1963).

6. See George Ross, "The Perils of Politics: French Unions and the Crisis of the 1970s," in *Unions, Change and Crisis: French and Italian Union Strategy and the Political Economy of 1945–1980,* ed. Peter Lange, Ross, and Maurizio Vannicelli (London: Allen & Unwin, 1982); William Andrews and Stanley Hoffmann, eds., *The Fifth Republic at Twenty* (Albany: SUNY Press, 1981); and Hoffmann, *Decline and Renewal* (New York: Viking, 1974).

7. Useful are Stephen Blank, "Britain: The Politics of Foreign Economic Policy," in Katzenstein, *Between Power and Plenty,* pp. 89–106; Richard Caves, ed., *Britain's Economic Prospects* (London: Allen & Unwin, 1968); Caves and Lawrence Krause, eds., *Britain's Economic Performance* (Washington, D.C.: Brookings, 1980).

8. See Stephen Bornstein and Peter Gourevitch, "Union in a Declining Economy: The Case of the British TUC," in Gourevitch et al., *Unions and Economic Crisis: Britain, West Germany and Sweden* (London: Allen & Unwin, 1984); Michael Stewart, *Politics and Economic Policy in the United Kingdom since 1964: The Jekyll and Hyde Years* (London: Pergamon, 1978); and John Goldthorpe and David Lockwood, *The Affluent Worker* (Cambridge: Cambridge University Press, 1969).

9. Cf. Derek Robinson, "British Industrial Relations Research in the Sixties and the Seventies," in *Industrial Relations in International Perspective*, ed. Peter Doeringer, Peter Gourevitch, Peter Lange, and Andrew Martin (London: Macmillan, 1981), and H. Clegg, *The System of Industrial Relations in Great Britain* (Oxford: Blackwell, 1979). On the effects of fragmentation of interest groups upon British economic policy see Mancur Olson, *The Rise and Decline of Nations* (New Haven: Yale University Press, 1983), and the critical review by Ronald Rogowski, "Structure, Growth, and Power," *International Organization* 37 (Autumn 1983), 713–38.

10. See Stephen Blank, *Government and Industry in Britain: The Federation of British Industry in Politics, 1945–65* (Farnborough: Saxon House, 1973); W. Grant and D. Marsh, *The Confederation of British Industry* (London: Hodder & Stoughton, 1977); and several works by Peter Hall: "The Political Dimensions of Economic Management" (Ph.D. diss., Harvard University, 1982); "Socialism in One Country: Mitterrand and the Struggle to Define a New Economic Policy for France," in *Socialism, the State, and Public Policy in France*, ed. Philip Cerny and Martin Schain (New York: Methuen, 1985); "Policy Innovation and the Structure of the State," *Annals* 466 (March 1983); and "Economic Planning and the State," in *Political Power and Social Theory*, vol. 3, ed. Maurice Zeitlin (Greenwich, Conn.: JAI, 1982).

11. For example, Zysman, *Government, Markets, and Growth*.

12. Those policies are outlined in Peter Katzenstein, *Small States in World Markets: Industrial Policy in Europe* (Ithaca: Cornell University Press, 1985).

13. See Andrew Martin, "Trade Unions in Sweden: Strategic Responses to Change and Crisis," in Gourevitch et al., *Unions and Economic Crisis*.

14. Walter Korpi, *The Working Class in Welfare Capitalism* (London: Routledge & Kegan Paul, 1978); Gosta Esping-Anderson and Roger Friedland, "Class Coalitions in the Making of West European Economies," *Political Power and Social Theory* 3 (1982); John Stephens, *The Transition from Capitalism to Socialism* (London: Macmillan, 1979); Michael Shalev, "The Social Democratic Model and Beyond: Two Generations of Comparative Research on the Welfare State," *Comparative Social Research* 6 (1983); and Peter Doeringer, Peter Gourevitch, Peter Lange, and Andrew Martin, *Industrial Relations in International Perspective* (London: Macmillan, 1981).

15. See Michael Kreile, "West Germany: The Dynamics of Expansion," in Katzenstein, *Between Power and Plenty;* Christian Deubner, "Industry and Politics in West Germany," *International Organization* 38 (Summer 1984), 501–36; and Edwin Hartwick, *The Fourth and Richest Reich* (New York: Macmillan, 1980).

16. Andrei Markovits and Christopher Allen, "Trade Unions and the Economic Crisis: The West German Case," in Gourevitch et al., *Unions and Economic Crisis*, 89–189.

17. David R. Cameron, "The Politics and Economics of the Business Cycle,"

in *The Political Economy: Readings in the Politics and Economics of American Public Policy*, ed. Thomas Ferguson and Joel Rogers (White Plains, N.Y.: Sharpe, 1984); and Douglas Hibbs, "Political Parties and Macroeconomic Policy," *American Political Science Review* 71 (1977), 1467–87. See also, by Neal Beck, "Parties, Administrations and Macroeconomic Outcomes," *American Political Science Review* 76 (March 1982); "Domestic Political Sources of American Monetary Policy: 1955–1982," *Journal of Politics* (August 1984); and "Elections and the Fed: Is There a Political Monetary Cycle?" *American Journal of Political Science* (forthcoming, 1987).

18. Felix Rohatyn, *The Twenty-Year Century* (New York: Random House, 1983).

19. Martin Shefter, *Political Crisis/Fiscal Crisis: The Collapse and Revival of New York City* (New York: Basic, 1985).

20. Alessandro Pizzorno, "The Individualistic Mobilization of Europe," *Daedalus*, Winter 1964, 199–224.

CHAPTER 6. *The Social Bases of the Autonomous State*

1. For a discussion of "historical trajectories," see Charles Tilly, *Big Structures, Large Processes, Huge Comparisons* (New York: Russell Sage, 1984).

2. On critical realignments, see V. O. Key, "A Theory of Critical Elections," *Journal of Politics* 17 (February 1955), 3–18, and Walter Dean Burnham, "The Changing Shape of the American Political Universe," *American Political Science Review* 59 (1965), 7–28.

3. The importance of elite cleavages in consonant with literature on other events. See, for example, Martin Shefter, *Political Crisis/Fiscal Crisis: The Collapse and Revival of New York City* (New York: Basic, 1985); Barrington Moore, Jr., *Social Origins of Dictatorship and Democracy* (Boston: Beacon, 1966); and Lawrence Stone, *The Causes of the English Revolution* (London: Routledge & Kegan Paul, 1972).

4. For literature on the alliance problems of labor, see Peter Lange and George Ross, "French and Italian Union Development in Comparative Perspective," in Lange, Ross, and Maurizio Vannicelli, eds., *Unions, Change and Crisis* (London: Allen & Unwin, 1982), 207–91, and Lange's contribution to John Goldthorpe, ed., *Order and Conflict in Contemporary Capitalism* (Oxford: Oxford University Press, 1984); Walter Korpi, *The Working Class in Welfare Capitalism* (London: Routledge & Kegan Paul, 1978).

5. For a discussion of the filling of "organizational openness," see Suzanne Berger, *Peasants against Politics* (Cambridge: Harvard University Press, 1972).

6. See Richard Hamilton, *Who Voted for Hitler?* (Princeton: Princeton University Press, 1982).

7. See Peter J. Katzenstein, *Corporatism and Change* (Ithaca: Cornell University Press, 1984), and *Small States in World Markets: Industrial Policy in Europe* (Ithaca: Cornell University Press, 1985).

8. On the role of organizational structure in economic policy, see Mancur Olson, *The Rise and Decline of Nations* (New Haven: Yale University Press, 1981), and criticism of this work by Ronald Rogowski, "Structure, Growth, and Power," *International Organization* 37 (Autumn 1983), 713–38. On the egostical bases of cooperative behavior see Robert Axelrod, "The Emergence

of Cooperation among Egoists," *American Political Science Review* 75 (June 1981), 306–18, and Robert Keohane, *After Hegemony: Cooperation and Discord in the World Political Economy* (Princeton: Princeton University Press, 1984).

9. See Ellen Comisso's very good formulations about the role of "differentiated political processes" in her "Introduction: State Structures, Political Processes and Collective Choice"; "State Structures and Political Processes outside CMEA: A Comparison"; and with Paul Marer, "Explaining Economic Strategy in Hungary," all in *International Organization* 40 (Spring 1986), a special issue on Eastern Europe, coedited by Comisso and Laura Tyson.

10. See Stephen Krasner's discussion of punctuated equilibrium in his "Approaches to the State," *Comparative Politics* 16 (January 1984), 223–46.

Index

Whigs, 122; Southern, 108, 110
Williams, William Appleman, 110
Wilson, Harold, 136, 193–195
Wilson, Woodrow, 48
Woodward, C. Vann, 122
World War I, 106, 113, 124, 127, 154, 160, 164, 226

World War II, 28–29, 64, 124–125, 153, 160, 169, 173, 175, 179, 186, 228, 237
Woytinski, Wladimir, 144, 240
WTB Plan, 144

Zero-sum conflicts, 42–43, 47–50, 128

Cornell Studies in Political Economy

EDITED BY PETER J. KATZENSTEIN

Collapse of an Industry: Nuclear Power and the Contradictions of U.S. Policy, by John L. Campbell

Power, Purpose, and Collective Choice: Economic Strategy in Socialist States, edited by Ellen Comisso and Laura D'Andrea Tyson

The Political Economy of the New Asian Industrialism, edited by Frederic C. Deyo

The Misunderstood Miracle: Industrial Development and Political Change in Japan, by David Friedman

Politics in Hard Times: Comparative Responses to International Economic Crises, by Peter Gourevitch

Closing the Gold Window: Domestic Politics and the End of Bretton Woods, by Joanne Gowa

The Philippine State and the Marcos Regime: The Politics of Export, by Gary Hawes

Reasons of State: Oil Politics and the Capacities of American Government, by G. John Ikenberry

The State and American Foreign Economic Policy, edited by G. John Ikenberry, David A. Lake, and Michael Mastanduno

Pipeline Politics: The Complex Political Economy of East-West Energy Trade, by Bruce W. Jentleson

The Politics of International Debt, edited by Miles Kahler

Corporatism and Change: Austria, Switzerland, and the Politics of Industry, by Peter J. Katzenstein

Small States in World Markets: Industrial Policy in Europe, by Peter J. Katzenstein

The Sovereign Entrepreneur: Oil Policies in Advanced and Less Developed Capitalist Countries, by Merrie Gilbert Klapp

International Regimes, edited by Stephen D. Krasner

Power, Protection, and Free Trade: International Sources of U.S. Commercial Strategy, 1887–1939, by David A. Lake

State Capitalism: Public Enterprise in Canada, by Jeanne Kirk Laux and Maureen Appel Molot

Opening Financial Markets: Banking Politics on the Pacific Rim, by Louis W. Pauly

The Business of the Japanese State: Energy Markets in Comparative and Historical Perspective, by Richard J. Samuels

Europe and the New Technologies, edited by Margaret Sharp

Europe's Industries: Public and Private Strategies for Change, edited by Geoffrey Shepherd, François Duchêne, and Christopher Saunders

Fair Shares: Unions, Pay, and Politics in Sweden and West Germany, by Peter Swenson

National Styles of Regulation: Environmental Policy in Great Britain and the United States, by David Vogel

International Cooperation: Building Regimes for Natural Resources and the Environment, by Oran R. Young

Governments, Markets, and Growth: Financial Systems and the Politics of Industrial Change, by John Zysman

American Industry in International Competition: Government Policies and Corporate Strategies, edited by John Zysman and Laura Tyson

Library of Congress Cataloging-in-Publication Data

Gourevitch, Peter Alexis.
  Politics in hard times.

  (Cornell Studies in political economy)
  Includes index.
  1. Economic policy. 2. Business cycles. 3. International economic relations.
I. Title. II. Series.
HD82.G623 1986   337   86-47631
ISBN 0-8014-1973-5 (alk. paper)